Time to Start Thinking

Also by Edward Luce

In Spite of the Gods

TIME TO
START THINKING

America in the Age of Descent

EDWARD LUCE

Atlantic Monthly Press
New York

Published simultaneously in Canada
Printed in the United States of America

FIRST EDITION

ISBN-13: 978-0-8021-2021-2

Atlantic Monthly Press
an imprint of Grove/Atlantic, Inc.
841 Broadway
New York, NY 10003

Distributed by Publishers Group West

www.groveatlantic.com

12 13 14 15   10 9 8 7 6 5 4 3 2 1

Contents

Introduction
THE GRADUATIONS
3

The Lonely Middle
WHY AMERICA'S MIDDLE CLASS CONTINUES
TO HOLLOW OUT
26

Leave No Robot Behind
WHY AMERICA'S EDUCATION SYSTEM
IS STILL FALLING BEHIND
71

The Golden Goose
WHY AMERICA'S LEAD IN INNOVATION CAN NO LONGER
BE TAKEN FOR GRANTED
100

Gulliver's Travails
WHY BUREAUCRACY IS HARMING
AMERICA'S COMPETITIVENESS
138

Against Itself
WHY AMERICA IS BECOMING LESS GOVERNABLE
176

CONTENTS

Maybe We Can't
WHY MONEY CONTINUES TO RULE WASHINGTON
214

An Exceptional Challenge
WHY THE COMING STRUGGLE TO HALT AMERICA'S
DECLINE FACES LONG ODDS
252

Acknowledgments
283

Notes
285

Gentlemen, we have run out of money. It is time to start thinking.
—Sir Ernest Rutherford, winner of the
Nobel Prize in chemistry

Time to Start Thinking

Introduction: The Graduations

The greatness of America lies not in being more enlightened than any other nation, but rather in her ability to repair her faults.
                              Alexis de Tocqueville, *Democracy in America*

THE SUN WAS shining. The last of the late spring cherry blossoms was still visible. All was well with the world. Or at least that is how it must have seemed to the three hundred or so graduating MBAs as they gathered for ceremonies beneath their university's clock tower. This being the Georgetown class of 2011, most of the graduates, including my wife's cousin Bikram Basu, who was my reason for attending, were keenly aware of the choppy economic waters into which they were heading. But on this day the positive was sure to be accentuated. Robert Solow, that year's distinguished commencement speaker, had other ideas. "I am sorry," Solow said to the graduates a few minutes into his bracing address. "I don't do motivational speaking."

Approaching ninety years of age, Solow is one of the few surviving American economists to have lived through the Great Depression, having been born five years before the crash of 1929. He won his Nobel Prize chiefly for identifying and measuring the technological underpinnings of economic growth, which, during the middle decades of his lifetime, created by far the largest and wealthiest middle class the world had seen. That same class has been under a grinding and, until recently, largely ignored siege for a generation or so. Having lived through the biting deprivations

3

of a genuine depression—and seen the difference—Solow would surely cast today's uncertainties in a reassuring light.

In the gentle and modulated tones of a true scholar, Solow set about doing the opposite. First he described the pronounced shift of America's wealth away from wages and salaries and toward business income in the past quarter of a century. Corporate profits as a share of the American economy had recently climbed to their highest level since the eve of the Great Depression and wages had fallen to their lowest, Solow observed. For most middle-class Americans this had meant years of flat, or declining, incomes at a time when the top one percent were reliving the Gilded Age. The causes of this skewing were complex and deeply rooted, he said. But its importance, he added, with an understatement beloved of economists, was "nontrivial."

"It might be that the balance of power in society is permanently shifting [toward the very wealthy]," said Solow. "If so, it is not going to be easily reversible—or reversible at all. If it continues, then your guess is as good as mine as to how society will respond." Society aside, I was curious to see how Solow's audience was responding. Few among the roughly equally divided American and international students and their relatives betrayed their verdict until Professor Solow had sat down. Georgetown's alumni were likely to be "among the favored part of the population," Solow reassured them. Then, as if to balance it out, he added, "It is by no means clear where you will all fit into all of this." The Nobel laureate was equally economical in his conclusion. "Good luck with all that," he said. "Thank you for listening." There was a moment of uncomfortable silence before the audience offered twenty seconds of tepid applause.

A day or two later I sought out Bikram for his reaction. Like many of his peers, Bikram had struggled to find a job before graduating, even though his credentials (and background in engineering) were excellent. "We were pretty much evenly divided," he said. Most of the foreigners, including Bikram, liked the speech for its honesty. But a lot of the American students were disappointed. "I think some of them wanted it to be a bit more uplifting," he said. Unlike his American friends, though, Bikram could always take the easy route back to his booming homeland if things didn't turn out well in America. "I would like to work in America for two or three more years before returning to India," he said. "But it isn't essential."

There was a time when the vast majority of foreign students in America, particularly those from Asia, who make up the bulk of the overseas intake, would have strained every sinew to become American. These days the picture is much more variegated. Not only do many of their home countries offer matching and sometimes more lucrative career opportunities but, since the September 11, 2001, attacks, it has become much harder for graduating foreigners to stay on in America.

This scissor effect—multiplying opportunities at home and declining ones in the United States—has tangibly slowed the brain drain from which America has profited so handsomely in the past half a century. The net effect amounts to a large American subsidy for her global competitors. Universities charge in fees only a fraction of the true cost of an advanced degree in most science and engineering subjects. As Fareed Zakaria, the Indian-born commentator, has said: "Every visa officer today lives in fear that he will let in the next Mohamed Atta. As a result, he is probably keeping out the next Bill Gates."

Some, like Michael Bloomberg, the mayor of New York, who refers to the post–9/11 U.S. system as "national suicide," have argued for a "staple act" that would automatically attach a green card to every university degree. But few, of whatever leaning, expect Washington to overhaul America's post–9/11 system any time soon. Barack Obama paid it only lip service in his first term. Even George W. Bush, who tried in his second term to push through an overhaul, was unable to bring along the majority of his Republican colleagues. Rahm Emanuel, Obama's pugilistic first White House chief of staff, said early on that it would be "a great second-term priority"—code for the kind of kamikaze mission undertaken by presidents not seeking reelection (Bush junior included).

What is true for immigration is even truer for the rethinking many believe Americans must make if they are to confront what increasingly resembles the onset of decline. Much has been made of America's mediocre public school system, which now consistently ranks below twentieth in the international tables in science and mathematics, and of the deterioration of so much of the country's infrastructure into second world status. Much has also been made of America's by now serial failure to capture the economic fruits of so many innovations that have sprung from its soil—not just in the rapidly widening sphere of renewable energy but also in robotics, jet propulsion, machine tools, nuclear energy, display systems, and batteries. Most of America's problems, including the mess in immigration, are easy to grasp in theory. Almost all are proving harder over time to address in practice.

Americans reflexively single out Washington, D.C., as the cause of their ills. As this book will explore, however, Washington's habits are rooted in American society. Blaming politicians has turned into a lazy perennial of modern American life. Even the politicians blame the politicians—bashing Washington is one of America's few remaining bipartisan talking points. Few candidates would campaign on the promise of changing the culture of America. Yet that is what any self-preserving candidate vows to do to Washington. Sometimes it seems Americans are engaged in some kind of collusion in which voters pretend to elect their lawmakers and the lawmakers pretend to govern. This, in some ways, is America's core problem: the more America postpones any coherent response to the onset of relative decline, the more difficult the politics are likely to get. Give or take a few years, China is set to overtake the United States as the largest economy in the world by 2020. Time and money are both in short supply. The appetite to mislay both remains unchecked.

Alexis de Tocqueville famously observed that Americans do not study much philosophy. But they tend to live by "philosophical method." In other words, foreigners, particularly the French, are obsessed with what works in theory, Americans with what works in practice. "America is therefore one of the countries in the world where philosophy is least studied, and where the precepts of Descartes are best applied," Tocqueville wrote. It is no accident that it was an American, Charles Sanders Peirce, who coined the word "pragmatism" to capture this philosophical method half a century after Tocqueville had described it. The word is distinctively American. But as this book aims to explain, America, at least in terms of how it governs itself, is no longer very pragmatic.

Among many liberals there is a resigned type of nostalgia that yearns for the golden age of the 1950s and '60s when the middle class was swelling and the federal government sent people to the moon. Breadwinners worked eight hours a day in the factory and could bank on "Cadillac" health care coverage, a solid urban or suburban lifestyle, and five weeks' vacation a year. Somewhat more mythically, among many conservatives the past is wrapped up in the godly virtues of the Founding Fathers from whom their country has gravely strayed. People stood on their own two feet and upheld core American values. It was a mostly small town place of strong families, where people respected the military and were involved in their community churches.

The right's nostalgia tends to be angrier. But in their different ways both tend to blot out the sunlight. When a country's narratives become this captivated by the past, they rob the present of the scrutiny it deserves. They also tend to shortchange the future. "America used to look ahead—we used to be good at that," Craig Barrett, the former chief executive of Intel, which could lay claim to being America's most consistently impressive company, told me. "Now we spend our lives reminiscing about the 'Greatest Generation' [i.e., that of World War II]. We can't stop looking in the rearview mirror."

Beyond the naval shipyard in Southeast Washington lies Fort McNair, America's third oldest continuous fort, which looks across the Potomac at the Reagan National Airport on the other side. Sacked by the British in the War of 1812, the fort is today better known as the home of the National Defense University—the descendant of the Industrial College of the Armed Forces that was set up in 1924 to prevent a recurrence of the procurement difficulties that had plagued the U.S. military during the First World War. It was also supposed to act as a kind of internal think tank for the military.

NDU was the place where promising officers were sent to prepare their minds for leadership. Dwight Eisenhower, after whom its principal redbrick building is named, graduated from here. By focusing on the resources needed to sustain the U.S. military, these midcareer officers think differently than others. They grasp the importance of a robust economy. "Without it we are nothing," says Alpha, a thoughtful air force colonel, who, as is the custom, is known by his military nickname (a name I have changed to protect his identity). "People forget that America's military strength is because of our power. It didn't cause it."

I had gotten to know Alpha in peculiar circumstances. Unusually for a foreigner, particularly one whose forebears once trashed the place, I was invited by the NDU to judge the school's annual exercise in national strategizing. Along with two other "distinguished visitors"—a label that has never before, and is unlikely again, to be bestowed on me—I was invited to assess a ten-year national security plan for America that the students had spent the previous two weeks thrashing out. The campus also conducts high-tech war simulations in which outsiders with military or diplomatic expertise are invited to participate.

This was an exercise in much fuzzier geopolitics. In short, what should America do over the next decade to sustain its global preeminence? I was intrigued to hear what these soldiers thought. Would they focus on defeating Al-Qaeda, pacifying Afghanistan, and disarming Iran? Or would they concentrate more on containing China as the emerging challenger to American power? As the saying goes, give a man a hammer and all he sees are nails. These people (I reminded myself) are the product of by far the most powerful military machine the world has ever known. Which nails were they seeing?

In what will qualify as another first and last, when I entered the room all its occupants stood and then, even more excruciatingly, sought my permission to sit down again. I momentarily thought about making a run for it. Instead we made our introductions. Of the sixteen members of the group, nine were in uniform and the remainder were mostly senior civilian officials from the Pentagon, the Department of Homeland Security, and the State Department. To judge from their accents at least half of them were from the South. Most had done combat duty in Iraq and Afghanistan. "I think you could still describe the U.S. military as a bastion of Republicanism," Alpha told me a few days later. "But it's a different kind to what's in fashion nowadays."

Over the following three hours this heavily bemedaled group laid out its blueprint. For the most part it was a highly articulate presentation. The only small exception was a tendency to stray into military jargon. Terms such as "off ramp," "kinetic," and "situational awareness" kept recurring. It reminded me of an American colleague at the *Financial Times* who, on his return from a briefing at the Pentagon, was asked what he had picked up. "I learned that situational awareness is a force multiplier," he said. "Which means if you know where you are, you don't need so many people." When I related this to Alpha he smiled. "We could have done with some more situational awareness when we went into Iraq," he said.

The group's premise was that America still had enough power to help shape the kind of world it wanted to see. By 2021 that moment would have passed. The country needed to act very fast and very pragmatically. "The window on America's hegemony is closing," said the officer selected to provide the briefing. "We are at a point right now where we still have choices. A decade from now we won't." The United States, he continued, was way too dependent on its military. The country should sharply reduce its "global footprint" by winding up all wars, notably in Afghanistan, and by closing peacetime military bases in Germany, South Korea, the UK, and elsewhere.

America should make extra sure not to go to war with Iran. "We have to be able to learn to live with a nuclear-armed Iran," said the briefer. "The alternative [war] would impose far too high a cost on America." In Asia, America should recognize the inevitable and offer the green light to China's military domination of the Taiwan Strait. In exchange for the United States agreeing to stand down over Taiwan, China would push North Korea to unite with South Korea. Finally, the United States should stop spending so much time and resources on the war against Al-Qaeda (the exercise took place about three weeks before Osama bin Laden was killed).

All this was a means to an end, which was to restore America's economic vitality. It would not be easy. It may not even be possible, they conceded. But it should be the priority. "The number one threat facing America is its rising debt burden," said the briefing officer. "Our number one goal should be to restore American prosperity." Intrigued by the boldness of their vision, I was unprepared for what followed. The briefer said they had all agreed on the need to shrink the Pentagon budget by at least a fifth, partly by closing overseas bases, partly by reducing the number of those in uniform by 100,000, but also by cutting the number of "battle groups"—aircraft carriers—below its current level of eleven.

Most of the savings would be spent on civilian priorities such as infrastructure, education, and foreign aid. None of this would be possible were the United States at war, or even under threat of war, they said. It could be pulled off only if America were effectively to cede—or share—its domination over large parts of the world. "We would need to persuade our friends on the Republican side that America has to share power if we want to free up resources to invest at home," said the briefer. "We tried really hard to come up with alternatives. But we couldn't find a better way to do this."

Led by my two "co-judges," we probed the fifteen men and one woman for signs of hesitation. Expecting some kind of a reaction, I suggested that their plan would be seen as dangerously radical in America's current climate. Pull out of Europe? Accept nuclear parity with China? Embark on a Marshall-style plan to revive the U.S. economy? The chances of anything like this happening were zero. "Nobody here thinks the politics in this town is going to change overnight," said an army colonel from Tennessee with a classic military buzz cut. "All we are saying is that we're in trouble if they don't." I heard his words and saw the person from which they were issued. It was still a struggle to match them up. "This isn't about ideology, it is about understanding where we are as a country," he said.

Later it occurred to me that what the group had laid out was within the mainstream of Republican tradition. In the 1860s Abraham Lincoln unleashed a series of investments that was to unify the continent into a single national economy—from the railroads to the public universities. In the early 1900s Teddy Roosevelt, another Republican, broke up the oil monopolies, introduced regulation of workplace conditions, and set up the first national parks to preserve American wilderness. Dwight Eisenhower, their fellow party alumnus, responded to the Soviet launch of Sputnik in 1957 with massive investments in public education, science, and road building. In a classic of unintended consequences, Ike also created the research agency that went on to develop the Internet.

Even Ronald Reagan, the undisputed icon of today's conservative movement, shepherded through an amnesty for illegal immigrants, closed down thousands of income tax loopholes, and set up a public-private partnership to defend America's embattled computer chip industry. Reagan once said, "I didn't leave the Democratic Party, the Democratic Party left me." Given the Republican Party's instinct to equate virtually any taxes with socialism nowadays, it looks like Lincoln's party has left the U.S. military—or at least its upper reaches.

Even with my grasp of polling methodology I knew a group of sixteen officers was too small a sample from which to draw any big conclusions. So it was with particular interest a few weeks after the session that I came across an article by the mysterious "Y" in *Foreign Policy* entitled a "National Strategic Narrative." The piece made much the same arguments—although with fewer specifics—as the NDU group. It was written in homage to the famous *Foreign Affairs* piece by George Kennan in 1947 that argued for a strategy of "containment" of the Soviet Union and which he published anonymously under the byline "X." In an attempt to get more attention, Admiral Michael Mullen, chairman of the Joint Chiefs of Staff and therefore the head of all the U.S. armed services, agreed to allow the names of the two "Y" authors to be revealed. These were Captain Wayne Porter of the U.S. Navy and Colonel Mark "Puck" Mykleby of the U.S. Marine Corps. Both were on loan to Admiral Mullen's Pentagon office when they wrote it.

The authors argued that the United States could not hope to practice "smart power" abroad if it did not practice "smart growth" at home. Unlike the fate of the Kennan's "Long Telegram" from which Kennan developed his piece, the article penned by Y generated virtually no response. Barring a few bloggers, none of the major newspapers or television stations saw it as newsworthy. Kennan had been compelled to reveal that he was X after a mounting campaign of public speculation. The authors Y elicited barely a shrug when they volunteered their identities. Yet their piece offered a key insight into the troubled mind-set of the U.S. senior military.

Much like the NDU group, Porter and Mykleby argued for a new spirit of "shared sacrifice" in America. It was Alpha who gave force to that phrase for me. Having patrolled the skies of Iraq—acting as the unblinking eye of the army—Alpha, like many of his colleagues, was disappointed with how the civilians managed that war. "In this country 'shared sacrifice' means putting a yellow ribbon around the oak tree and then going shopping," he said, in reference to George W. Bush's infamous call for Americans to hit the ski slopes and the shopping malls after 9/11. The memory clearly still bothered him. "Taxes are the price we pay for civilization," he said, in quotation of the jurist Oliver Wendell Holmes.

America's ability to reverse her fortunes could come about only through being admired around the world, rather than feared, Alpha said. There was a thin line between being feared and being mocked. "Should we be seen as a hegemon that imposes its will on others or as a beacon?" he said when I asked whether America should regain its appetite to promote democracy overseas. "The best thing we can do for democracy around the world is to change our act here at home."

Alpha's group had also recommended lifting the foreign aid budget by $30 billion a year entirely at the expense of the Pentagon. "We know there's no lobby in Washington for foreign aid," he said. In a poll by World Public Opinion a few months earlier, the American public estimated that one quarter of the U.S. federal budget was spent on foreign aid. In fact Washington spends little more than a dollar on aid for every ninety-nine dollars it spends on something else. The gap between perception and reality is occasionally stunning. In practice, and given the patchy record of the aid industry around the world, it is unlikely more money would buy the kind of goodwill that Alpha's group would expect for America. Development is a complicated business. But that seemed beside the point. What I took from Alpha and his colleagues was a visceral concern about America's future.

I picked up the same concern from Admiral Mullen in an interview that he gave me three months before retiring as head of the U.S. military. Mullen was in a talkative mood. In 2010, in the midst of overseeing a 30,000-troop surge to Afghanistan, Mullen had vented alarm about growing U.S. national debt, declaring it the country's number one threat—greater than that posed by terrorism, by weapons of mass destruction, and by global warming. He had since repeated his point. We met amid the rolling high drama that led up to the last-minute decision in August 2011 to raise the U.S. national debt limit by more than $2 trillion.

Perched at his utilitarian semicircular desk, with a bank of television screens behind him, the admiral munched happily through two hot dogs, both of which he had drowned in mustard. It did not slow his word rate. "We are borrowing money from China to build weapons to face down China," he said. "I mean, that's a broken strategy. It may be okay now for a while, but it is a failed strategy from a national security perspective."

Mullen spoke of the need for Washington to make more effective decisions at a time when America is entering a lengthy phase of fiscal austerity. It was clear Mullen did not think authorities in Washington were up to the task. Many still hadn't made a proper account about the events that led up to the September 2008 meltdown following the collapse of Lehman Brothers. Nor was there strong reason to be confident that such a meltdown would not recur. "Where were the overseers, as opposed to the finger pointers, which is what they became?" he asked. "Where was the oversight, the helpful, regulatory, legislative oversight to keep us in limits? Because it wasn't there. It wasn't there. Where the hell is the accountability for this?"

Mullen's concerns reminded me of Eisenhower's famous farewell address in 1961, just before John F. Kennedy was inaugurated as president, in which he warned of the dangers posed by America's emerging "military-industrial complex." The world has turned at least a half circle since then. Nowadays people in Mullen's position spend more time worrying about the foreign sources of components that go into U.S. military equipment. The global supply chain is a growing reality for the Pentagon. In such a hyperintegrated world, very little is made purely in America.

The world is changing rapidly, Mullen continued, and America cannot be expected to do all the heavy lifting. Much of America's industrial base, including the naval shipyards and certain kinds of missile-building systems, was now in a "critically fragile" state, he said. "Once you lose that capacity it's hard to get it back. We're going to have to have something like a global security strategy that involves our allies and our alliances so that our industrial capacities are complementary." In short, America's allies should share much more of the economic burden. "There is not a country in the world that can do this alone any more," Mullen said.

A few weeks after the NDU course finished Alpha went back to Afghanistan, to a war in which he believes America has again set its heights too high. "We should be more modest in what we think we can achieve," he said. "The American military was never supposed to be an aid agency." For Alpha, as for Mullen, America's recent history offers a lesson in overreach. The U.S. military forces have been asked to pull off the impossible in faraway places. But whatever they have learned only reinforces their skepticism about what they can achieve.

In contrast, America's soldiers can at least imagine America surmounting some of its bigger domestic problems. For the most part these are not obscure. But the will to confront them appears to be missing in action. For Alpha the biggest puzzle remains Washington's reluctance to address the festering morass in America's immigration system. As a nation of immigrants, America is supposed to attract people. "We take the world's smartest kids and we give them the best education available and then we put them on a plane back home," he said. "How smart is that?"

Don Riegle rose very early in the morning to give himself enough time to write the commencement address he was due to give later that day. "This isn't an easy speech to give," he said as we were driving to the venue. He continued to scribble notes throughout the morning. We had both stayed at the Holiday Inn Gateway, the only decent hotel in Flint, Michigan, which, perhaps appropriately, is located next to an interstate highway several miles out of town. As Michael Moore showed in his famous (to many in Flint infamous) documentary *Roger and Me,* the town has been in economic decline for many years. Today it serves virtually as a museum of American deindustrialization—the collapse of middle-class neighborhoods and the institutions that came with it.

From the robust public school system to the social clubs and voluntary associations that Edmund Burke called America's "little platoons," Flint has lost virtually all texture of a functioning city. Large tracts of it, including the neighborhood in which Riegle was born and raised, turn into shooting zones at night. In spite of having a population of only a hundred thousand Flint had sixty-six documented murders in 2010, giving it the seventh highest murder rate (by population) among American cities. The same year there were 517 acts of arson. Yet over the previous three years Flint's police department had been cut by a whopping two-thirds[1]. On some Friday or Saturday nights there are fewer than ten police personnel on duty and just one patrol car to go around. Flint's police headquarters is "closed weekends and holidays," leaving a largely desolate urban landscape to its own fate.

A former Democratic senator for Michigan who stepped down in 1995 after having served thirty years on Capitol Hill (finishing his career as chairman of the Senate banking committee), the seventy-three-year-old Riegle was back in Flint to give the graduation address at the local community college. He invited me along so that he could show me what had happened to his hometown. Riegle, whose father was briefly mayor of Flint in the 1950s, grew up in a lower-middle-class suburb within earshot of the factory whistle that would issue each dawn from the adjacent Buick plant, signaling the start of the morning shift. Every Buick made in America was produced here.

During World War II the auto plants in Flint, like most of the rest of Michigan and the surrounding Midwest, were converted into Franklin Roosevelt's so-called arsenal of democracy. General Motors and Ford turned into the world's most efficient military suppliers. At one point half of the world's industrial production took place within a three-hundred-mile radius. This was the epicenter of the machine that rolled back Japan and helped defeat Hitler. Flint's workforce also helped to keep Britain afloat during the darkest days of the war, when the United States was still hoping it could stand apart.

Today, Riegle's formerly bustling neighborhood reminded me of the strangely pockmarked streets of Bosnia that I saw in the mid-1990s. Ethnic cleansing in Bosnia had left some houses perfectly intact and others totally burned out, like a mouth with pearly white teeth except that half of them had been removed. Riegle drove me through the streets of his youth. At one moment you would see a nicely kept picket fence bungalow. "These are the people who are keeping things together but are locked in because they can't sell their home," said Riegle. The next you were staring at an empty lot where the house had been burned to the ground.

"These are the people who went for the insurance," he said. The pattern repeated itself for block after block.

Most of the trees that had once given these streets their intimacy had been stripped for fuel. At regular intervals local residents had nailed wooden makeshift signs to whatever trees were still standing. "This is a Kid's Zone, not a Hoe's Zone," says one. "Prostitutes keep out!" says another. "One thing we don't want to do is get out of the car," said Riegle. It was eleven in the morning. Flint has had it bad, but this could have been Cleveland, or Detroit, or any number of economic sink zones in the American Midwest. For Riegle, however, the sight was visceral. He hadn't been back in several years. At various points Riegle would point at a boarded-up shop or a smoke-charred ruin and say, "That was a ten-cent variety store," or "That was where the Coney Island restaurant used to be, my dad used to take us there," or "This block was what we called the Hungarian Village."

When we reached his childhood home at 1814 Franklin Street, Riegle's expression saddened. The modest single-story house looked like it had seen better days. It was still possible to picture the busy community that had surrounded it. "It is almost an out-of-body experience," said Riegle, driving at a crawl past his house. "To think of the epic, compressed change that has hit this neighborhood. To think of how totally things can fall apart." Gesturing at what was clearly a crack house a few doors down, he continued, "For better or worse, it was this town that made me into who I am," he said. "If you're born here nowadays what chance do you have?"

In spite of his parents' modest financial means, Riegle had enough parental support to make it to college in Michigan and then into Harvard Law School in the early 1960s. Riegle also credits his local public school for his subsequent success. "Most of the teachers were women and if they got married they were fired," he said chuckling. "It sounds quaint in today's context. But the system worked." We were heading for an indoor hockey rink to celebrate the eleven hundred people graduating from Mott Community College. "The one thing I'm not going to dwell on is the state of the economy," said Riegle, who had been mulling over what tone he should strike. "On the other hand I don't want to paint an unrealistic picture. Are there any jobs for them?" After some thought, he added, "These kids have beaten all the odds to pick up a skill and I want to make them feel good. They deserve it."

Before the ceremony we ate a buffet lunch with members of the college board in an upholstered campus residence. Richard Shaink, the nationally recognized college president (Mott was ranked by the college association among the top ten of the 1,167 in the country[2]), described the condition of the students when they arrive to begin their two-year associate degree. More than two-thirds fail to pass an eighth-grade reading test, which means the large majority of Flint's high school graduates are stuck at or below the reading age of a thirteen-year-old. Mott requires students with deficiencies in reading, writing, or basic maths (and sometimes in all three) to take crash courses before they are allowed to go any further. A majority of the students drop out before starting their chosen degree. It reminds them too much of high school.

In an area with more than 20 percent official unemployment— almost double that in real terms if you include those who have dropped out of the labor market or who cannot find full-time work—Mott's graduates have a fighting chance of getting jobs. "The people who are graduating today have stuck at it through thick and thin and really accomplished something," Shaink said to us. A large number were qualifying as nurses, dentist's assistants, or social workers. Others were picking up certificates in more tailored fields. A few had been trained to work in nail salons, many more to work on IT help desks, and there were a wide range of electricians, auto-repair workers, and paralegal assistants. "In most cases they are the first people in their family to graduate from anywhere or with anything," said Shaink.

The stadium floor was covered with lines of empty chairs that would be filled by the students at the end of the opening procession. The stands around it were packed with expectant relatives. The buzz they gave off was the kind you hear before a sporting event. Some of them had brought *vuvuzelas*. They erupted in cheers when the choir launched into "America the Beautiful," which signaled that the students were starting their procession. Dressed in ceremonial black gowns and mortarboards, each bore a different colored tassel or sash, conveying the subject field in which they were graduating. I flicked through the event brochure, which listed the rules governing the pageantry for community college graduations, including the colors you are permitted to wear and in what form. There was "apricot" for nurses, "golden yellow" for the sciences, and "citron" for social workers. Amusingly—and I wondered if it was intentional—"drab" was assigned to those graduating in accounting.

At a guess, about two-thirds were women. Some flashed smiles and waved both hands at their families in the stands. Others took pictures of their classmates. There was a small but consistent trickle of middle-aged men and women, most of whom seemed a little less exuberant. "Keep your eyes on the women's shoes," said the lady sitting next to me as they shuffled past in single file to collect their degrees. "Aren't they the best?" Like many Europeans (and a smaller minority of Americans), I am not a fan of having to stand up and sing patriotic songs. But there was something very moving about the undisguised pride written on so many faces as they entered the arena to "America the Beautiful." For the first time I paid close attention to the words. *O beautiful for patriot dream / That sees beyond the years / Thine alabaster cities gleam / Undimmed by human tears / America! America! / God shed His grace on thee / And crown thy good with brotherhood / From sea to shining sea.*

After the posting of the colors, the audience settled down for Riegle's address. Having heard him mull over its contents earlier on, I felt an unearned stake in his performance. I was curious to see how it would be received. Riegle started on the economy. "These are hard economic times for people in America and particularly for the people of the Midwest," he said. But the people of Flint—or the "Flintstones" as they have more recently become known—had been through even tougher times than this. Riegle described the

Flint into which he was born in 1938, when it was just emerging from the Great Depression and the bitter factory lockouts that had scarred the auto industry through the 1930s. It culminated in a climb down by management and the creation of the United Auto Workers union. "Many of our citizens died in poorhouses," said Riegle. "But we were a hardscrabble town, probably the toughest in America."

Then came the Second World War, which turned Flint into a critical piece of the war machine that defeated fascism. The experience helped to cement one of the tightest knit industrial communities in the nation. When the town was devastated by a tornado in 1953 it pulled together. "Within two weekends the people of Flint rebuilt ninety-five percent of the houses—everybody pitched in. It was in our DNA. It is in your DNA," he said. Riegle quoted Franklin D. Roosevelt and John F. Kennedy.

Then he turned to the present. He told the graduates that they had climbed a big mountain against steep odds and the expectations of society. "Some people think Flint doesn't have what it takes to survive and succeed," he said. "But you have shown with your courage that you have what it takes." Without painting a false picture of the world that awaited these graduates, Riegle's words showed heart and knitted skillfully with the pride of the occasion. Apart from the loud chatter from children in the stands, the adults clearly appreciated it. "What did you think?" asked Riegle as we got into the car. I said he had pitched it perfectly. "I'm not so sure about that," he replied.

Many economists would argue that what has happened to Flint and so much of the Midwest is a sad but necessary feature of America's dynamic economy, the country that has most closely tracked the cycle of "creative destruction" set out by the early-twentieth-century political scientist Joseph Schumpeter. In Schumpeter's society dying assets are liquidated more rapidly, making way for a more rapid investment in the next cycle of production. The old dies so that the new can be born.

There is accuracy to the observation. But a city is also a home. And cities never really die. Detroit's population today is less than half its peak of 1.8 million in 1950. Places such as Toledo, Flint, and Cleveland have experienced similar drops in what demographers say is the greatest urban population decline since the Black Death in thirteenth-century Europe. But that still leaves more than 700,000 people trapped in Detroit, many of them in homes they can never hope to sell. Will they be buried with their assets? "It's easy to say now but I guess the moral of the story is you've got to diversify," says Riegle.

The slow-burning plight of America's Midwest is no longer something that can be swept neatly, if unhappily, into a side category. People used to see America's rust belt as a tragic but unavoidable casualty of America's transition into a dynamic service economy. But the rust continued to spread into other corners of America. Since 2000, America has lost another 5 million manufacturing jobs, which is roughly a third of what was left. The new service economy jobs that replaced them don't pay the same rates. Nor do most of them come with health care benefits or pensions. Five-week holidays have almost vanished. For the first time in modern history the majority of American households were poorer at the end of a business cycle than at the beginning (2002 to 2007). Since then things have gotten worse.

A nation the size of America can handle the fates of a few Flints and Detroits. But how many declining suburbs and exurbs can it absorb before some kind of tipping point is reached? Many Americans attribute their country's success to a unique set of virtues that qualifies the United States as exceptional in world history. In economic form, such values include self-reliance, a small state, low taxes, and free trade. All of these are freighted with some elements of myth. America's deepest virtue may lie in its rich tradition of pragmatism. How soon, and with what effect, that quality will resurface is a "nontrivial question," as Professor Solow might say.

This book will not predict America's collapse. But it will prove skeptical about America's ability to sharply reverse her fortunes. Its title, *Time to Start Thinking,* implies that America has not yet begun to think seriously about the consequences of where it is headed. Nowhere is this deficit more apparent than in American politics. If America is to restore its competitiveness it will need to do many things, few of which will be possible without a much more effective federal government. In today's world, smart government is a critical ingredient of national competitiveness. Unless America can address government's role in a more pragmatic light, it may doom itself to continued descent.

The first chapter, "The Lonely Middle," looks at the changing structure of the U.S. economy, in which the impact of technology and globalization has reduced the earnings potential of a large share—and possibly most—of the workforce while catapulting the most productive elites into a different hemisphere. It will ask whether it is possible to revive a jobs-rich American manufacturing sector, as many, perhaps somewhat optimistically, believe is still possible. And it will assess the growing bewilderment of America's economic elite, who have been hit by a crisis they were the last to see coming. They have yet to find a new paradigm.

The second chapter, "Leave No Robot Behind," looks at America's steep challenge in overhauling public education. It also asks whether America can refurbish a system of worker training that is shortchanging most of America's labor force. Chapter three, "The Golden Goose," looks at the health of American innovation and takes a neutral stance on America's chances of remaining the world's leader. Silicon Valley continues to be the most dynamic place on the planet to start up a company and the likeliest parent of disruptive technologies. But if the valley's secret sauce is to be found in its distinct blending of place, money, and talent, only "place" can be firmly relied upon to stay put.

Chapter four, "Gulliver's Travails," looks at waning prospects for overhauling the U.S. federal government, which, in spite of repeated efforts at reform, remains part of the problem. Chapter five, "Against Itself," looks at what is driving the continued polarization of America's politics. The bitterness in Washington might be seen as an analogue to the polarized economy outside the Beltway. So, too, is its disorientation. It has become fashionable to talk of America's "broken politics." Unlike most fashions, this looks to be more durable. The lessons taken in states such as Texas and California are not encouraging.

Chapter six, "Maybe We Can't," looks at the increasingly debilitating effect of the "permanent [election] campaign," a trend Barack Obama has exacerbated and in many ways come to embody. The final chapter, "An Exceptional Challenge," looks at America's dwindling options in a world where the pace is increasingly being set elsewhere. Many Americans believe it is still within their power to determine whether the country retains its global preeminence. That is probably wishful thinking. But it is within America's power to reverse its increasingly plutocratic internal character.

The book therefore concludes where it begins, with America's shell-shocked middle classes. Can their fortunes be revived? Must we await another shock, along the lines of the 2008 Wall Street meltdown, for America to stir itself into action? American history is rich with examples of shocks that galvanized big change (the Great Depression, Sputnik) and others that prompted much darker responses (the McCarthyite Red Scare and the invasion of Iraq). Who can say whether the next tipping point will be positive or negative? "It is conventional wisdom in Washington to say, 'We need another crisis. That's when we'll get things done,' " Michael Bennet, the senator from Colorado, told me. "I'm not so sure about that. What would it look like? Shouldn't we be careful what we wish for?"

In what had been a summer of graduations, I still had one to go, the event to which I had been most looking forward: the 2011 Princeton Class Day for my talented nephew Nikhil Basu Trivedi. At just twenty-two, Nikhil had already secured his first job at a private equity firm in Manhattan, at a starting salary that discretion forbids me from disclosing. The previous winter I had visited Nikhil at Princeton to talk to his peers about the jobs they wanted. My chief curiosity was to see whether the

2008 meltdown, which took place when Nikhil's class was in its sophomore year, had made any impact on the career aspirations of Princetonians. Chiefly via a Facebook posting and a Tweet, Nikhil pulled together an articulate cross section of about twenty of his peers.

We sat around a dining table for a couple of hours talking about their career plans. Roughly a third of this self-confident, bright, and diverse group of young men and women were planning to study for MBAs at places such as Harvard and Wharton. Some were applying to Teach for America—the philanthropic movement that places highly motivated graduates into some of America's toughest schools for two years. And most of the rest, in one form or another, including Nikhil, were heading into the financial sector and into nonfinancial business.

My unscientific poll may have understated how little had changed, however. A large chunk of college graduates who do MBAs go on to Wall Street. And a large share of those who join Teach for America go on to study for MBAs. Given that Wall Street had been through only a year of suppressed bonuses before bouncing back to its precrash heights, most of Nikhil's peers agreed that the 2008 financial cataclysm had not radically altered their outlooks. The price signal from Wall Street was almost as loud as it had been before the bubble burst.

Six months later on a sweltering day in early June I watched them graduate. Having supplied nine of the fifty-five attendees to America's constitutional convention, Princeton rivals Yale and Harvard in Ivy League prestige (they had five and four apiece). For commencement days, the president of Princeton is always the speaker, unless, that is, the U.S. president is available. That day's chief dose of reality came from Shirley Tilghman, Princeton's first female president and a renowned molecular biologist. She gave some tongue-in-cheek advice to the young graduates.

Tilghman warned that Princetonians of the class of 2011 would find themselves in a world that operated under different rules once they had left "the orange bubble." Outside the bubble, you will not be rewarded for doing your work with free Kettle corn and pancake breakfasts," she said. "You will be rewarded by not being fired." Tilghman's advice provided a lighthearted reminder of how enjoyable life at Princeton had been. "In the real world using printers, getting massages, and going on trips to the Galápagos Islands actually costs money," she said.

In her humorous way, she also chided the outgoing class for where most of it was likely to be headed—barely a forty-five-minute car ride away. "And so," she concluded, "we are proud to have you carry Princeton University's name into the farthest reaches of the upper west and upper east sides of Manhattan." Everybody laughed. They laughed, too, on the previous day when Michael Bloomberg dropped by to speak at yet another Princeton graduation event. The mayor of New York had also done some unscientific polling. Like most graduation speakers, he felt obliged to dispense career advice. That is one thing graduation speakers seem to have in common. "As you venture forth into your chosen careers, whether it be in finance, or . . . Oh wait," said Bloomberg, pausing. "I think that pretty much covers it."

I

The Lonely Middle

The best political community is formed by middle class citizens.

Aristotle

A SMALL CROWD JOSTLED at the entrance, straining for a glimpse of the contents within. The ten-by-thirty-foot space, which was shrouded in inky darkness, contained what looked like bubble-wrapped furniture in the front and a pile of nondescript boxes farther back. Since the room was in darkness, the only way of guessing the value of its contents was to scan it by torchlight from the entrance. At any moment there were seven or eight beams frantically sweeping the room hoping to isolate a telling detail before being asked to make way for others. The scene gave off a macabre disco effect except that the floor was piled with inanimate objects rather than dancers. Toward the back you could make out what could have been the handles of a concealed motorbike. Or perhaps they were attached to a lawn mower. It was hard to tell.

The company, ezStorage, insisted on payment in cash only for all of its auctions, which are straightforward fire sales of the belongings of people who have defaulted on their storage rent. It took bids in increments of $25. After about seven minutes the bidding for this unit stopped at $475. The auctioneer took the money and moved down the corridor to the next one. A desultory gathering of roughly fifty people trailed behind him. "After you've done this for a while you get a sense of which rooms might have valuable stuff and which are full of junk," said Chad Shanholtz, a journeyman carpenter from Winchester, Virginia, with a goatee, a wealth of tattoos, and now the owner of the contents of room 1321.

Chad said he once paid $500 for a unit that was piled up to the ceiling with boxes. When he opened them up he saw they were stuffed full of Longaberger baskets, worth between $10 and $100 apiece. He made thousands of dollars that day. One of his friends once found an old Mercedes-Benz buried under a pile of carpets and bric-a-brac. Another said he had discovered cartons of virtually untouched toys from China that he took home for his children. But these were rare exceptions. "Sometimes you find a lot of personal stuff and keepsakes. I've found a few birth certificates," said Chad. "None of that stuff has monetary value."

Over the past quarter of a century America's storage industry has grown almost tenfold and now generates revenues of almost $25 billion a year.[3] At every busy intersection in the country, and in every strip mall, it is hard to miss the hulking white boxes sporting names like Public Storage, U-Store It, and Extra Space. In 1984 there were six thousand storage centers in the United States. Now there are almost ten times that number. In addition to the national chains, thousands of mom-and-pop centers have sprung up all over the country. Whether you own a chain or run a stand-alone center, the industry's future looks stellar. "This business is one hundred percent recession proof," said the manager at the ezStorage center in Glen Burnie, a suburb of Baltimore. "It doesn't matter if the economy is going through good times or whether it's in the doghouse, we just keep growing."

Over the past few years, since before the onset of the recession, storage companies have seen a sharp rise in defaults. Most of their cash flow comes from the monthly rent for the units. Often proceeds from a fire sale fall short of the renter's arrears. Under Maryland law, storage companies are required to wait for two months before posting the notice. Requirements vary from state to state. But the trend is national. After the notice goes up, renters are barred from returning to their units unless they pay up. Neither they, nor their relatives, can attend the auction. "We call it the five Ds—debt, divorce, displacement, death, and disinterest [uninterest]," said the branch manger, who was formally prohibited from speaking to the media but happy to help me out. "If we're auctioning your unit, then you're going to be one of those Ds."

Most of the storage renters had likely lost their homes through bank foreclosure. Many dump their things in storage until they can find a new home. Others, in what often amounts to the same thing, have acquired too many possessions. There were also ghosts of small businesses. One of the units contained what looked like the contents of a clerical operation, from the desktop computers to the office crockery and the wall hangings. Another was piled high with garden furniture and equipment, the leftovers perhaps from that large suburban house garden that is now in the bank's possession. "For the biggest rooms we only charge $240 a month," said the manager. "If you can't come up with that kind of money then you've got to be desperate, or dead."

Watching this crew of dollar-store managers, flea market vendors, private collectors, and fortune hunters move from one unit to the next, torches in hand as they picked over the carcasses of people's lives was an unsettling experience. Everything about the scene, from the long semilit corridors to the CCTV cameras, smelled of loneliness. There was nothing menacing. Just an undertone of deracination. A large share of those with whom I spoke said they either worked part-time jobs or were self-employed. A small hard core moves almost continuously from one auction to the next. Some will drive up to four or five hours to get to auctions in Maryland, southern Pennsylvania, Washington, D.C., and Virginia. Everyone was friendly. But not always about each other. In particular, the hard-core group complained about the "amateurs" who had begun to inflate their numbers.

In 2010 A&E launched a reality TV show called *Storage Wars*, which netted several million viewers a week. Its popularity spawned a rival show, *Auction Hunters,* which is featured on the Spike channel. "Since that show people have been turning up thinking they'll find a Picasso or a $200,000 collection of baseball cards like they saw on TV," said Jerry Wilkinson, a former railway engineer who now runs a stall at a flea market in Cumberland (about a two-hour drive from Baltimore). Like many of the others Jerry, whose large ruddy face is crowned by a mop of graying blond hair, was wearing shorts, a T-shirt, and flip-flops. The show clearly rankled him. "It took them [A&E] two years to shoot six episodes. But if it's on TV then it *must* be true," he said.

Unaware until then of *Storage Wars* I downloaded a couple of episodes. It offered a somewhat different picture than what I had seen. To the backdrop of "Money Owns This Town," the show's husky theme song, the featured bounty hunters are introduced one by one walking toward the camera, their designated monikers flashing up sequentially on screen: the Gambler, the Mogul, the Young Gun, the Collector. "You don't know what you're going to be up against," says the Collector, assessing the coming auction as though talking about a gunfight. "When I see a room, I want to see dust on the boxes, no footprints, no evidence anyone has been there [to remove their valuables]."

Each time someone wins a bid it is posted on-screen next to the actual value of the room's contents. The latter is usually a multiple of the former. One of the characters reveals he paid $2,700 for a unit that contained a collection of comic books worth $130,000. Another discloses that he has four Picasso sketches at home that he found in an auction. To succeed in this game, he says, you need cojones. "A lot of people are just collectors," says the Mogul. "The only thing I collect is Benjamins [dollars]." The show left an imprint. Had I not already been to a couple of auctions, I might have been tempted to buy a pair of Stetson boots and head for the nearest showdown. It was harder to shake off what I saw in Glen Burnie.

Since the 2008 financial meltdown Washington has lapsed epi-
sodically into feuds over the chief causes of the subprime bubble.
How could so many cash-strapped Americans have convinced
themselves they could repay the 100 percent and even 110 percent
home mortgages they took out? Millions were persuaded to sign up
for so-called Ninja loans ("no income, no assets"). On the ground-
level causes of the bubble, most of the Democratic Party focuses
on the brokers who tricked people into signing loans that buried
the interest rate kickers in the small print. They also highlight the
unwillingness, or inability, of the U.S. Federal Reserve and other
Washington agencies to regulate housing finance.

In contrast, Republicans continue to blame high-minded and/or
self-enriching bureaucrats in charge of the Federal Housing Administration and at Fannie Mae and Freddie Mac, the government-
sponsored mortgage providers, for allegedly stuffing mortgages
down the throats of the urban poor. Their culprits are the liberal
class of social engineers, an abiding phobia of the conservative
imagination. In spite of the sharp philosophical differences between the two, they both place heavy emphasis on regulation or
its absence. What they see is what they get.

In contrast, both parties, but in particular the Republicans, tiptoe
softly around what readers will forgive me for describing as the
giant elephant in the room, specifically, the sharp rise of economic
insecurity among the American middle classes of the past generation or so, of which the subprime housing bubble was merely a
symptom, albeit a very dangerous one. In contrast to the "golden
years" of the 1950s and '60s when almost a quarter of Americans
were in secure manufacturing jobs, life has become steadily less
predictable for the middle class over this period; the median income has largely stagnated in real terms since 1973 while simultaneously the economy's ability to generate new jobs has been
steadily contracting.

Manufacturing now accounts for less than a tenth of private
sector American jobs, its lowest share since the early twentieth
century. Moreover, the service sector jobs that have arisen in their

place often come without health and pension benefits. People who move from manufacturing to the service sector take a pay cut of more than 20 percent, according to the Bureau of Labor Statistics. Based on what they had earned, rather than what they borrowed, or what they thought they owned, few Americans would have been able to participate in America's long consumer boom.

According to the Economic Security Index, which tracks the number of Americans who experience a drop in their annual income of at least a quarter, the rate has almost doubled since Reagan was president.[4] In 1985 just over one in eight Americans suffered an income loss of a quarter or more. By the time the financial meltdown hit, almost one in five Americans were affected. Since then, that number has grown sharply. Losing your job is not the worst that can happen—more bankruptcies are caused by medical emergencies.

Since one year's casualties are mostly different than the next, much more than one in five Americans now live in semipermanent fear of falling off the precipice. In the decade leading up to the collapse of the subprime market, more than half of Americans experienced an income loss of a quarter or more in one or more of those years. Think of the General Motors worker with his pension and health care plan. In the 1960s he earned $60,000 a year in today's prices. Walmart, which as the largest employer in the United States is GM's equivalent in today's economy, pays its 1.1 million mostly female employees on average $17,500 a year, most of them without attached pension or health care benefits.[5] One may imagine that many of Walmart's "associates" have their possessions locked up in storage.

There was a time, until relatively recently, when belonging to the American middle class brought with it a basic level of security. Many of those certainties have gone or continue to erode. Yet there has been little appreciable decline in the cultural yen to consume. "We live in an overwhelmingly consumer-driven society that is marked by levels of capriciousness and insecurity we haven't seen since the 1930s," says Jacob Hacker, a Yale professor who helped devise the Economic Security Index. The change, in his view, was the result of the continuing morphing of the U.S. economy over the past thirty years from one based on investment to an economy driven by consumption.

It is an economy in which most Americans have had to borrow in one form or another—particularly against their homes—in order to be able to join the game. With the collapse of the long property boom in 2008 that option is now closed. The credit has run out but the problem of stagnating income is deepening. As Warren Buffett once said: "When the tide goes out you see who has been swimming naked." Much of the debris from the age of easy credit is piled up in storage centers around America. "Over the last thirty years we have progressively shifted more and more of the big risks in life onto the individual, which has resulted in a steady atomization of American society," says Hacker. "Play the lottery, watch reality TV, hunt for bargains in the mall. But don't expect secure health care or a comfortable retirement. Those luxuries have gone."

Carl Camden has met the future and she works; indeed, she seems to be working almost all of the time. She no longer takes paychecks from a company but is working alone, sometimes from home, and is often self-employed. She is also arranging and increasingly funding her own, almost continuous, technical education, often by doing online courses at night. Much of what she picked up in community college or university five years ago is obsolete. She needs to upgrade. The future holds fond, mostly borrowed, memories of the days when employers used to look after her. But she knows—for better or worse—that she is basically on her own.

I first spoke with Camden, chief executive of Kelly Services, America's second largest staffing agency (formerly known as temping), over a glass of California wine in a bar in downtown Washington. We spoke many times after that. Everyone has a view of how to respond to the deep structural changes in the character of the U.S. economy. Camden, whose industry has grown nearly as fast as the storage business over the previous two or three decades, can think of little else.

Although hardly reassuring, Camden's view may be better grounded. The era of secure employment is over, he said. Welcome to the era of mass casualization. It is still in its early days. "If you are smart, entrepreneurial, and highly educated, the new world offers you more options than ever before," said Camden. "For everyone else, I feel pessimistic." Something of a former hippie, Camden is a rare type of chief executive. He studied linguistics rather than for an MBA and is more libertarian than conservative. Yet these days, his abiding fear of big government is outweighed by rising concern over its incompetence.

Camden's company, which is headquartered in Troy, Michigan, no longer farms out coiffured "Kelly girls" to do the typing in executive offices. Those days have faded into sepia. "You'll be flying high as a Kelly girl earning top pay!" states a corporate leaflet from 1950. "Stenos, Typists, Machine operators or Girls with any office skills. Start now for that Easter Bonnet or those vacation expenses!" Today, with 530,000 people on its books and annual revenues of $5 billion, Kelly Services plays an intimate role in the operations of some of America's leading companies.

Many large U.S. companies no longer do their human resources in-house. Instead they pay Kelly Services, or its larger rival Manpower Services, to hire new employees, manage their payroll, and process their tax returns. Companies also routinely outsource "talent management" and warehousing to staffing agencies like Kelly. They even offload entire projects. When Camden started at Kelly in the mid-1990s, the agency was winning $50 million in business contracts. Now $1 billion is normal. "On some of our contracts you can work on the full life-cycle of a project without ever meeting someone from the company that you're working for," says Camden.

In this rapidly evolving world everything keeps getting "leaner," more "flexible," and "streamlined." If companies cannot replace an employee with automation or a less expensive hire from Asia, they will farm the permanent job out to a contractor. If improving quarterly margins is the continual and overriding goal, as is the case for almost all listed U.S. companies (only an exceptional few, such as Intel and Google, can ignore the Wall Street analysts), shrinking the head count will be an equally unending pursuit.

Nor is this confined to manufacturing, where there has been a net worldwide reduction in jobs since 1990 in spite of their sharp growth in China and other countries. Many of America's larger companies, such as Microsoft and IBM, have more full-time independent contractors working for them than permanent staff. Whether it is the janitor at the door, or the chief engineer on an oil drilling platform, companies today are increasingly driven by the need to shrink overheads.

Robert Gordon, the renowned economist from Northwestern University in Illinois, describes the human effect of this as the "rise of the disposable worker." From the corporate angle, McKinsey Global Institute describes it as the "any place, any time" mind-set —companies want maximum legroom to do what they want when they want. It marks a revolutionary shift from the in-house ("vertically integrated") company of America's postwar decades. It has also brought with it an accelerating metamorphosis of the character of the world in which Americans live and work.

In the old days temps did the menial work. Now Kelly girls have been supplanted by Kelly lawyers, Kelly scientists, Kelly accountants, and Kelly engineers. "I know well-paid engineers at big companies whose only role is to think up of new ways to reduce the head count," said Camden when I met him at his headquarters in Troy. "They want to ramp up an operation and then ramp it down at high speed without bothering with all that HR stuff."

In today's world the average American has done twelve jobs by the time she reaches her forties, says Camden. Her parents, most likely just her father, had done only one or two. "There is no such thing any more as loyalty in either direction—the company owes you nothing and you owe the company nothing," says Camden. It is a theme that obviously plays to Camden's interests. The more "noncore competencies" that companies farm out, the more business there is for Kelly Services.

This is also backed up by the data. Instead of blaming manufacturing companies for offshoring to China or Brazil, people should look at why they are doing it, says Camden. In the United States it costs $2.38 an hour to pay for an employee's health care coverage. In the remainder of the rich world it costs just 98 cents. For most companies, including Kelly, health care costs often exceed profits. "America is begging them to take jobs someplace else, or find a robot that can do it instead," he said.

Camden's view of where the future is going may sound hard-edged. Yet it has led him in some unlikely directions. In spite of being a libertarian, and thus deeply suspicious of any government intervention in the economy (or the bedroom), Camden joined with an unlikely group of chief executives that put its shoulder behind the wheel of President Obama's health care reform effort in 2009. The group included Lee Scott, then the chief executive of Walmart, who earned more in two weeks than the average Walmart employee does in her lifetime. In their view America's health care system was undermining its competitiveness.

Their hope was that President Obama would put an end to America's unique employer-provided health care system. In one form or another they wanted to replace it with something that looked a bit like all the others. In the event, Scott, Camden, and his colleagues did not get anything near what they wanted. The group, which included Andy Stern, then head of one of America's largest unions, the Service Employees International Union, was outgunned by the powerful health care lobbies.

Hemmed in by the realities of politics in Washington, which were then exacerbated by the White House's tactical mistakes, President Obama decided that he had little choice but to work with the system as it was. Instead of severing the link between health care and employers, Obama's 2010 health care act stayed within it. In short, Obama took America's complex and expensive system of health care and made it more humane (as well as more complex). "It was like adding a new wing to a dilapidated house," says Camden. "I give it a C minus. It was still better than nothing."

That missed opportunity, in Camden's view, will only deepen America's crisis of competitiveness. America already spends much more on health care per head than other wealthy countries—almost triple the level of the British and double the French. Yet Americans continue to die earlier and spend more time disabled than their peers in Europe and Japan. And that gap is getting worse. The average life expectancy of Americans has been virtually stalled at seventy-eight years for more than a decade, at a time when several wealthy countries, including Japan as well as the Scandinavian nations, have edged up to eighty-two or eighty-three years.

Camden believes that the growing costs of American health care also accounts for the decline in business start-ups over the past decade. Rising costs have blunted the entrepreneurial impulse of educated Americans in their thirties and forties, who are at the likeliest stage in life to take risks. A large majority of the people at staffing agencies such as Kelly are either in their twenties or in their late fifties and sixties—and not many in between. They have either chosen or been forced to pursue a career without health care benefits. Those in their twenties do not worry much about their health. Those approaching retirement are on the cusp of qualifying for Medicare, which they still hope will offer them reliable health care coverage until they die.

The people in between—that key demographic in their thirties and forties—are caught in a "job lock." Their employer-provided family health care package is just too valuable to give up. It is a tall order to expect those in that key age group fortunate enough to be in secure jobs to inject the entrepreneurial energy America needs. "When you start up a small business you are putting your capital, and even your reputation, on the line," says Camden. "And then on top of that we expect you to risk your kids' health care?"

In Camden's view the growing gap between how businesses and the government think and act is one of the biggest threats to America's future. In some respects still a libertarian, Camden

sketches his preferred future for America. It is a place where individuals would be in control of their fates, no longer having to bury
their identities within the stultifying matrices of big organizations.
They could choose their path in life and keep changing it. In such
a world, people would be far better able to "self-actualize."

Alternatively, it could consist of an America where the elites in
the top 10 percent continue to thrive and where most of the rest
are left standing on sinking ground, constantly hopping from one
dry patch to the next. It is a future that bears a heavy resemblance
to America's present. For Camden, the most important difference
between these alternatives is effective government. He is clearly
angered by the growing probability of the second.

Camden's own achievements, he pointed out, were grounded
in the public education and scholarships he received when he was
growing up in Ohio in the 1960s. If the self-employee of the future
is going to thrive as a capitalist—and venture things that would
benefit others (such as starting up a small business and making sure
her children are well educated)—she would require a government
that enabled her to be one. "We can't expect people to survive
let alone thrive in this new world unless we have much smarter
government," he said.

Having presented his vision of the future, Camden then introduced me to the past, in the form of Bill Lichtenberger, an impec-
cably polite and reflective retired lawyer who was born at the end
of the Great Depression. An old-school type, who is economical
with his words, Lichtenberger also offers a foretaste of the future.
In spite of having spent thirty years building up a handsome pension and health care plan as a machine operator and then a lawyer
at General Motors, Lichtenberger lost most of that when GM was
restructured (before it went bankrupt). "Looks like I might still be
working when I'm eighty," he said.

Driving to see him on Michigan's highways reminded me of
Venezuela. The roads are cracking up, half the traffic lanes are
closed, and most of the cars around you look like they were bought
twenty years ago. Lichtenberger, who lives in Farmington, a leafy

and largely white suburb of the war zone in Detroit, apologized for my journey. At the best of times Michigan's roads tend to crack up in summer because of all the salt they take during the winter snows. Nowadays Michigan can afford only to repair, rather than to upgrade, its roads. "Looks like that's turning into a full-time job," said Lichtenberger.

We met at Farmington's large and well-equipped public library, where Lichtenberger spends a lot of his time. We were only a few miles from some of the most dangerous, and bleak, urban streets in the world. We might as well have been on a different planet. "Let's take one of the studios," Lichtenberger said, leading me through the periodical stands and the computer room to a small soundproof room. We met to talk about Lichtenberger's future. But I was mesmerized by his past. It sounded so familiar. Yet it had all but vanished.

When Lichtenberger was twenty-seven and working as a journeyman machinist at Goodyear, the tire company, he got a letter from GM offering him a job for life. "The letter said: 'We will take care of you until you're sixty,' or words to that effect," says Lichtenberger. Now turning seventy, Lichtenberger spends most of his days doing legal work on contract for Kelly Services. The medical bills for his wife, who has a worsening liver condition, keep mounting. Lichtenberger totes up for me the cost of the co-pays Medicare requires for his wife's heavy cocktail of medicine. "We both spent forty years paying into Medicare thinking it was an insurance program that would cover our retirement," he said. "Doesn't feel that way right now."

Lichtenberger says that in the absence of another medical crisis, the two could get by on their pensions and savings. But they cannot afford that risk. He also wants to help his children save for his grandchildren's college education, an outlay that keeps getting more expensive. Thus, every morning, as he has been doing for half a century, Lichtenberger puts on his suit and tie and heads to wherever work happens to be. The chances that one or other of them would suffer another health condition are just too great.

"When you're my age you just can't take that kind of risk," he says. "You can't bank on anything any more, even Social Security."

Every now and then I had to remind myself that this was America we were discussing. Over the course of his working life, Lichtenberger's employers had provided whatever means Lichtenberger needed to move up from the working class to the middle class. Having started out life as a blue-collar machinist, he ended it as a lawyer with an MBA. It was a typical pattern. "When you're hiring people for life, it makes sense to invest in them," says Lichtenberger.

When Lichtenberger left Goodyear in 1968, it was to study labor economics at Akron University in Ohio, his first degree. Goodyear funded him. His experience of tensions between the shop floor and management "gave me a thirst to know more." Before Lichtenberger had graduated he was poached by GM. Under what it called the Tuition Refund Assistance Program, GM funded Lichtenberger to train as a lawyer in the early 1980s. He took three years off work to complete his studies. "I had no idea how good a decision that was," he said.

The same story—of getting your employer to fund a continuous career-long upgrading of your skills—held true also for many of Lichtenberger's friends and siblings. One went to work for Cargill, the agribusiness giant, in Minnesota. Another went into management in the tire industry, where Lichtenberger's father had worked all his life on the shop floor. All of them were educated, often in multiple fashion, by their businesses.

Having started his career on the shop floor, Lichtenberger took early retirement at fifty-seven with enough degrees to cover half a wall—all of it at the expense of his employer. Alas, much of it was illusory. "Well, you play the hand life dealt you," Lichtenberger said. Other than America's most globally competitive companies, such as GE and much of Silicon Valley, it is harder and harder nowadays to find American companies that invest in their employees. As the saying goes, the past is another country. "The idea that your employer would pay you for what you are going to do in the future, rather than for what you did over the last two weeks, is a fantasy," says Lichtenberger. "I tell my grandchildren: Loyalty is a one-way street. Invest in yourself. No one else will."

Like so many older members of America's fraying middle class, Lichtenberger looks longingly back on the days when manufacturing was booming. Lichtenberger's father, an immigrant from Hungary, eked out a kind of Steinbeckian living during the Great Depression. But then he got a job on the shop floor at Goodyear. In spite of having left school at sixteen he never looked back and retired on a pension that kept him secure until he died. "That's what people did in those days," says Lichtenberger. "They retired without a mortgage to the shores of Lake Michigan and never did another day's work in their life."

From the Great Depression to the Great Recession, Lichtenberger's family rode the roller coaster of American manufacturing. At the time it seemed as though the big factories that propelled America into its remarkable period of dominance were a permanent feature of the American landscape—the unending assembly lines of cars, washing machines, tanks, machine tools, steel, telephones, computers, and patented drugs. But history will look back on it as a brief, if extraordinary, flowering of collective employment on the road to the more automated and globalized America of today.

Many Americans believe they have been duped of their birthright by unfair competition from Japan, South Korea, Taiwan, and now China and India. Much of the intellectual property theft, especially in Japan and now China, would have been recognizable to Alexander Hamilton, the architect of the American system on which the nation's early fortunes were built. What is new is the speed and the scale of today's shift. The combined impact of the rise of a billion or more Asians into the global consuming classes over the past generation evokes no precedent from the past. The only likely parallel will come in the next generation when the still more numerous remainder of Asia starts to catch up with its booming cities.

At the "economic ground zero," where so many Americans live, this "epic, cataclysmic change" described by former senator

Don Riegle is generating an accelerating shock. Lichtenberger is more fortunate than most people in Michigan. But he shares with many in the Midwest an abiding rancor for what has happened to America's heartlands. He apportions roughly equal blame to the U.S. government, big American corporations, and Asia—in particular to China. "These are American-made," said Lichtenberger pointing to his hand-stitched loafers. "I make sure always to buy American shoes."

When Lichtenberger was in his youth, America produced half the shoes in the world. Now it has only two remaining shoe-producing companies: Allen Edmonds in Wisconsin and Red Wing in Minnesota. As a child in Ohio, Lichtenberger helped out in the local shoe shop. "When customers saw that we were stocking Japanese-made shoes, they turned around and walked right out of the store," he said. "Even if America stopped making shoes, I will never buy shoes made in China." With a modest chuckle, Lichtenberger added that if he extended the same principle to any electronic or consumer product he could imagine, he would have to quit American suburbia for the wilderness.

Whether Carl Camden's future turns out to be a bright or a bleak place to live and work it is unlikely to offer much employment in manufacturing. The economics just don't add up. According to a study by Michael Spence, a Nobel Prize–winning economist from Stanford University, and his co-author, Sandile Hlatshwayo,[6] all of America's net job creation since 1990 has come in the "nontradable sector" in services industries. Between 1990 and 2008 the United States added 27.3 million jobs, of which almost every one was in services.

Almost half of these jobs were in health care or government, both sectors in which productivity growth is virtually zero. Conversely, manufacturing's impressive productivity growth has tracked its shrinking head count. For economists, productivity is the ultimate measure of an economy's IQ—more important, in some respects, than the annual number for growth in gross domestic product. That number, which accelerated sharply after the 2008 meltdown, is sending an increasingly counterintuitive signal. Some argue that U.S. productivity growth has been massively overstated.[7] Others argue that it has become a benchmark of pain. But the overall pattern is clear: most of America's jobs are in low productive sectors.

If there is an explanation as to why U.S. middle-class incomes have stagnated this is it: whatever jobs the United States is able to create are in the least efficient parts of the economy, the types that neither computers, nor China, have yet found a way of eliminating. That trend is starting to lap at the feet of more highly educated American workers. "The tradable side of the economy is shifting up the value-added chain [with jobs shifting abroad] especially to the rapidly growing emerging markets," write Spence and Hlatshwayo. "The latter themselves are moving rapidly up the value-added chains. . . . Higher-paying jobs may therefore also increasingly leave the United States."

America is seeing growth in two types of job. On the one hand there are the top 10 percent who continue to do well. These are the Wall Street financiers, Silicon Valley developers, managerial and intellectual elites, and doctoral engineers and physicists whose salaries are more aligned with global than domestic growth numbers. Then there are the low-end service jobs that employ people in every other educational category, from high school dropouts to a growing share of those with only an undergraduate, or vocational, degree, as opposed to postgraduate education. They are the nurses, domestic aides, food preparers, janitors, call center workers, IT help deskers, skin care specialists, auto-repair workers, nutritionists, and dental assistants. Their numbers will grow while their incomes will most likely continue to tread water or submerge.

David Autor, the MIT economist, describes this phenomenon as the "missing middle": the economy increasingly requires people with very high skills or very few. The far more numerous jobs requiring "middle" skills that could be learned principally on the job are disappearing. In a stark report,[8] McKinsey forecast that U.S. manufacturing would not add any net new jobs to the U.S.

42

economy between 2011 and 2021—and that was according to its "positive scenario." Under its "neutral scenario," manufacturing would continue to shrink in its share of total U.S. employment. What few manufacturing jobs are likely to be created in the United States in the coming years will be largely for highly educated people, those who have acquired knowledge that cannot be learned on the job, such as robotics, advanced engineering, or biochemistry.

In contrast to Washington's continued love affair with agriculture, which retains many of the subsidies from the 1930s when dust storms were spreading across the plains, few with influence in Washington talk about subsidizing manufacturing. Unlike farming, however, most factories and plants can shift lock, stock, and barrel to other parts of the world at remarkably high speed. "Our federal subsidies don't make a whole lot of sense," Gerald Abbott, the head of the industrial defense program at the National Defense University, told me. "You can dismantle and reassemble an American factory, brick by brick, on the other side of the world. But you cannot transplant the cornfields of Nebraska to China."

Barring a sea change in American politics, the structure of the U.S. economy is likely to continue to bifurcate in troubling directions. The middle is likely to get only lonelier. Whether, or how quickly, the U.S. economy is able to recapture its precrash annual GDP growth rates of around 3 percent a year, most of what it generates will be cornered by Professor Solow's fortunate few. In the last full American business cycle, between 2002 and 2007, the top one in one hundred Americans captured almost two thirds of all growth[9] while the top one in one thousand Americans (0.1 percent) captured more than a third of the economy's growth. Meanwhile, the median American household, which accounts for the bulk of America's workforce, saw its income decline by $2,000—the first time in the modern era that the bulk of Americans were worse off at the end of a business cycle than they were at the beginning.

It makes for what could be a destabilizing future, one that Lawrence Katz, the renowned Harvard economist, described to me as the emergence of an "inelegant America." Its chief characteristic would be of the many serving the few. "What we [America] are on track to becoming is a place where the top tiers remain wealthy beyond imagination, and the remainder, in one way or another, are working in jobs that help make the lives of the elites more comfortable—taking care of them in old age, fixing their home Wi-Fi systems or their air-conditioning units, teaching or helping with their kids, and serving them their food," he said.

Katz was agitated by the prospect of the continued decline of the American middle class. "It is a society that, in my view, is starting to belie the promise as a land of equal opportunity in which the place that you were born was not as important as the talents that you were born with," Katz said. I asked what the political consequences might be. "My fear is that it will create an increasingly ugly political culture in America," said Katz. "That will make it even harder to address these problems."

The future sketched out by Katz, which differs only in the details from that offered by Camden, is a prospect with which Lichtenberger and many others are already well acquainted. Lichtenberger says it helps to draw on some of the values that his father tried to impart to him—occasionally via the sting of his leather belt— and also the vocabulary. Lichtenberger uses words such as "frugal" and "thrift," which have seemingly vanished from the American lexicon. For younger men, in particular, the transition is hard, Lichtenberger says.

On some of his jobs for Kelly Services, the septuagenarian lawyer rubs shoulders with people in their twenties and early thirties. Some of them are frustrated law graduates trying to pay off heavy tuition debts. Others, including a number of former electrical workers and machinists, have lost their jobs on the shop floor at companies such as GM, U.S. Steel, Caterpillar, or GE. They do occasional clerical work.

"Some of them say, 'It's too late now but I should have trained to be a nurse,'" says Lichtenberger. "I tell them it's not too late. They have their whole lives to get new qualifications." Lichtenberger seemed to have internalized the new reality. But he worried a lot about the younger generations. They lacked direction. In his laconic midwestern way, he added, "I don't like what is happening any more than anyone else. But it is what it is."

Henry Ford notoriously said, "All history is bunk." Since Ford was at the forefront of a new industrial revolution, his attitude was understandable. Oliver Wendell Holmes was closer to the mark when he said, "An ounce of history is worth a pound of logic." Most economists don't study history and most historians don't study economics, which is a pity for both disciplines. It may be a serious handicap in Washington, D.C. Too many of the town's economic opinion formers are hazy about America's past. This may help explain why so many are so unsure of how to interpret the shattering challenge the 2008 meltdown posed to their worldview. The old model died in the rubble of Lehman Brothers. The new has yet to be born. Many still hope the corpse can be revived.

In the book *No Apology: Believe in America,* which Mitt Romney released before he entered the 2012 presidential race, the Republican candidate summarized the conventional wisdom on the values that had propelled his country's rise to global dominance. Those who forget what made America great, he wrote, were condemned to lead it astray. "They simply do not believe in America as it was shaped by the Founders," he wrote. "They do not believe that the principles and values that made America a great nation still apply . . . free enterprise, free markets, and free trade."

America's Founding Fathers disagreed sharply among themselves on many subjects, including the economy. So it is always enjoyable to speculate which of the founders a politician has in mind when he or she cites them in support of an argument (or whether, in Sarah Palin's case, she struggles to remember the name of any). It is unclear whether Romney had a specific one in mind. But if it was Alexander Hamilton, America's first treasury secretary who viewed free trade as a luxury the young Republic could not afford, then Romney would have been mistaken.

On matters economic, Hamilton, who was the coauthor, with James Madison and John Jay, of the Federalist Papers, was the giant among the founders. Describing America's early economic philosophy without Hamilton would be like recounting the Revolutionary War without George Washington or the Declaration of Independence without Thomas Jefferson. If Jefferson was the poet of the revolution, Hamilton was its economist. It was Hamilton who led the way in devising the pragmatic ideology that propelled America from an agricultural backwater in the 1790s to the world's foremost industrial power by 1900. Today, anyone looking at the main details of what was widely known in the nineteenth century as the "American system" could mistake it for China's industrial policies in the early twenty-first century.

Brilliant though he was, Hamilton developed his "industries in their infancy" argument (a term he first coined) only after having studied Britain's industrial rise. From the reign of Henry VII, who resolved that England should challenge the stranglehold of the big textile centers in Flanders, England had continually over the preceding three hundred years pulled itself up by its mercantilist bootstraps. Henry VII imposed escalating tariffs on the export of wool to the continent in order to keep the raw material at home for England's infant textile sector. This was then converted by Elizabeth I into an outright ban on all raw wool exports, a step that was to cripple towns such as Ghent and Bruges.

Over the next two centuries English parliaments passed a series of navigation acts that resulted in a total ban on any foreign vessel carrying out trade in English waters. As Hamilton was to start doing for America in the 1790s, England built a large edifice of tariffs around its infant industries in order to nurture their development. Through trade, and especially via its control of the colonies in America and India, England very consciously chose to prohibit its American colonies from manufacturing.

In 1770, just as the American rebellion was really starting to brew, William Pitt, Britain's prime minister, said, "The New England colonies should not be permitted to manufacture so much as a horseshoe nail." In addition to Britain's many provocations—from the Townshend and Stamp acts to the notorious levy that sparked the Boston Tea Party—London's abiding mistake was to insist on an agrarian status for America while continuing to deny it a voice with which it could argue back. In rebelling against this, the American colonists were as much economic as political renegades against the crown.

The two qualities fuse best in the person of Alexander Hamilton who very consciously adopted Britain's methods for America. Starting with the "Report on Manufactures," which Hamilton submitted to Congress in 1791, the young treasury secretary set about erecting the protective walls that were largely to prevail until the Second World War. The British fought tooth and nail to stop America from creating a manufacturing capacity. After 1787, Britain tightened domestic laws that had already banned British skilled artisans from overseas travel and stopped the export of any patented machinery. Both were criminal offenses.

Hamilton responded by offering large inducements to skilled British artisans to cross the Atlantic. He even sent a commercial spy, Andrew Mitchell, to travel around England posing as a gentleman tourist. Mitchell returned with George Parkinson, an artisan who had apprenticed with Sir Richard Arkwright, who then set up what Hamilton dubbed Parkinson's Flex Mill in New England.[10] The leadership in today's China would be more than familiar with Hamilton's methods.

Many of the recommendations in Hamilton's exhaustive 1791 report were put into effect only after the Anglo-American War of 1812, in which the sacking of Washington, D.C. by British troops gave lawmakers a smoldering reminder of America's vulnerability to her former sovereign. In the aftermath of that war the city of Washington embarked on a vigorous bout of internal improvements, helping to underwrite the system of canals that was to crisscross the East Coast and paving the way for the extension of the American frontier. The government in Washington also imposed high tariffs on English manufactured imports—duties that escalated as the nineteenth century progressed. Toward the end of the American Civil War, Abraham Lincoln raised average tariffs up to a range of between 40 and 50 percent, a level around which they would fluctuate until the middle of the twentieth century.

Britain had long since turned full circle and switched to a system of laissez-faire. When it repealed the Corn Laws in the 1840s, it became the sole standard-bearer of free trade, almost single-handedly over the next seventy years upholding the global commons in what was dubbed the age of Pax Britannica. America, meanwhile, like Bismarck's Germany in the late nineteenth century, or China in the late twentieth and early twenty-first centuries, continued to take its cues from a very different phase in Britain's history.

Then, as now, mercantilism was the preferred route to development. Countries seem to imbibe Adam Smith's free trade philosophy only after they have reached the economic summit. Until such point, it seems, they prefer Alexander Hamilton. China's politburo seems far better acquainted with America's history than does Mitt Romney. To be fair to the former governor of Massachusetts, the same holds true for many other politicians and economists in America today. The United States has never quite descended to the zero tariff levels of Victorian Britain. But successive U.S. administrations over the past seventy years have ensured America remains the indispensible force behind the only conscious project in the history of global trade liberalization.

To judge by the schooling of today's opinion formers in Washington, including those advising Barack Obama, it would be fairer to say that the founding fathers of their minds were Friedrich Hayek, Milton Friedman, and Joseph Schumpeter, the neoclassical descendants of Adam Smith and David Ricardo. What Hamilton called the American system most U.S. economists today would dismiss as "industrial policy"—a suboptimal allocation of resources that subtracts from global welfare. Whether it was the Bush (senior and junior), Clinton, or Obama White House, the idea of supporting strategic industries has been largely repudiated even if it was a critical feature of America when it was on the way up.

Yet since 2008 those verities have gradually lost their luster. The longer the United States takes to recover from the financial meltdown, the more the critics of the established model gain traction. H. L. Mencken, the mordant journalistic wit from Baltimore, once wrote, "For every complex problem, there is an answer that is clear, simple and wrong." What was an axiomatic worldview before the great recession becomes less sure of itself as time goes on. The more you delve into the sometimes rancorous debate about the future of U.S. competitiveness, the more the uncertainties open up.

Broadly speaking there are two groups: those who hold on to the conventional wisdom, including most of Washington's leading economists, but with waning ardor; and those who challenge it with an increasingly conventional alternative of their own. The latter includes many business leaders, such as Jeff Immelt, of General Electric, and numbers more public scientists and engineers than economists. They believe that America can maintain its global economic supremacy only if it regains an innovative—and jobs-rich—manufacturing sector. Sometimes, such as on the need to overhaul U.S. education, the two camps overlap.

Their biggest gulf is over industrial policy. Those arguing for the alternative conventional wisdom have gained little ground. But they have become more strident as America's great contraction continues. Immelt even slapped down Jack Welch, his legendary predecessor, who infamously boasted about GE's ability to shift jobs overseas at a moment's notice. "Ideally, you'd have every plant you own on a barge to move with currencies and changes in the economy," Welch said in 1998.

It took me a while to get an interview with Immelt, who became more wary of such requests after the *New York Times* published a piece breaking down GE's minuscule annual tax payments. The company's army of lawyers and tax advisers had used every loophole to ensure that GE paid a grand total of zero federal taxes on its $5.1 billion of U.S. profit in 2010.[11] The company even claimed a rebate from the Internal Revenue Service. That's what a thousand-strong tax department can do for its employer.

As the chairman of Barack Obama's council on jobs and competitiveness, which had been set up with some fanfare after the Democratic Party's stinging defeat in the 2010 congressional elections, Immelt was also a juicy target for allegations of double standards. The launch of the council was timed to coincide with Obama's 2011 State of the Union address in which he unveiled the goal of "Winning the Future." Obama put forward a relatively modest short-term agenda as a down payment on a much more ambitious drive to ensure America would once again "outeducate and outinnovate" the world.

By the time I spoke to Immelt it was clear that the bulk of Obama's agenda was at best likely to gather dust until his second term began in 2013—assuming, of course, that he was reelected. Immelt took my question on why it had stalled as a cue to strike out at Washington in general. He reserved a particular barb for economists. "If you even whisper the phrase 'industrial policy' in Washington, D.C., today then, within twenty-four hours, you will be stoned to death," he said. "I mean, China is out there eating lunch out every day but we still won't challenge the orthodoxy."

Immelt described to me his routine two-hour conference call with GE's executives around the world in which he gets feedback about multiplying growth opportunities all over the place except from America (and presumably Europe). Of the world's ten largest airlines, all of which are key potential customers for GE's aviation unit, only one—Southwest—is American. The same story repeats itself in sector after sector. Like any other company, GE goes to where its customers are. None of the wind turbines GE produces in its plant in Greenville, North Carolina, are sold in America. "Every time I speak to my colleagues, I am reminded of how much the U.S. economy has decoupled from the world," said Immelt. "We are no longer the only act in town."

By now hard to get off topic, Immelt described how in his view the mind-sets of America's business leadership and its political classes had swapped places since America's golden decades after World War II. In those days, U.S. chief executives rarely bothered to leave American shores. America's booming middle classes provided the overwhelming source of their revenue growth. Washington's policy elites, on the other hand, were busy containing and rolling back communism around the world. They traveled all the time. The shoe was now on the other foot. "We [business leaders] spend half our lives flying around the world because that is where the action is," said Immelt. "If you look at Washington some people don't even have passports. Do I think Washington gets how fast and far America's role is shrinking in the world? Doesn't seem like it to me."

Immelt reeled off the almost metronomically familiar reforms the United States needed to make, such as investing more in infrastructure and scientific education, as was in Obama's State of the Union speech. Then he went a step further and issued an attack on the conventional wisdom in Obama's Washington. "It is okay not to believe in industrial policy when you are the only player on the world stage," Immelt said. "But when your biggest competitor is China then you are confronted with industrial policy on steroids. . . . Should you continue in the belief that industrial policy is only for the weak? I guess we'll find out the answer in the next ten years."

Among Immelt's implicit targets were economists such as Lawrence Summers, who was Obama's senior economic adviser during 2009 and 2010 and who has always been impatient with any hint of industrial policy. But Immelt could have meant any number of others. To judge by the strength of Immelt's feelings, the less tutored ones should tread warily when they next meet him. "I read all of these Washington reports and think tank studies that say, Let the market work, except that the guys who are writing the books in China think it's f***ing bullshit: 'Pease let those guys in Washington, D.C., keep reading those books. Things are going just fine.'"

By the standards of most modern-day business leaders, Immelt's words were forceful, even if they seem to clash with what Immelt himself has done at GE. In spite of disowning his predecessor's unsentimental approach to the U.S. labor force, Immelt has only extended the globalization of GE that Welch had begun. More than half of GE's workforce of nearly three hundred thousand are now employed outside of America—up from a third when Immelt took over in 2001. Immelt argues that he has had little choice. "I would like nothing more than to create more jobs in America," he said. "But we have to pay attention to where the markets are."

Immelt's views are readily echoed across the most high-tech sectors of America's economy. Among these perhaps the most persistent is Andy Grove, the legendary former chief executive of Intel, which, with the exception of IBM, is America's most enduringly successful high-tech company. Grove, too, along with his successor Craig Barrett, has developed cold feet on free trade. Grove believes America must abandon what he caricatured as the attitude of "potato chips, computer chips. What's the difference?" Another commentator lampooned it as, "We will buy your cars and you will buy our poetry."[12]

Pointing out that Foxconn, the Chinese computer and mobile phone manufacturer, employs more people than Apple, Dell, Microsoft, Cisco, Intel, and Hewlett-Packard combined, Grove had argued in an article in *Bloomberg Businessweek*[13] that America's policy elites were blind to the virtues of a strong middle-class economy. "Our fundamental economic beliefs, which we have elevated from a conviction based on observation to an unquestioned truism, is that the free market is the best of all economic systems—the freer the better," wrote Grove. Such a belief was flawed, he believed. America needed to take radical action, including imposing a tax on the offshoring of U.S. jobs, to re-create a decent job market at home. Left to its own devices the market would continue its relentless march eastward. "If what I am suggesting sounds protectionist so be it," wrote Grove.

When I caught up with Grove, he seemed even gloomier. He reeled off a list of clean energy companies that had moved their manufacturing operations to Asia. Without domestic plants, U.S.-headquartered companies turn into mere wholesalers, said Grove.

The company's ability to innovate tends to shift to the place where it is making its products. At the Defense Advanced Research Projects Agency (DARPA), the Pentagon R&D unit that is responsible for much of what has powered Silicon valley, there is a saying: "To innovate, you must make."

Later in the book we will look at the continually rumbling debate about how to sustain, or revive, America's global lead in innovation, a debate so conflicted it often fails to agree on how to define "innovation." Grove's definition bears his own imprint as an engineer, a scientist, and a manufacturer—all types that think very differently than economists. Engineers are fond of pointing out that China's Politburo Standing Committee is dominated by engineers (seven out of nine members), almost nobody can name an engineer in the Obama administration. "This debate is too important to leave to the economists," Grove said. "We are in the middle of a titanic economic war for global supremacy. We shouldn't be carrying on as though it's business as usual."

That titanic struggle may already be lost. China is set to overtake the U.S. economy as soon as 2020, according to the latest projections. In truth, the precise date when that will happen is a distraction. What counts is the momentum. On this, history offers no guide to what America should do. But it may offer a relevant parable. In his widely cited book *The Weary Titan*, which looks at the British debate around 1900 as it was dawning on Britain's elites that she was being outstripped by the United States and Germany, Aaron Friedberg, the Princeton scholar, found some unsettling parallels.

Whether it was chemicals and metallurgy in Bismarck's Germany or the invention of electricity and the internal combustion engine in the United States, Britain was being left behind. Should Britain abandon its long-standing, but still lonely, regime of free trade? Ought it to establish a German-style network of vocational schools to reinstill a native proficiency in science and engineering? Or should it trim its sails to a world where she may no longer be first among equals?

This intensive debate, which lasted from 1895 to 1905, concluded with a period of budget cutting after the draining costs of the humiliating Boer war in South Africa. There are very clear echoes in today's marathon fiscal debate in Washington following America's equally costly and controversial wars in Iraq and Afghanistan. It may be what accounts for the noteworthy reemergence (and reprinting) of Friedberg's 1988 doctoral thesis. "The [British] debate seemed to have changed remarkably few minds," wrote Friedberg. "Britain was fortunate in the trials ahead to have more advanced friends on whom it could rely."

Like the United States today, Britain under the Conservative prime ministership of Arthur Balfour debated what to do about the seemingly inexorable drift of industrial capacity elsewhere. The prime minister's reckoning contained what qualified as an Edwardian-style dig at the economics profession. "I am a free trader," wrote Balfour. "[But] it is irrational to suppose that what is good for the wealth-producing capacity of the world may necessarily be good for each particular state."[14]

By the standard measures, Britain's total wealth and "diffused well-being" were greater than ever. Yet the "commercial optimists" may well be missing the currents beneath the surface, he wrote. Britain was being overtaken on mechanics, chemistry, steel, and even shipbuilding. "The ocean we are navigating is smooth enough," Balfour continued. "But where are we being driven by its tides? Does either theory or experience provide any consolatory answer to this question?"

At the end of 2010 Larry Summers gave a farewell speech[15] as he left the White House to resume academic life at Harvard. The outgoing chief architect of Obama's economic policy expressed optimism about America's ability to remain the world's top dog. I pay a great deal of attention to what Summers thinks. There are few better bellwethers of America's economic worldview.

Today's "declinists" were wrong, he argued. These were the "self-denying prophets" of American doom who had kept the republic on its toes for more than two centuries. Examples included the late-1950s panic that the Soviet Union was pulling ahead of the United States. Another was the so-called Japanic of the late 1980s in which the Cold War was declared over and Japan and Germany had won. Each forecast looked comically wrong in retrospect.

America had always had its share of Cassandras. But if it could sort out its politics the economy would be fine. "Predictions of America's decline are as old as the republic," Summers said in the speech. "I submit to you that as long as we're worried about the future, the future will be better. We have our challenges. But we also have the most flexible, dynamic, entrepreneurial society the world has ever seen."

This was Summers's version of Winston Churchill's oft-quoted observation that "America will always do the right thing after exhausting all the alternatives." In addition, Summers was also conveying his variant on American exceptionalism, the idea that the United States is uniquely endowed to excel. Churchill never went that far. But his fellow Britons radiated a timeless optimism about their place in the sun.

"The number one country is always the most complacent,"[16] says Paul Romer, another renowned economist, but one who is more unorthodox than many. "America is a bit like a company," he said. "As a start-up, it was nimble and sharp. Then it grew into a behemoth that was able to dominate and shape the world. Now America is so stuck in its habits that it gets harder and harder to change its way of doing things."

Having been Larry Summers's speechwriter when he was treasury secretary during the late stages of the Clinton administration, I know that I lack anything close to an ability to take him on in an economic argument. Summers's intellectual reputation is richly deserved. So, too, is his reputation for ebullient self-confidence. Although he has trained himself to be less combative in his conversational style—and with some success—he still knows he is the smartest person in the room.

Yet for all his acuity Summers has got a lot wrong. Take the collapse of the U.S. property bubble in 2007, which key actors such as Alan Greenspan and Ben Bernanke, who replaced Greenspan as chairman of the Federal Reserve in 2006, wholly failed to anticipate. Contrary to what Dick Cheney, the outgoing vice president said in January 2009 ("nobody saw it coming"), many were aware of the impending bust and had issued repeated warnings. "They weren't asleep at the wheel," said Barney Frank, a senior Democratic congressman. "They took us over the cliff with their eyes wide open."[17]

Among these were Raghuram Rajan, the Chicago professor and former chief economist at the International Monetary Fund. Rajan delivered a paper, "Has Financial Development Made the World Riskier?," at Jackson Hole in 2005 in which his clear—and prescient—answer to the question he posed was yes. Both Greenspan and Summers were sitting in the audience. Rajan highlighted the risk that complex derivatives would trigger a systemic crisis. He was dismissed as an antimarket Luddite. Speaking afterward Summers said that he found "the basic, slightly lead-eyed premise of [Mr. Rajan's] paper to be misguided."

Another was Elizabeth Warren, the Harvard law professor, whom President Obama was powerless to make head of the fledgling consumer finance regulatory agency in 2011 because he knew Republicans would block her nomination. Warren has a taste for lampooning "the best and the brightest." Much like the Ivy League brains who took America into Vietnam, today's leading intellectual lights have led America into an economic quagmire, in her view. "People talk about the meltdown as though it was some kind of once-in-a-century natural disaster, like a tsunami or a flood," Warren said to me. "It wasn't a natural disaster. The bubble was man-made."

As a scholar of bankruptcy, Warren had spent years ringing the alarm bell about the mounting level of U.S. credit card debt, which, between 1980 and 2010, had almost quadrupled to 14 percent of the average American household's income—and that was just the monthly interest. Warren also blew the whistle on its corollary, America's plummeting rate of household savings, which dipped into once unimaginable negative territory during the bubble of the "aughties." "We kept saying, 'The middle class is in crisis. Most of our consumers are going to go bankrupt. They can't afford to own what they own,'" she said. "None of the important people were listening, or if they were listening they didn't agree."

As late as 2005, when the collapse of the subprime bubble was only eighteen months away, Greenspan publicly declined to use the Federal Reserve's authority to regulate the subprime mortgage market. It was a decision upheld by Bernanke until after the bubble collapsed. These were the sins of omission. But there were also sins of commission. Perhaps most egregiously, both Greenspan and Summers were instrumental, in 2000, in helping pass a law that deprived Washington of the ability to regulate most financial derivatives. Among the over-the-counter derivatives that were excluded from regulation was the credit default swap, the mother of all financial weapons of mass destruction and the instrument by which Wall Street both enriched itself and brought the rest of America to its knees.

Some, including Brooksley Born, who headed the Commodity Futures Trading Commission, issued loud warnings in the late 1990s about the consequences of failing to regulate financial derivatives. Her warnings were publicly slapped down by both Summers and Greenspan. To be in favor of regulation was to be against innovation, they argued. I remember that well because I was the speechwriter who pulled together* the address Summers gave in November 2000 in which he called on Congress to pass the blandly named Commodity Futures Modernization Act. The bill, which was passed a few weeks later, essentially gutted Washington of the power to regulate derivatives.

---

*The words in Summers's speeches were usually his own. He would often dictate large chunks of what he wanted to say, which I would then transcribe. On the occasions he extemporized at length only minor editing was required.

Today its assumptions sound dramatically misplaced. First Summers explained why America was booming. "These are prosperous times for America," he told the Securities Industry Association, one of Wall Street's biggest lobby groups. "I am convinced that an important part of the credit ... goes to the unparalleled strength and dynamism of our financial markets." Summers then listed Wall Street's key attributes. "No other financial market is so open to foreign competition or so quick to innovate, whether it be in the area of securitization, financial derivatives, high-yield debt, or equity finance."

He then warned that we should all be on our guard against "toxic" risks in the market. The solution was for the government to get even more out of the way than it already had. Washington should leave financial derivatives to the experts. "As I have stated before, it is the private sector, not the public sector, that is in the best position to provide effective supervision," Summers said. "Creditors have more knowledge of their counterparts, more skill in evaluating risk, and greater incentives than any public regulator will ever have."

Summers's assumptions proved to be very mistaken. To be fair he gave many speeches urging the United States to continue achieving federal budget surpluses during the good times so that it had firepower to act during the bad—sound advice that was fatefully ignored by the Bush administration. On this, Summers looks good in hindsight. Clinton bequeathed to George W. Bush a larger fiscal surplus than any in U.S. history before or since. It was rapidly wasted. But on many other questions Summers now looks to have been on the wrong side of history.

After the meltdown, I began to detect what might have been a very different Summers from the ebullient proselytizer for deregulation we saw in the late 1990s. Although still skeptical of regulation, he was in favor of strong public action to counter the fallout. "The risk of doing too much is outweighed by the risk of doing too little," he said in the early months of the Obama administration. "Americans have learned that it is not okay to love your country and to hate your government." In the months before Obama's election, Summers had also written in the *Financial Times* of his concerns about the "anxious middle," which he worried was increasingly indebted, insecure, and vulnerable to shock.

A few months after Summers left the White House I got on a plane to visit him in Boston where he now holds a prestigious chair at Harvard's Kennedy School of Government. Following his having escaped what he referred to as twenty-four-hour "looney tunes" in Washington, I wanted to see if he had acquired a different perspective. What I found was a much more philosophical, and conflicted, Summers than I had anticipated. But I found little evidence his worldview had altered radically.

On the one hand, the American middle class was in crisis, he said. On the other, it had never had it so good. Politics was "vastly less corrupt" than it used to be. Yet rent seeking by special interests in Washington had never been more profitable. America's innovative ingenuity was in robust health. But most of America's workforce was unlikely to benefit much.

"Go to any place with sales, walk into any dealership, and ask them what fractions of the cars are sold by the best twenty percent of their salespeople," he said. "The answer is eighty percent." On strictly economic grounds—as measured by productivity—America's growing inequality was a natural result of its underlying distribution of skills and aptitude. "What is happening is that in a world that is getting economically larger and where people have more choices, there's more and more pressure pulling pay toward productivity," Summers said. "People are being linked to the market more and more and it's turning out that since the eighty/twenty rule is true, things aren't that great for the eighty percent."

On top of these economic trends, there was a large and growing sociological problem with men—first they lost their jobs in manufacturing and then in construction. Whether it was about the declining "honor and dignity" of work or growing insecurity in whatever jobs they had, men, for some reason seemed far worse affected than women. "The people who think if only we could bring back manufacturing all would be well are deeply confused," Summers said. "The truth is that a reasonable amount of manufacturing will come back but it won't involve jobs."

There was not much else that could obviously be done to sort out this growing conundrum. Even if American politics was in better shape and able to take action to shore up the "anxious middle," it was not clear whether spending more on labor force skills, for example, would get the desired results. "Am I in favour of community colleges?" he asked. "Yes. Do I think that in an economy that transfers a trillion dollars to the top ten percent every year that it would be desirable to spend more on community colleges? Yes. It would probably help at the margins. But I am not sure how efficacious it would be until we have seen the end of this recession." Summers was talking almost eighteen months after he and his colleagues in the Obama administration had declared the recession over.

Nor was Summers quite so sure how bad things were for American middle classes; he seemed of two minds on this as well. He said he was still concerned about the future of America's anxious middle but he was unsure whether there was much that could easily be done about its stagnating earnings. The problem had also been overstated, he said. Americans today had iPhones, flat-screen TVs, and other technologies that had been far beyond their budgets in 1973. Most consumer goods were far cheaper in relative terms than they ever had been. Whatever problems the middle class was experiencing, the remedies were not within easy reach. "There are good things we can do at the margins," he said. "But on a lot of this, I just don't know."

It was the increasingly shrill looney tunes tone of American politics that most troubled Summers. Life in Washington looked destined to get only worse. Even here, however, Summers admitted to being agnostic about what was driving the polarization of U.S. politics. Was it the public's growing cynicism about the power of business lobbies in Washington, D.C., who were extracting ever greater rents from the federal system "at a shockingly low cost"? Or was it the increasing tyranny of public opinion that had been squeezing decision makers of whatever leeway they had to take unpopular but necessary decisions? Perhaps it was both. "Either we need to take Washington back from the corrupt politicians, or Washington has become corrupt because we've taken it back from the politicians," Summers said chuckling. "There's something to both those views."

Compared to Alan Greenspan and Robert Rubin, the other two in the trio that *Time* magazine memorably dubbed "the Committee to Save the World" in a 1999 cover story, Summers is much more modest than he was beforehand. Rubin, who was Summers's predecessor as treasury secretary, earned $126 million from Citibank after he left Washington, having pushed through the abolition of the Glass-Steagall Act, which had kept deposit-taking banks separate from investment banks since the 1930s. This enabled Citibank to merge with Travelers and sharply inflate its bottom line. In spite of being the chief architect, and one of the biggest beneficiaries, of financial deregulation, Rubin has not let slip a hint of self-doubt for the decisions he made. That has held true even after Citibank went bankrupt in 2008 when he was still a senior director (having briefly been chairman).

Greenspan, meanwhile, confessed to a sense of "shock" in 2008 at the failure of the "efficient market hypothesis." The theory had not worked as well in practice as he had expected, he conceded in a hearing on Capitol Hill. Three years later, in an article for the *Financial Times*,[18] Greenspan abruptly recanted his recantation. We should not allow the 2008 crisis to panic us into actually *regulating*, he argued. In what may go down as one of the most myopic subclauses in history, Greenspan then said that, "with a few notable exceptions," deregulated financial markets always tended to work well. Greenspan might perhaps have added that, with one or two breathers, the twentieth century was free of world wars.

By these standards Summers was self-doubting. But our conversation left me feeling uneasy. America had great challenges.

Yet there was nothing to either suggest that it would meet those challenges or know what to do if it tried. In a curious way, Summers's passivity reminded me of Arthur Balfour, who wondered whether "either theory or experience could provide any consolatory answers" to his question on how his country should respond to the rise of others. Free trade theory taught Balfour that economics was not a zero-sum game. Nations do not compete. But he also sensed that his country was losing power in tandem with its draining industrial capacity. He concluded there was not much he could do about it.

I asked Summers whether he now thought America was in competition with other countries. Here, too, he gave signs of partial rethinking. Strictly speaking, nations don't compete, he said. "It's not like GM and Ford, or Pepsi and Coke. If more people become literate around the world that's good for America, not bad." But if political elites think their nation is in competition with others, then that can have a big impact on how they act. "It's a shocking fact about human nature that even the most sophisticated and high-quality and well-trained athletes run faster if someone is pacing them," he said. "It is true of horses and it is true of people. It makes sense, therefore, to think it is also true of societies."

Summers offered no forecast as to when or whether America would summon the resolve it would need to address the burgeoning question mark over its competitiveness, in whatever way one defines that. Some believe America needs another good crisis. Others shudder at the thought. But nobody, including Summers, believes they have the answers or even whether the question is entirely valid. "The answer is that I'm not really sure what I think about that," Summers said on several occasions and then with great felicity weighed up the competing explanations. Events and time have given Summers a degree of intellectual humility. Some still cling tenaciously to old nostrums. Whether you are a masterful synthesizer, like Summers, or a latent defiant, like Greenspan, the facts have changed. (Ben Bernanke seems to be in between.) With the changing facts has come a realization of the narrowing ability of America's best and brightest to shape the world around them. Summers acknowledges that. When he and his colleagues were confronted with global financial crises in the 1990s they had few doubts. Now that there may be a need for a Committee to Revive America, the world seems a lot more complicated.

In the foyer before you go onto the factory floor there is a large chart on the wall that no employee working at Marlin Wire could miss. Drew Greenblatt, the company's single-minded chief executive, calls it the "skills matrix." For a few it must seem more like the Doomsday Book.

The names of each of Marlin Wire's thirty employees are posted along the horizontal axis, while the vertical lists the twenty-eight separate skills each employee could learn. For each skill they possess, which can range from using an oxygen acetylene torch to milling (surfacing) electrodes, the employee gets up to five points. Some of them are clearly possessed by the devil—their total points exceed a hundred. Others have fewer than ten. "Yeah, I would be worried about my future if I was him," said Greenblatt pointing to someone with five points against his name.

The exercise sounds brutal. But it is also realistic. Basic skills are no longer enough to keep you in a decent job in America. You have to keep climbing the skills ladder. Marlin Wire, which makes precision steel-wire baskets for the companies Honeywell, Genentech, Novartis, and others, is based on an estate in an otherwise nearly forgotten industrial outpost of Baltimore. Many of the other buildings look unoccupied. Tall grass has broken through cracks in its concrete entry road. But Marlin Wire's small corner is booming.

Greenblatt, who is a staunch Republican and who has testified several times on Capitol Hill about the difficulties facing small business owners, admits that his obsession is robots. The more he can substitute technology for employees, the better he can control rising costs. A stocky man with a friendly laugh, Greenblatt listed the transaction costs just of doing the paperwork for each employee—their health insurance, retirement funds, IRA returns, and many more. He then added the cost of workers' compensation insurance, which amounts to 4 percent of their salary, and it added up to a tidy sum, enough to hire three to five more employees.

"Think about it. That's ten percent of my workforce that I'm not hiring," said Greenblatt. "And that's just the cost of the paperwork. I'm not even complaining about health care premiums." Greenblatt then marched me across the factory floor to a robot in the middle of the room. He explained what it could do. "We paid $700,000 for this," he said gesturing proudly at a large glass and steel processor. It could create 431 wire rings a minute. I did not dare ask how many people used to be employed to weld rings. "It is worth every dime," he said.

In fact, Marlin Wire's head count had expanded since Greenblatt bought it in 1998. Its output had multiplied and by 2011 it was in its fifth consecutive year of profit. The big difference was that most of the employees Greenblatt inherited had low skills. Now a quarter had postgraduate degrees, mostly in manufacturing design. And most of the rest had taken Greenblatt's hint and were trying to improve their scores on the skills matrix chart. "When I took this over, there were a lot of men on the shop floor with big biceps," said Greenblatt. "Now it's robots and people with skills."

The march of the robot would probably have continued at the same pace even without Greenblatt's expensive paperwork. But the nonwage cost of hiring full-time employees in the United States is starting to touch European levels. Perhaps uncoincidentally, the average duration of unemployment in the United States is also Europeanizing. Which means that employers are increasingly moving in one of two directions. One group, typified by the big box retailers, keeps most of its labor force casualized to avoid the overheads that come with hiring full-time employees.

The other large category of employers, which includes America's more competitive manufacturers, are aiming for fewer and fewer employees, who, in turn, will need to have increasingly impressive qualifications. Unlike in parts of Europe, notably Germany but also the Scandanavian countries, there will be precious few incentives for American manufacturers to be labor-intensive. "The system here screams at you: Don't hire more people—it's really, really expensive," said Greenblatt. "Every time I think of hiring someone I think, 'I wonder if a robot can do that.' "

In its stark and widely read 2011 report on the future of work in America, McKinsey reported that more than half of American employers it had surveyed said they planned to move more into part-time, casualized hiring in the next few years—on top of the large wave that has occurred in the past ten. Between 2000 and 2009 America lost 5 million manufacturing jobs and it gained nearly 4 million jobs in health care. Even under its "positive scenario" over the following decade, McKinsey stated there would be zero net growth in manufacturing jobs. The neutral and negative scenarios showed further decline. It urged people without college degrees to think about becoming "welders, nutritionists and nursing aides."

Even if America were able to return in the next few years to the annual growth rates it achieved before 2008—a prospect McKinsey treated with skepticism, given how long it takes to recover from a "balance sheet" recession—this would be insufficient to create new full-time jobs. America's labor problem was structural. In addition to weakness of demand in the U.S. economy, there was also a growing supply-side problem—a shortage in skills.

In other words, the conventional approach of priming demand when the economy is contracting and managing demand when the economy is booming is no longer sufficient to return to full employment. The labor market must first be cured. "High skill. High share. High spark. High speed. It's a recipe for success for the U.S. economy," McKinsey concluded. "Yet if the United States [continues to] allow job creation to be merely a by-product of other policy choices—rather than a focused, high priority in its own right—then jobless recoveries will indeed become the new normal."

There can be no better illustration of McKinsey's worryingly plausible "new normal" than what remains of America's incredibly lean steel sector. The last steel mill I visited was in 2005 in the province of Jharkhand in eastern India. In some respects, the Nucor mill in North Carolina reminded me of that. Each converted volcanic quantities of molten lava into shiny steel plates and ingots. Both put on a flickering orange *son et lumière* from their hulking satanic furnaces. And both feed the same world market.

Yet there was one key difference: the size of the labor force. As I toured Nucor's plate mill it was sometimes hard to spot human beings. In India, I could have been walking through a busy market. Nucor employs just four hundred people at its Hertford mill, which sits in a heavily forested part of North Carolina near the border with Virginia. With more than one hundred times as many employees, Tata Steel's plant in Jamshedpur made only three times as much steel as Hertford (about 5 million tons). That means that Nucor, which is one of only two remaining large U.S. steel companies, produces more than thirty times as much steel for each of its employees as its Indian competitor.

And yet no matter how lean Nucor becomes America's share of world steel production continues to fall. With just 153,000 steelworkers, America produces 7 percent of world steel production.[19] Until the 1970s America was the largest producer in the world. China now accounts for more than 40 percent of global output. India is expected to rival China as a steel power within the next fifteen years.

This means that Nucor's employees, many of whom earn more than $100,000 a year, roughly two-thirds of it in profit sharing and team bonuses, will continue to think of ways of squeezing their numbers (or of getting more with the same numbers). That might be tough on the plant's surrounding area, which has suffered the closure of a Ford plant in nearby Norfolk, Virginia, and the bankruptcy of a local paper and pulp company. Other than a naval base Nucor is about the only good employer around.

From the safety of the pulpit—a control room overlooking the furnace, which is protected by heat-resistant glass—the mill goes from Dickensian to futuristic. The heavily tattooed crew seemed a little perturbed by my accent. Glancing periodically at a bank of computer screens, each monitoring some aspect of what was happening in the blinding furnace below us, Leonard "Lemonade" Mendes, the shift leader, explained that his earnings were almost entirely pegged to productivity. "Twenty years ago you would have had forty or fifty people on one shift," Lemonade shouted above the maddening clamor of the furnace siren. Now there were fifteen.

Those numbers dwindle through each of the five following stages of production, which stretch an unbroken mile through an increasingly cathedral-like hush. Amid the towering stacks of steel bars and sheets, and the beginning tracks of the railway line, the clearest thing you hear once you have reached the finishing department is the sound of your own footsteps. I never thought you could feel spiritual in a steel mill.

I visited Hertford because I wanted to meet Dan DiMicco, Nucor's fire-breathing chief executive. Although DiMicco is famously outspoken, particularly about Washington's alleged indifference to the hollowing out of U.S. manufacturing, he is surprisingly difficult to meet. One of the preconditions was that I visit one of Nucor's mills before talking to him. I am glad I did. It reminded me how much the modern economy still weighs.

The mill produces steel entirely from scrap metal. At its start there is a large yard where trucks and trains and even canal barges converge from across America's eastern seaboard to dump shredded cars, construction beams, factory shavings, and other scrap metal to be converted into steel. There is a world spot market for scrap metal and little is wasted. Nucor is now the largest recycler in America. Among other destinations, Hertford's final product goes into wind towers, rail cars, fuel tanks, and automated teller machines.

Watching this process reminded me that America still makes things. It also reminded me that however "weightless" America's cloud-based new economy might be the old one on the ground still consumes vast mountains of metal (Nucor also supplies steel to some of the energy-hungry data centers that companies such as Facebook maintain across the country). It is a point that DiMicco, whose company's slogan is "A Nation that makes and builds things," is fond of repeating. "Do these idiots think we can survive by pushing paper around?" he said more than once.

Interviewing DiMicco is not like talking to other chief executives. Unlike so many of his Fortune counterparts, DiMicco is an engineer rather than an MBA. In addition to the plain speaking, DiMicco's appearance is proudly blue collar. With his droopy mustache, New Jersey Italian accent, and a generous stomach overhanging his jeans, talking to DiMicco feels more like an encounter with James Gandolfini's Tony Soprano. They even talk alike. "You gotta identify the problem, or else you're just f★★★ing yourself," he said about America's manufacturing decline. The problem was China.

We were sitting at Nucor's headquarters in Charlotte, about a five hours' drive south of the Hertford mill, overlooking a green canopy of trees from his top-floor executive suite. DiMicco mentioned the people advising Obama and their connections to Wall Street. Then he mentioned the kinds of chief executives whom Obama likes to consult—those, such as Jeff Immelt of GE or James McNerney of Boeing, who are shifting more and more of their company's production offshore. Taking advice from them, said DiMicco, was like talking directly to Beijing.

"These multinationals don't speak for the American worker, or the American economy, they speak for China," he said. "They say, We don't just want you to come here, we want all your suppliers. Then it happens. And we're surprised when China eats our lunch." DiMicco held out his open palms and lifted his shoulders in mock exasparation. "I mean what the f★★★?"

Since he is a member of the Commerce Department's advisory council on manufacturing, DiMicco also has a chance to put his views to Obama and his people. His core point is that if you let the "bread and butter" commoditized manufacturing go, which is what has happened, the higher-value stuff begins to follow. With the high-end value innovation also goes. Although manufacturing now barely reaches double digits as a share of the U.S. economy, it accounts for almost three-quarters of private sector R&D spending in the United States.

At a meeting with Joe Biden, the vice president, in 2009, DiMicco and some colleagues urged him to become Obama's chief czar for manufacturing. "Biden just laughed at us, like we were making a joke or something," said DiMicco. "The guy actually thought we were joking," he repeated. Then, at a small lunch with Obama, DiMicco urged the president to spend more on infrastructure. China was spending $750 billion, he said. America was rusting. The president told DiMicco that he would love to but "we just can't afford it." DiMicco again showed me his open palms.

DiMicco later conceded that he might have been unfair to Immelt and McNerney, both of whom had developed more skeptical views of China than they once had. But he felt the United States remained a captive of "free trade ideology" in spite of all that has happened. China's currency manipulation, he said, had been allowed to persist unchecked under Obama. "I watch what that guy does rather than what he says," DiMicco said of Obama. "I mean free trade is nice but so is world peace. Here are how things work in the real world: antelopes get eaten by lions."

Attributing America's manufacturing jobs decline to Chinese mercantilism might be simplistic, even exaggerated. But it is a deeply held view across broad swathes of America. DiMicco's company gives it expression—"a nation that makes and builds things." It is a worldview that fits into neither Republican nor Democratic talking points. But it better captures popular sentiment than either. A lot of people believe America should be making more things. A lot of economists tell them they are missing the point. Which is catching up with which? "The food preparation industry cannot sustain a middle class," said DiMicco. "We need to have a skilled labor force. We need machinists and electricians."

I thought about the many counterarguments to what DiMicco was saying. I also detected in him a somewhat romantic view of how much sway Washington could have over deep-seated global and technological trends. Yet in listening to DiMicco despair about Wall Street's continuing grip on the mind-set in Washington, D.C., I found myself, like much of America, in sympathy with his tone. Some of the nation's best scientists were still getting snapped up by a taxpayer-bailed-out Wall Street, said DiMicco. Meanwhile, Wall Street was pouring large sums of cash into both party's election coffers. After all that had happened not much has changed. "We need to get back to making things and employing people to make things," DiMicco said, looking steadily more like a Soprano as the interview went on. "If we lose our capacity to innovate, then we're really f★★★ed."

2

Leave No Robot Behind

If a nation expects to be ignorant and free, in a state of civilization, it expects what never was and never will be.

Thomas Jefferson

THERE IS ROOM for only six passengers in the Beechcraft Premier I— one of the smallest yet one of the most sophisticated light jets in the world. Only highly qualified pilots are allowed to fly it alone. To master the Beechcraft's fly-by-wire controls, it helps to love engineering. It must be even better, as is the case with Dean Kamen, who was our solo pilot for the flight, to have a passion for physics. We were taking off from a small municipal airport in Frederick, Maryland, on a one-hour route to Manchester, New Hampshire, running the gauntlet through the most crowded air corridor in the world.

Fortunately Kamen, who is one of America's foremost inventors, and probably its wealthiest, is more than familiar with the aerial cross talk along America's eastern seaboard. The man who invented the iBot—a wheelchair that can walk up and down stairs—relishes his encounters with air traffic control. "We start with Frederick, then D.C., then Baltimore hands us over to Philadelphia, then New York, then Boston, and finally Manchester," said Kamen, after we had put on our headphones. "None of them will want us above forty thousand [feet]." Kamen's plan was to talk them into it.

Dressed in blue jeans and denim shirt Kamen looks about forty-five. Technically he is sixty-one. But as I glimpsed in the way he flies and from the decor of what one profiler described as his "Willy Wonka" home,[20] Kamen is still a teenager. His original passion is to invent things. Deka, Kamen's Manchester-based company, is working on a prosthetic limb for DARPA that people could learn to control by thought. The latest prototype, which would be meant initially for military veterans, was stowed in the plane's small underbelly. Potentially it would exceed the impact of the Segway, Kamen's self-balancing human transporter on which one occasionally sees airport police, and American urban tourists, whirring innocuously past. "The Segway is what made Dean famous," said a Deka engineer who was seated next to me. "But it is not his best invention."

In addition to the engineer and me, there was one other Deka employee on the flight and two of Kamen's friends, who would be staying at his hexagonal Westwind mansion for the weekend. On condition of keeping silent, we could tune in to the air traffic frequency in which Kamen was sparring with one air traffic control tower after another. They spoke to each other in an incomprehensible mix of latitudinal coordinates, Whiskeys, Tangos, and Foxtrots, and what could have been a forgotten dialect of Eskimo. As we took an unnervingly steep ascent, the *Star Wars* theme wafted back from the cockpit. "He always plays that on takeoff," said the engineer.

Kamen's second passion, and now his most time consuming, is to save America's public education system from itself. Through his annual FIRST world championship (For Inspiration and Recognition of Science and Technology), which is evolving into a kind of Super Bowl for self-confessed teenage geeks, Kamen is trying to trigger a cultural revolution in American education. His target is a K-12 system that by global standards no longer graduates large numbers of high school leavers with either an aptitude, or appetite, for science.

Kamen's enthusiasm for what the U.S. education system could become is matched only by his despair for how he sees it today. In a 2010 poll, a small majority of Americans revealed that they did not realize that humans and dinosaurs never coexisted.[21] Another showed that almost half of Americans thought the sun revolved around the earth. The United States now frequently falls below twenty in international school rankings for math and sciences, and the country is alarmingly low on language proficiency measures. "We are becoming a stupid country," Kamen said to me later, "where the kind of thing that most people seem to care about is what I call the Stupid Bowl."

Most of America's "education billionaires," including Bill Gates, whom I interview later in this chapter, blame schools for the relative decline in America's educational performance. Their solutions are rendered in the dry bullet points of MBA-speak and are focused chiefly on bringing about a managerial overhaul of education. For Dean Kamen, who comes from a Jewish New York background, the problem goes deeper. Declining schools are one facet of what he sees as the broader atrophying of the American mind-set. Kamen's language is anything but dry. He can point to a growing list of heavyweight sponsors, such as Boeing, NASA, Siemens, DARPA, and Kleiner Perkins, Silicon Valley's biggest venture capital firm, who share his fears about the vanishing of a skilled U.S. middle class.

Something of a rock star of robotics, and an evangelist of engineering, Kamen has a following that swells year by year. A couple of weeks earlier I attended Kamen's 2011 FIRST championships at the gigantic Edward Jones Dome in downtown St. Louis, Missouri. More than 60,000 mostly schoolchildren (also teachers and a large number of parents) had turned up to pit each team's self-designed robots against others in various contests. Each school team, which came from every state in the United States and from as far as China, Argentina, Britain, India, and New Zealand, had their own mascot name and uniform. Amid the thicket of Viking helmets, green Mohican wigs, cowboy hats, and red devil's horns you could read off the team names Say Watt?, Lord of the Screws, Semper Fi, and Beasty Bots.

Kamen had persuaded the superstar rapper Zuper Blahq, otherwise known as will.i.am, to give a concert at the end of the championship. Blahq, who wrote the viral 2008 "Yes We Can" rap song that was taken from Obama's speeches, turned out to be something of a geek himself. "My music takes me all over the world," he told the children at an event the day before he gave his concert. "What I see is that so many other countries are getting suited and booted for the future. When I compare them to what is happening in America it gets me depressed." The rap star, who personally footed most of the $1.1 million bill to stage the concert, said that FIRST had rekindled his hope in America's future. "Looking at bright and skilled students like you, I wouldn't miss this for the world," he said.

The idea of recruiting will.i.am had struck Kamen when he watched the rap star's thirty-second appearance during a break in the 2011 Super Bowl. Although I am usually impervious to any whiff of religious-camp revival, there was an infectious energy to the FIRST championship. Among the school teams was an African-American group in which one of the teenage girls had taken a knife in her abdomen after she told members of her gang she would be designing a robot for the next few months. Beneath the cheering and team chanting every child was committed.

"When I talk to classes I tell the kids to look to their left and to their right," says Woodie Flowers, a professor of mechanical engineering at the Massachusetts Institute of Technology and a FIRST board member. "Then I tell them that each of their neighbours will lose their jobs to Watson [the IBM supercomputer that can beat humans at *Jeopardy,* the nation's favorite quiz show]," he said. "Watson can do most things better than humans. It can even understand sarcasm."★ Behind Flowers was the hive of mini-arenas ("pits") on the vast Dome floor, where teams of robots competed

---

★Given my own nationality, and profession, this had been a source of nagging concern.

to see which would pick up the most hoops and deposit them on elevated pegs. Flowers pointed to the look of utter absorption on the kids' faces. "Building a robot gives them a real, worthwhile sense of self-esteem," he said. "They can start to imagine a very different kind of future."

Periodically, Kamen threaded through the pits with visitors such as John Doerr, Silicon Valley's biggest venture capitalist, and had animated conversations with the players. In a talk to the parents, Doerr described the event as "the rock concert of innovation." Many of the children wanted Kamen to autograph their shirts. The impression was of a suppressed yelp of liberation by science-minded teenagers against the world of cheerleading and high school football around them. "FIRST gives these kids an antidote to all the pressures in the other direction," Kamen said to me after the event. "We live in a society where kids follow idols like Britney Spears and watch reality TV shows that make a spectator sport out of humiliating people. We are trying to fight back." In spite of FIRST's success—it started with just a handful of teams twenty years ago—Kamen knows that at one level he is involved in a battle of educational cults. The other cults are much bigger.

In terms of resources, one of the biggest rivals to STEM (Science, Technology, Engineering, and Mathematics) education is the sporting cult. At the relatively prosperous Round Rock school district I visited in Texas in early 2011, Jesus H. Chavez, its wonderfully named superintendent of education, explained why the state's budget cuts were leaving high school sports, particularly football, relatively unscathed. "The families around here worship football," said Chavez, a soft-spoken man whom I guessed would prefer a good game of chess, "We have to respect what the parents want." Chavez was too tactful to add that in most schools the athletics director gets paid a lot more than the director of arts. According to the *Austin American-Statesman* the average salary for a high school sports coach in Texas is $73,000, versus $42,000 for a teacher in any other field at the same grade.[22]

In many schools the athletics director is paid more than the principal. In some schools the coach goes on to be the principal. "Their salaries don't come at the expense of other teachers," Chavez was keen to underline. When a team advances in the playoffs, the district gets more money. In the plush and sturdy environs of suburban Texas, Kamen's rival looks well entrenched. Kamen told me that at many of the thousands of schools that now field a FIRST robotics team, the principal refused to pay $3,000 for their team's assembly kit. Most would think twice before cutting sports coaching positions. "It is what it is," said Dr. Phil Warrick, principal of Round Rock High, about football's untouchable status. "We have a saying at this school: 'Don't pass, don't play.' "

Doerr, whose investments over the years helped create Sun Microsystems, Google, and Amazon, laid it out statistically. Of the 4 million students entering America's school system in 2011, he said, just 70,000 would graduate in engineering. "Football isn't a career. Using your brain is a career," said Doerr. "Less than one percent of kids who win athletics scholarships to college go professional." In contrast, kids who had competed in the FIRST championships were twice as likely as other Americans to graduate from college with a degree in a STEM subject.

Looming even larger than football is what Kamen describes as the excessive cult of self-esteem in American homes and schools. Some have dubbed it the "good job" approach to parenting and teaching. The proportion of teenagers who check the box "I think I am a special person" versus those who check "I am no better and no worse than anybody else" has gone off the charts since the 1980s, according to Jean Twenge, an educational psychologist at the University of San Diego. And the incidence of narcissistic personality disorder—delusional levels of self-esteem—among American students has more than doubled. "In America today, there are few values more fiercely held than the importance of self-admiration,"[23] wrote Twenge, who is also coauthor of the book *The Narcissism Epidemic.*

More than a quarter of American students drop out of high school. Many of the rest present a different kind of challenge. Teachers avoid issuing verbal reprimands for errant behavior (to avoid disciplinary action). Parents remonstrate with teachers if their kids get C grades. And every child gets to win some trophy or other at school prize day ("effort" and "punctuality" are my favorite perennials). So sheltered have American middle-class teenagers become that the deans of small American colleges have recently begun using the phrase "tea cups" about incoming freshmen.★ The shock of moving from the high school world of Lake Wobegon, where everyone is above average, to a world that can dispense failing grades makes them fragile. As Wendy Mogel, a child parenting expert, puts it, at high school every child "is either learning-disabled, gifted, or both. There's no curve left, no average."[24]

It is little wonder that almost half of America's students fail to complete their college degree in the allotted time. Almost a third drop out and nearly half of those taking four-year college degrees fail to complete in the allotted time. Parents also find it harder these days to let go of their kids once they reach university age. In an attempt to stem the tide of "helicopter parenting," the University of Chicago recently created a bagpipe processional on opening day to lead the parents away from their children. At the University of Vermont "parent bouncers" are hired to keep the lingerers off campus. "By trying so hard to provide the perfectly happy childhood, we're just making it harder for our kids to actually grow up," says Lori Gottlieb, a psychologist who writes about education.[25]

At Kamen's FIRST championships, there is no prize for runner-up. Only one team gets to win each competition. And the spirit is

---

★At the induction meeting for its 2011 summer intern program, State Department officials in Washington were stunned to hear what the students wanted. "We don't like to be criticized," said one. "It is really motivating to get praise." All the others assented. This exchange was related to me by one of the program's organizers. "I could not believe what we had just heard," said the State Department official. "To say upfront, 'Please don't criticize me'—I've literally never come across this before."

channeled toward a "rational self-esteem" that comes from figuring out how to build an agile machine that can handle objects with rapid precision. "We tell kids at FIRST that nobody can take away their passion for knowledge—they should feed that with everything they have," said Kamen.

If you stand back and compare America's reality to the dramatic changes advocated by Kamen and his supporters, some may believe their task is hopeless. But there is something about Kamen—a mix of restless energy and an almost childlike optimism about technology— that achieves unlikely things. To wander around Kamen's self-designed home is to leaf through the mind of a very American inventor. It reflects Kamen's personality—childlike, impatient, nostalgic, brilliant. Much of it is cluttered with electronic memorabilia. There are neon Coke signs, 1950s jukeboxes, and flashing slot machines. Like so many others, Kamen seems to yearn for the era of midcentury American optimism.

Most of Kamen's wind-powered home, which is hidden from the road on a small hill surrounded by pine trees, serves as a museum to the industrial age. Its entire open-plan shape—from the hexagonal base via its spiral staircases to a miniature cupola-topped observation room at its summit—pays homage to the exhibits inside. At its center, and cutting through two floors, sits a hulking and beautifully polished twenty-five-ton London steamship engine once owned by Henry Ford.

On one of the walls hangs a row of small portraits painted by Kamen's father. They start with Francis Bacon, the Elizabethan philosopher-scientist, then move on to Newton and Descartes, and run all the way to Edison and Einstein. These are Kamen's heroes. In the basement, beneath all the toys and artifacts and next to the hangar where Kamen keeps his two helicopters, is the atelier, where he works on his next inventions, such as the Stirling engine-based system pump that he hopes will simultaneously be able to generate power and purify water. It is meant for villages in the developing world.

It is a home built by an American, an optimist and a scientist. It is the last place you expect to find pessimism. Yet even he is not immune. Perhaps this is the essence of what Kamen fears America is losing—the self-fulfilling energy that is born of naïveté. "We have become like the latter-day Romans," said Kamen. "We worship the gladiators and we have forgotten the architects and the philosophers." A decade ago that sentiment might have been confined to history professors at Yale or literary editors of highbrow periodicals. Yet in one form or another since around 2006 I have heard variations of it from Fortune 100 chief executives, U.S. military chiefs, senior government officials, and big Silicon Valley investors.

Few, even among America's crowded field of big education philanthropists, have as much experience at the coalface of education as Kamen. None share Kamen's passionate following (Bill Gates is too technocratic to lead a grassroots movement). But even Kamen sounded out of touch when I asked him about where his educational vision would lead. What jobs would all these scientifically minded students be going into? "It's always jobs, jobs, jobs. Americans should stop talking about jobs the whole time," Kamen said. "Was Edison looking for a job? If people set their sights on the gutter that is where they will probably end up." He added: "We need to focus on creating lifelong careers that are rewarding and sustainable—not 'jobs.'"

When we touched down in Kamen's jet at Manchester airport earlier that day, Kamen was smiling broadly. In spite of the threat of storms, unusually busy skies, and argumentative air traffic controllers, we had stayed above 40,000 feet and taken a direct route. As we were beginning our descent one of the engineers asked Kamen about the plane's design. Kamen explained some of the Beechcraft's wizardry and why it was such a delight to fly. Then he added, "A few years from now we'll have robots flying these planes."

When we landed, Kamen alighted the plane clutching a remote control. With the handheld device, he opened the door to his hangar, summoned a small towing device from within, elevated the plane's front wheel onto the towing platform, and swiftly maneuvered the plane into its parking place inside. Kamen had barely flinched a muscle. IBM's Watson may one day put every air traffic controller on the eastern seaboard out of a job. Watching Kamen twiddle his remote control, however, had left me dumbfounded. "A few years ago you would have put a lot of effort into that," said Kamen, as the hangar door closed behind us. "Now you can do it with your thumb."

Obama's big aim in his Winning the Future agenda was for America to "outeducate and outinnovate" the rest of the world. Everybody needed to pitch in. By 2020, Obama said, the United States would again lead the world in the ratio of graduates in the workforce. "We need to teach our kids that it's not just the winner of the Super Bowl who deserves to be celebrated, but the winner of the science fair," said the president. Obama built on the theme a year later in his fourth State of the Union address, "An America Built to Last." Dean Kamen certainly approved. Like Bush junior, Clinton, and Bush senior before him, Obama squarely diagnosed the problem. In just one generation, the United States had fallen from first to ninth in the proportion of its young people with graduate degrees, and it was still falling (in fact the United States ranks twelfth among all nations[26]). Parents, or their absence, should share much of the blame, said Obama.

Yet there is only a limited amount an American president can do about America's schools. With the exception of Switzerland, no other Western democracy diffuses power to the same degree as America. In addition to the separation of powers, the United States has a robust federal system. No single policy area is as decentralized as education. With fifty states and more than fifteen thousand elected school districts around the country, Washington in most years contributes less than a tenth of national spending on public education. That number also serves as a rough estimate of the degree of influence a U.S. president normally has over what happens in the nation's schools. "If you want to change education, you have to do it by demonstration," said Bill Gates, whose foundation has poured $3 billion into U.S. education since 2000. "You need to establish what is best practice and then work to spread that across the country."

With the support of Gates, Kamen, the Eli Broad Foundation, the Walton Foundation, Irwin Jacobs, and most of the other so-called education billionaires, Obama in 2009 launched Race to the Top—a very imaginative way of using what money the federal government had to persuade states to change their education policies. "Restoring American competitiveness is our North Star—it guides us in everything we do," Arne Duncan, Obama's highly rated education secretary, said in an interview with me at the time. "If America is to succeed, our schools cannot keep failing."

Duncan invited each state to compete for a pool of $5 billion. At a time of acute stringency in the capitals, state governments bent over backward to qualify. Although only a handful were rewarded, more than forty amended the way they run their schools in an effort to get a slice of the "competitive funds." At the heart of Duncan's reforms was the goal of weakening the teachers' unions and moving to merit-based pay—ending the "last in, first out" seniority culture and ushering in an unprecedented level of teacher evaluation. Given the campaign donations the Democrats get from the teachers' unions, it was a bold step for a Democratic president to take.

But Race to the Top won Obama approval across most of the opinion-forming classes, and especially with wealthy liberal philanthropists. People had read about New York's infamous "rubber room"[27] in which teachers who were fired for disciplinary reasons, including sexual harassment, continued to draw their salaries as they whiled away their tenure. Even the liberal think tanks were happy to see Obama take on the unions. Given all the polarization in Washington, it offered a rare instance of consensus. "The effect of Race to the Top has really been a very pleasant surprise," said Robin Chait, an education expert at the Center for American Progress, a liberal think tank. "Nobody would have expected that you could leverage so much change, so rapidly, with such a small pot of money."[28]

It may take years to find out whether Race to the Top gets the results it intends. To judge by the charter school movement, which has been heavily sponsored by the Gates Foundation and which strongly influenced Race to the Top, the outcome may be disappointing. The movement, which is publicly funded but is free of most of the bureaucratic requirements that plague public schools, set itself the same goals adopted by Duncan—to eliminate the grip of the teachers' unions over America's schools. Since the first charter school was launched in the mid-1990s, the movement has gone from strength to strength. There are now five thousand across America.

One key advantage is that many charter schools can avoid devoting as much time as their public school counterparts to "teaching to the test"—a scourge of teachers up and down the country since the No Child Left Behind Act was passed in 2002. George Bush's signature education reform was intended to lift standards by requiring constant tests of how much students had learned in math and English. In the process it has changed teachers' lives into an unending pursuit of numerical targets, in which data inquiry teams run down their checklists of which "learning goals" teachers have reached. Since the tests are the only thing by which schools are judged, teachers teach to the tests, an exercise in priming children to answer multiple-choice tests. Many consider it to be a travesty of what education should be about.

Nor are the results widely trusted. Bush's reform, which he took from a similar system he had passed when governor of Texas, offered no definition of the proficiency students were supposed to achieve. That subjective definition was left up to the states and cities. It remains an easy system to game. Between 2003 and 2007 proficiency scores in New York City, which was under the management of Joel Klein, now Rupert Murdoch's senior adviser, soared in most schools. But tests conducted by the National Assessment of Educational Progress showed that students' level of knowledge had not increased.[29] Similar manipulations took place in Tennessee, Washington, D.C., and elsewhere.

The act offers what Professor Diane Ravitch described as a "cramped and mechanistic" vision of education. Several years after Bush had pushed the reform in Texas, studies showed that children excelled at passing the reading tests. But they could not write in English. "They had mastered the art of filling in the bubbles of multiple choice tests but they could not express themselves," said Ravitch.

It has also made teaching a much less attractive career. More than a fifth of new teachers leave within three years.[30] Not only has creative possibility been squeezed from their timetables, their pension and health care benefits can no longer be taken for granted. In Phil Warrick's relatively prosperous district, which is a plush outpost of Austin, the Texas capital, a teacher with a PhD and thirty years' experience is paid $62,000 a year.[31]

In spite of their greater freedom from bureaucratic targets, most charter schools have failed to offer either an effective alternative to public schools or an attractive career for teachers. If the data is to be believed, charter schools have benefited from an extraordinarily overhyped media. "On average, charter middle schools that hold lotteries are neither more nor less successful than traditional public schools in improving student achievement, behavior, and school progress," according to an exhaustive 2010 study by Duncan's own department of education. "Participating schools had no significant impacts on math or reading test scores either a year or two years after students applied."

The report was published three months before the widely celebrated 2010 documentary *Waiting for Superman*, which honized the charter school movement. The documentary, which was praised by liberal and conservative critics alike, made no mention of the fact that charter schools had on average failed to outperform public schools. *Waiting for Superman* identified teachers' unions as the problem and charter schools as the solution, with not much else in between. It included very few skeptical voices.

Part of the movie's popularity among America's educated elites was its high-quality production values—and its skill at manipulating an audience's emotions. The film followed the stories of several inner-city children who had pinned their life's hopes on winning a place at a charter school by putting their names into the lottery. Unlike most school lotteries, these were staged publicly rather than online. Along with the actual participants, whose close-up reactions were caught on camera, the movie's audiences whelped with joy when a name was called and wept when they weren't. The emotion was brilliantly cinematic. No one could fail to be moved.

Some of the movie's appeal reflected the growing unpopularity of teachers' unions, a lot of it deserved. In the post-McCarthy era, few understand why teachers should have lifelong tenure when almost no one else does. Nor, in spite of the difficulties in evaluating their work, do most people accept that there is a good argument against paying teachers on merit. There are grounds, however, for doubting whether everything can be laid at their door. Study after study shows that the biggest factor in children's performance is their socioeconomic background. The more the U.S. economy bifurcates its middle class, the more problematic educational disparities will become.

Discrepancies in the movie's chief argument—that unions are chiefly to blame for America's stagnating education results—were also pointed out. For example, America's union-free southern states have the worst school results in the country. Schools in the highest-ranking nations, such as Finland and Germany, which outclass the United States on virtually every measure, are fully unionized. Both countries have much lower income disparities than does the United States. On education, Britain, whose income disparity is closest to that of the United States among the advanced economies, ranks worse than most of its European neighbors on education. "What infuriated me about *Waiting for Superman* is that it blames schools for the problems of society," said Richard Rothstein, a professor of education at UC Berkeley. "The fact is that good teachers get bad results in poor zip codes and bad teachers get good results in wealthy zip codes. That should be the starting point for any debate about performance."

Rothstein and others point to a third reason for the movie's success—the influence of America's education billionaires. In her 2011 book *Death and Life of the Great American School System,* Diane Ravitch, a former education official in George Bush senior's administration and now a professor at New York University, points out that pretty much every advocacy group involved in U.S. education had been funded by the Gates Foundation. Ravitch cited a survey of Gates's donations printed in *Education Week,* which itself received money from the foundation. "Never in the history of the United States was there a foundation as rich and powerful as the Gates Foundation," she wrote. "Never before has a foundation given grants to almost every major think tank and advocacy group . . . leaving almost no one willing to criticize its unchecked influence."

Given the diversity of America's education policy community, Ravitch may have been unfair both to Gates, who has funded contrarian voices, and to his recipients, many of whom needed no persuading, having themselves clashed with America's powerful education bureaucracies. Yet the breadth of consensus behind charter schools is nevertheless remarkable. So, too, is its resilience in the face of largely mediocre outcomes. "Gates and all the others are missing the point," said Rothstein. "You cannot address the problem with American schools and ignore the world beyond the school gates."

To his credit Bill Gates, who has been working on U.S. education for more than a decade, has often been ready to admit shortcomings. I met him at his private office in Seattle, which he keeps separate from the foundation's large downtown headquarters. His office provides a sweeping view of Lake Washington, a few miles inland from Puget Sound. "Looks like the sun's coming out again," Gates said as an opening gambit at the beginning of our interview. "Oh, dear, it seems to be raining again," he said at the end. Seattle makes me feel at home.

Like Mark Zuckerberg, the founder of Facebook, whom I have not met, Gates has occasional difficulties interacting with others— some observers say they have detected traits of Asperger's syndrome, a mild form of autism. Had I not been aware of that, I might have mistaken Gates's moments of animated gesticulation and pacing around as anger. It was his way of emphasizing a point. What Gates most wanted to put across was the need to rectify the "lack of good data" on what distinguishes a good from a bad teacher. We still did not know enough: the U.S. education sector lacked an R&D arm, he said. That was what Gates was trying to offer with his foundation. "We spend a lot of money on education in this country and we don't measure properly how it is spent," Gates said. "We've got to fix that."

Gates said the main project was to set up a "personnel data system" to collect information about what teachers do in the classroom and how they do it. Teachers around the country had allowed Gates to install full-time cameras with which to observe their methods. It was unclear how the cascade of video footage would be quantified. Nor was it clear how usefully the data could be mapped onto teacher pay awards or whether merit pay could reflect the income level of the district in which they were teaching. These are tough problems to crack, Gates conceded. But he was convinced it should be the top priority. "Can you control a classroom?" asked Gates. "How do you stop a class from getting bored? What is it that makes a great teacher? Until we can collect more data about what makes a teacher great, we are groping for the right solutions."

Gathering data is a good thing, particularly when it is accurate, even more so when it is useful. As the saying goes, if you torture the statistics long enough eventually they will confess. Perhaps more informatively, Albert Einstein famously observed: "Not everything that can be counted counts, and not everything that counts can be counted." What would Gates be able to count? It was a question I had put to Allan Golston, a former senior auditor at KPMG Peat Marwick, who now heads the Gates Foundation's education program. Golston was even readier to concede mistakes than Gates.

In 2008, the foundation abandoned eight years of focus on promoting smaller schools and made a "pivot" to teacher effectiveness. The foundation had thrown a lot of money at its small schools program and concluded it was a failure. In one instance Gates sponsored the breakup of a large public school in Denver called Manual. Each of its three progeny morphed into a separate enclave—one of them was dubbed the "Asian gang" school, another as "preppy white." The balkanized faculties squabbled with each other over the division of resources they had once happily shared.[32]

"We realized we didn't know nearly enough about what works," said Golston. I took that as Golston's way of saying that it had been a dud hunch. Now the foundation was returning to the drawing boards. "Just because you can't measure everything, or because your measure isn't perfect, doesn't mean you shouldn't try to build a picture," Golston said. "And just because socioeconomic factors are relevant, that shouldn't stop you from trying to change what you can change."

Critics, including Ravitch, say that Gates and his fellow philanthropists share a tendency to believe that if only they applied what worked in the businesses they once ran—in Gates's case Microsoft—then schools would turn around. That explained the emphasis on competition, choice, incentives, and deregulation. "These were not familiar concepts in the world of education, where high value is placed on collaboration," said Ravitch.

But they were highly familiar to Washington. Nowadays America's nonbusiness elites converse fluently in Gates's language. More than twice as many graduates do MBAs as science doctorates.[33] In a very different context, Jim Messina, Obama's 2012 reelection campaign manager, had said, "If you can't measure it, then it doesn't count." Obama himself is very much a data-driven president. "Frequently the president asks: Where is the data on this?," said a former adviser to Obama. "He doesn't feel briefed if he hasn't seen the best data."

A number of critics claim that the foundations harbor a stealth agenda to privatize the U.S. public education system. Many are particularly suspicious of the Walton family, which has made its $90 billion fortune from Walmart. But it would be unfair to accuse

Gates of concealing an ideological agenda. If a passion for metrics can be described as an ideology, the godfather of geeks wears his on his sleeve. Yet more than eleven years after getting into education, Gates seems genuinely puzzled about how little we still know about what works. "The truth is that we don't know enough yet," Gates said more than once. Golston said, "We are no longer at zero knowledge. But we aren't halfway either."

America now spends twice as much per student in real terms as it did in 1973. Yet according to the National Association of Educational Progress, which measures knowledge as a constant rather than via grade results (which are subject to inflation), results have hit a very long plateau. The average American score on the mathematics test was 306 (out of 500) in 2010, against 304 a generation ago. The same is true in other subjects. Like the middle class wage earner, America's schools are suffering from a prolonged bout of stagnation.

"Since the early 1970s we've added money, teachers, and administrators and we haven't budged an inch," said Michael Kirst, who heads education policy for Governor Jerry Brown of California. "Which is another way of saying we have zero productivity growth in education. That is the heart of our problem." One way to boost productivity is to lower labor costs, which is a priority at most charter schools. Another would be to reduce the number of teachers by better integrating technology with instruction, which is a Gates passion. A third is to extend the school day and open schools on Saturday mornings, which most charter schools also do.

People such as Kirst, who is also a professor emeritus at Stanford, are increasingly questioning the model. Kirst even goes so far as to describe charter schools as "sweat shop factories." To control costs, most charter schools hire enthusiastic graduates, often via Teach for America, at very low wages, sometimes as little as $20,000 a year. "The burnout rate is really high," said Kirst. "The charter school hasn't solved the productivity problem. They have taken the existing model and shifted it to Bangladesh." After toying with whether or not to say it, Kirst added, "These kids aren't teachers. They're missionaries."

So, in their own ways, are Bill Gates and Dean Kamen. Yet they share something in common with Kirst, Rothstein, and other skeptics that takes a while to become apparent: a growing willingness to admit they do not know the big answers. Forget public education budgets. Any company, including Microsoft, that spent as much as Gates has on R&D would expect some kind of a product by now. "We are forty years into this and we still don't know what we can do with technology in the classroom," said Kirst. "Do they use classroom iPads in Finland [the country that tops the rankings]? Could we aspire in California any time in the near future to have Finland's education budgets?" The answer is no.

Perhaps the most candid evaluation I have heard is from John Hennessy, president of Stanford and winner of the prestigious von Neumann medal. In addition to running Stanford, which remains one of the key generators of ideas and start-ups in Silicon Valley, Hennessy sits on the boards of Google and Cisco. He has his own perspective on America's schools. It is not a happy one.

Teachers should be more meritocratic, he said. And parents, among other things, should read to their children much more. It did not sound as though Hennessy was expecting rapid progress. More than a fifth of American adults have a reading age of fifth grade (eleven years old) or below. Just over half of Americans read books to their young children.[34] "There is no magic bullet that will suddenly fix our schools, the problem is too deeply embedded," said Hennessy. "We took decades to get into this problem, and it is going to take decades to get out of it."

How many electricians does it take to change a lightbulb? None. They are too busy hooking up your catheter. That may sound unlikely. But in Michigan, where hundreds of thousands of mid-career men have lost their jobs in the auto plants, nursing is one of the few alternatives on offer. Health care provides Michigan with by far the largest (and largest growing) source of new jobs—as it does for America as a whole. Men still account for less than a tenth of the intake for nursing schools. But that is a multiple of where it was a few years ago.

Some people talk about the feminization of the U.S. workplace. Others about the rise of the "disposable worker."[35] This might also be dubbed the age of retraining. Just as America's schools are in a state of almost permanent confusion, so, too, are community colleges, the worker training centers that are often left to cope with the consequences of school failure.

"My friends taunted me all the time after I said I was going to be a nurse," said Kenneth Swint, a forty-four-year-old electrician who used to work at General Motors. Swint, who is a gentle-spoken, bespectacled African-American, is studying nursing at the Oakland Community College in east Michigan. The teasing had no impact on him. Swint told his friends to look at the changing world around them.

"Those jobs, you know, where you didn't have to work very hard, and you earned a hundred grand a year, have gone for good," Swint told them. "Now if that's your preference, you can sit around and wait for the tooth fairy to visit, or you can wise up to what is happening." A small number were beginning to adjust their outlook, he said. "It's very hard for most men," said Swint, who talks in that reassuring manner you would want from a nurse. "They get hung up over this pride and dignity thing."

The decision to get a new skill had come to Swint in unfortunate circumstances. A few years ago his wife was diagnosed with breast cancer. The prognosis was worrying and there was nothing Swint could say to console her: "I was helpless to do anything about it." Then he observed how effectively the nurses lifted his wife's spirit. Her prognosis turned out to have been too bleak and she was now in remission. But in the meantime her mother had died of breast cancer. Swint helped to care for his mother-in-law in her last days. "I became very close to her in those months," he said.

Both episodes had convinced Swint that he wanted to do the kind of job where he could help people. He chose to specialize in oncology, psychiatric, and geriatric nursing, skills that would enable him to look after people who had "fallen by the wayside" and "people who had been misunderstood." On weekends he was also volunteering at a hospice in Detroit, where his two passions—Sudoku and chess—occasionally came in handy. "If I can help make people comfortable and give them some dignity at that stage in their lives then I feel I am contributing something."

If every former electrician thought like Swint, America's Midwest would be turning the corner. But even the best-funded community college—a relative term in the post-2008 American economy—would find it impossible to teach its students what Swint has learned. Much like America's public schools, community colleges derive a large chunk of their funding from local property taxes. That funding model brings two big disadvantages. First, it means community colleges are also a victim of "zip code apartheid"—the lower the property values in an area, the less money there is to train the workforce or educate the children.

Second, it means that community college budgets shrink just when society needs them to expand, that is, during a downturn and particularly after a mass home foreclosure crisis. Because of America's decentralized fiscal system, places like Michigan have far weaker "automatic stabilizers" than they need. "It is absurd that we withdraw support from the community colleges just when they most need it," said David Autor,[36] the MIT labor economist. "At a time like this, with a labor market in this condition, community colleges are too valuable a tool to waste."

Some of the best community colleges in the United States, such as Nova in northern Virginia, which President Obama has visited and where Jill Biden, the vice president's wife, teaches English, have kept their heads well above water. Washington's property boom takes in a generous radius. But most community college budgets have taken a nosedive at a time when worker demand for retraining has surged. At Oakland there has been a 25 percent surge in applications since 2008, much of it from people coming out of high school; it is cheaper to attend community college from home than it is to move to a university campus. Over the same period its budget has fallen by a fifth.

"It's like a scissor effect," said Sharon Miller, who heads work-force development at Oakland and who is always on the lookout for more support from the private sector. "Demand is coming at us from all angles and supply is shrinking." Miller was heartened in 2010 when the county voted in favor of a community college "millage"—local surtax—by a big margin. "We held our breaths but then it passed two to one," she said. The overall budget still went down a fifth. Since many homes in Oakland County are likely to remain underwater for some time, Miller does not see the picture improving rapidly.★

Like many of her peers, including Dick Shaink, who heads Mott Community College in Flint, which played host to Don Riegle's graduation address, Miller is alarmed by the low aptitudes of many college entrants, particularly among midcareer men seeking new skills. She is also troubled by their resistance to change. Some of the applicants require a whole year to relearn basic math and English. Fewer than 10 percent make it to the end of their remedial year. This is a shockingly bad ratio, which hints at a deep underlying crisis in the U.S. labor market.

"If it's not connected to what they came to study, they lose interest very quickly," said Miller. "We are trying to make it more interesting but there's only so much you can do." Many drop out of the labor force altogether. America's economic participation rate—a far truer picture of the labor market than the jobless number—has fallen from 64 percent of the total population in 2000 to a postwar

---

★American mobility has fallen sharply in the past quarter century. In the 1960s, one in five U.S. households changed residence every year. That had steadily fallen to one in ten households by 2010, according to McKinsey. Some of this derives from the rise of the dual-career household—it's tougher for two to make a career move to another city. And some of it comes from the spread of negative equity.

low of 58 percent in 2011.[37] Some are on disability benefits. Others are in jail. Still others drop off the economic map altogether. They are beyond the reach of the community colleges.

Even those who make it to college, and stick through remedial boot camp, find it tough to acclimatize to the world of working. Unlike previous recessions, when the turnover from trough to peak had been fairly rapid, Americans are staying unemployed for far greater spells than ever before. All the evidence shows that the longer you remain without a job, the more deskilled you become. Eventually, you become unemployable. Alarmingly, the same "lack of work ethic," in Shaink's words, is increasingly prevalent among school leavers.

"We get feedback from employers and it is very dispiriting to hear," said Shaink, who half jokingly compared what had happened to places like Flint with the sudden environmental collapse of Easter Island. Employers complain of a poor work ethic. What this means in practice is that they often talk on their cell phones, turn up with a hangover, argue with coworkers—there are even complaints about personal hygiene, said Shaink. Many fail the preemployment drug test.

Mott recently sent a group of Help Desk graduates to local employers to perform simple tasks on the telephone and computer. "The employers came back and said to us, 'Could you please send us some different people? We need workers who can talk in clear English.'" Both Miller and Shaink emphasize that the problem is acute among males. "Women are just better able to adapt. We never had a golden age of secure middle-class jobs to feel nostalgic about," said Miller.

Women are also increasingly favored by the new types of jobs that are becoming available. Among the most important attributes in the future workplace will be in what economists call the "soft skills"—the ability to communicate, basic cognitive understanding, punctuality, appearance, and flexibility. Here are the first six jobs on the Bureau of Labor Statistics' top ten list for rapid employment growth in the next decade: registered nurses, home health aids, customer service representatives, food preparers, retail sales people, and office clerks. Manufacturing is nowhere to be found. In most of the growth areas women have a better track record of getting and keeping their jobs. "Women have fewer dignity issues," said Miller. "They tend to be more pragmatic about getting whatever job will get to the paycheck."

America's pronounced and growing gender divide is a great puzzle to economists; their models cannot explain it. Yet the more you look for it, the more visible America's prolonged "mancession" becomes. Since 1979 the median wage of a male worker has fallen in real terms by more than a quarter, a huge drop. Entirely because of women's entrance into the workforce (a trend that hit a plateau in the early years of the twenty-first century), the overall median wage rose slightly over the same period.[38] Nor is the problem confined to blue-collar professions. Males with a four-year college degree saw their earnings decline by almost 10 percent between 2000 and 2010, while it rose for female graduates. The median earnings of young male graduates (aged twenty-five to thirty-four) fell by a staggering 19 percent in the same decade.[39]

Women now also make up a clear and growing majority of America's students, recently overtaking men to become the majority studying law. Some colleges have even started to institute an informal quota for men to ensure their ratio does not fall below 40 percent of the intake, according to Autor. "What is happening to men in America is a very significant and serious problem that I'm not sure we fully understand," he said. "As economists we need to consult sociologists, criminologists, and other disciplines a lot more than we do now to get a better grip on what is going on."

The most important thing on which all disciplines agree is that the earlier you intervene in a child's education, the more effective you will be. By the time a person gets to community college it is too late. "There are some states where if a boy cannot read by third grade then you know he has a higher probability of going to prison than getting a job," said Autor. "You need to get them before they are six or seven." As is so often the case, America has a wealth of impressive early-learning projects that never appear to "scale up."

The world has also turned upside down for the white-collar Michigander. As is true across the country, community colleges are trying to figure out how to retrain the office worker for life beyond the corporation. Oakland Community College was hit not just by the closure of big manufacturers but also by Pfizer's 2007 decision to close its sprawling campus in Ann Arbor, the nearby university town on the shores of Lake Michigan. Instead of offering the usual tax breaks to persuade companies to stay or relocate to Michigan, its first-term Republican governor Rick Snyder wanted to turn Michigan into a hub for small start-up companies.

Some believe it is utopian to imagine Michigan as a hive of entrepreneurship. It is probably more realistic than hoping for the return of big employers. Oakland's only remaining large employer is the William Beaumont Hospital. "Competing on tax rates is like hunting," said Sharon Miller. "Promoting entrepreneurialism is gardening." Much of Miller's life now involves figuring out ways to convert the mind-set of corporate man (and sometimes woman) into being a risk taker. The program Shifting Gears is backed by Snyder. "You have to remove the corporate smell," said Miller. "People who say, 'Call the IT department' and 'That's not my job' or 'Let's deal with that at the next meeting' have to change their attitude. A lot of people need a lot of scrubbing."

For some, Shifting Gears is too harsh an adjustment. A lot of its participants are middle-aged men who have lost their jobs and are attempting to make a Hail Mary pass to succeed as entrepreneurs. "They keep telling us to follow our passion," said Randy deVelbiss, a former teacher, university administrator, and fund-raiser now training to be an entrepreneur. "At the end of the day, though, you need to put food on the table." DeVelbiss, who is fifty-six and has had "lots of training at being unemployed," is one of those rare diamonds who has the stamina—and hope—to get him through all the self-help classes, networking opportunities, and mentoring programs that are required.

In his résumé is the white-collar analogue of what has happened to blue-collar America. An English major from the University of Michigan, de Velbiss taught at middle school for several years before quitting teaching to become a university administrator. "Teaching crushed my spirit," he said, which, given his lively mind, I found hard to believe. A dexterous fund-raiser, which is a skill he says more and more people are going to need, de Velbiss decided to break away from administration and set up his own company. It failed. He now works for a company that works on contract for community colleges. Many find it hard to anticipate what skills employers will need and when. De Velbiss's employer helps them to fill gaps quickly. "Right now employers can't get enough of hybrid engineers," said Miller, pointing to GM's new hybrid Chevy Volt, which was inaugurated by Obama. "The only predictable sources of demand are for IT and health care."

De Velbiss, about whom I had a strong hunch would succeed in his next start-up, said Shifting Gears was too much of a cultural shock for too many people. The idea that you multitask and do everything yourself is alien, he said, particularly for those over fifty. They are used to thinking of fixed annual budgets. When the trash can is full, they expect someone else to empty it. Teaching risk taking is hard when the people you are teaching have had risk thrust upon them. Yet a third still get jobs within three months of completing the sixteen-week course. "I guess everybody's got to lose their sense of entitlement," said de Velbiss. "I tell my fifteen-year-old daughter to pay attention to the business climate. Be nimble. Don't get hung up on one passion, or another, because tomorrow the demand will have shifted."

As a former educator who loves to read, de Velbiss has all the traits of a classic liberal Democrat. But his experiences as a teacher and as a father have changed his outlook. As the saying goes, "a conservative is a liberal with a daughter in high school." For de Velbiss, as for so many Democrats, including those who are invest-ing their hopes in the charter school movement, America's big-gest problem originates from what they see as the warped values of its public education system. It is a line that is echoed by other lapsed liberals, such as Miller and Shaink, who, in common with American colleges everywhere, face the growing strain of having to cope with the output of a failing public school system.

They would still argue strongly for other center-left priorities, such as progressive taxes and generous spending on education and training. But in their different ways each believes the 1960s revolution left unintended cultural damage in its wake. That decade helped break the bonds of racism, sexism, homophobia, and other social prejudices—much-needed changes that remain incomplete. Yet in its interstices the 1960s also bequeathed a value system in which self-esteem somehow became a near universal barometer of a child's progress. The battle to self-actualize branched off into a culture of self-worship. In this world, it is the children, rather than the teachers, who have the upper hand.

For de Velbiss it was the parents who prompted him to quit his safe and secure career as a teacher. "Parents will be the death of America," he said. Now an independent, rather than a liberal, de Velbiss would make a very good school entrepreneur. "I left teaching because I couldn't stand it any more," he said. "If I failed a child, the parents always complained. If I reprimanded a child, the school would threaten disciplinary action. I figured out there were better things I could do with my life."

Although he taught in a middle-class suburb, de Velbiss said only a fraction of the eleven- and twelve-year-old children that he taught English had attained the reading age requirements. Since discipline was off-limits, de Velbiss had to dumb down his act in order to get the children's attention. On Fridays he would focus on the lyrics to pop tunes or the dialogue from a popular TV show as a substitute for English texts. For a man who loves great works of literature, which have all but vanished from most schools, the experience was too painful to sustain. "I had to become an entertainer," he said. "If it wasn't pop culture then it wasn't entertaining."

To rub salt into the wound, de Velbiss would get the blame if he failed a child. Eventually he figured out what it is that teachers do to survive. "It doesn't matter how bad it is, if the child shows any effort then you give them a pass," he said. For all but the most hopeless cases, children must be pushed up a class a year, no matter how comprehensively they should have been failed. That expectation had bred a deeply unrealistic view of what life would be like after school. "We keep telling children they are a success when they are not succeeding," said de Velbiss. "People come out of school thinking they have a skill set when they don't. Then we are surprised to find out that we have a problem with our labor force."

Some college heads, such as Shaink, and some private sector leaders such as Jeff Immelt and Carl Camden say America has a lot to learn from other countries about how to run its public schools. Germany usually tops the list. In particular, its system of apprentice-based vocational education is attracting a growing amount of envy in the United States. One New York–based foundation sponsors German-lite "career academies" in inner-city schools through which teenagers are given frequent experience in the workplace, whether it be on a production line or in a chef's kitchen. Studies show that male graduates from the career academy are far likelier to keep a job and to get married. They are also far likelier to make it through community college. "It is usually too late by the time most kids get to community college," says Shaink, whose job involves clearing up the mess. "We need to change what happens to them before they get here."

Yet even supporters of creating a vocation stream in the United States handle their arguments gingerly. Selecting whom among fifteen- or sixteen-year-olds will go to university and which will go the vocational route is much easier to handle in a less diverse society like Germany. In countries where ethnic and socioeconomic divisions are strong—and where social trust is usually lower—the whole notion can more easily be attacked. "To a lot of people there is something un-American about it. It seems to clash with the principle of equality of opportunity," said Autor, who is a strong supporter of career academies. "If we were to be honest with ourselves, it is unrealistic to expect every American to go to college. We have to think in more practical ways."

Every now and then you come across Americans like Kenneth Swint, the male nurse, or Randy de Velbiss, the teacher and serial entrepreneur, who are thinking in heroically practical ways for themselves (and others). But they are the minority. Since 2008 American employers have complained of a growing difficulty in finding qualified applicants. In 2011 there were still five unemployed people for every job available. Yet American businesses in 2011 reported more than 3 million job openings[40] they had been unable to fill because of a skills shortage. Somehow the message isn't getting through to the labor force: the market signals aren't working.

Whether that can be blamed on society, schools, community colleges, employers, or Washington is ultimately an academic question: a solution is needed. Unless America can sharply boost the proportion of its workforce that is skilled—whether from college or vocational studies—a growing share will face the probability of spending their lives in low paid work. As Autor and others keep reminding us, America's job market has a "missing middle": jobs are going either up or down. Right now, most of that flow is in the wrong direction.

Swint said he sees too much of that among his friends and former colleagues. Some of them hang around at home, not knowing what to do with their lives. They still found it hard to believe the old way of doing things was not coming back. "We're still going to need electricians," said Swint, who joked he never wants to change a lightbulb again, "But a lot of them are going to need PhDs. We are entering a whole new world."

3

The Golden Goose

WHY AMERICA'S LEAD IN INNOVATION CAN NO LONGER
BE TAKEN FOR GRANTED

We are the nation that put cars in driveways and computers in offices; the nation of Edison and the Wright brothers; of Google and Facebook. In America, innovation doesn't just change our lives. It is how we make our living.
Barack Obama, "Winning the Future"

EVERY U.S. PRESIDENT pays homage to America's inventive genius. From the age of electricity and the internal combustion engine at the end of the nineteenth century to today's continuing IT revolution, America has dominated human technological advancement for more than a century. The United States continues to lead the world in many strategic areas, notably software, biosciences, social media, and most computer chip technology. In some others, such as aerospace and satellites, America now shares the lead with Europe and Asia.

In many areas, however, including robotics, flat panel displays, lithium ion batteries, nuclear power, high-speed trains, memory chips, and most fields of clean energy, the United States has given up the chase. In some fields, such as flat panel displays, America lost its lead gradually through the shift to Asia. In others, such as clean energy, the United States has almost willfully pushed away what was originally a huge first-mover advantage. Even in computing, Americans cannot rely on keeping an indefinite edge: in 2010 the Chinese built the fastest computer in the world.

Citing America's genius for invention, or what David Roth-kopf, a former Clinton official, now Washington commentator and author, describes as "America's get out of jail free card," is a standard way for politicians to reassure people that things will always turn out all right. "Once we tap into this unique dimension of the U.S. character those Chinese and other Asian robots won't be able to hold a candle to us," says Rothkopf, tongue in cheek. But is it true?

Many of the big inventions that are attributed to Americans are not as clear-cut as they may seem. For example, Edison "perfected" the lightbulb. It is fairly certain he did not invent it. That merit goes to either Humphry Davy or Joseph Wilson Swan of Britain. Innocenzo Manzetti of Italy and Charles Bourseul of France did most of the invention of the telephone. But Scottish-born Alexander Graham Bell got the U.S. patent in first. Charles Babbage and Alan Turing of Britain built the early models for the computer. And a German, Philip Nipkow, invented the television. Not to mention the camera (Monsieur Daguerre of France), and penicillin (Alexander Fleming of Scotland).[41]

America's key advantage has been its superiority at turning invention into commercial application. As Abraham Lincoln observed, the U.S. patent system adds "the fuel of interest to the fire of genius." But the U.S. system is no longer quite as unique as it once was. The idea, for example, that the Chinese are able only to replicate rather than invent is belied not only by its history— where would we be without the compass, printing, and paper money?—but also by the present.

In the view of Dean Kamen, the successful inventor, China is rapidly reacquiring its ability to innovate. China's share of citations in international scientific papers is projected to overtake America's by 2020, based on the trends since the turn of the century, reported the UK's Royal Society in a recent survey. In 2006, China overtook the UK to become the second most prolific scientific publisher in the world. "People reassure themselves that it's not in China's culture to innovate," said Kamen. "Striving to succeed didn't used to be in China's culture either. Things change."★

That rule of thumb also applies to the United States. Some scholars argue that America's culture of innovation is exogenous to its political economy. Innovation is baked deep into American society. Washington may be bringing the sky on its head, but as long as America's courts uphold property rights entrepreneurs will continue to thrive. It is a comforting thought. But the truth is that no discipline, particularly economics, can fully explain what causes innovation. It remains a subject of contentious debate. Even defining the word is controversial. (Is it invention, its application, or some point in between?)

There are growing reasons to doubt whether America's innovative advantage is immune to the broader health of society. The goose that lays the golden eggs is not oblivious to what happens around her. Readers disapproving of journalists inventing parables can skip to the next paragraph (it won't happen again). Picture a traditional homestead in Iowa. In the center of the farmyard sits a small barn where Mother Goose lays her golden eggs. The large family around her starts to descend into squabbling. They move into different wings of the house. Their main dispute is over how to share the golden eggs. The tussle gets noisier. Mother lays fewer eggs. Efforts to calm her fall prey to the same divisions that split the family.

What puzzles so many observers of America is the extent of the family's dispute. Only the willfully unseeing would disagree that America offers the friendliest culture in history for risk takers, and in many respects it still does. Not only is it socially acceptable to fail. In some parts of America it is a badge of pride. On top of that, America also built the world's most robust climate for innovation. Its vital attributes included the ability to attract the world's best

---

★In his book *Bad Samaritans,* Ha Joon Chang has some amusing descriptions of how British travelers to Germany in 1800 wrote about the "indolent," "sloppy," and "over-emotional" character of the people they found. Cultural mind-sets change. Who today would describe the British as having a stiff upper lip?

brains, a deep pool of venture capital to fund the best ideas, the most generous spigot for private and public R&D, a pragmatic tradition of public policy, the most robust system of patent protection, and the best universities.

With the exception of the university system most of these advantages are being whittled away. And even here, Asia is investing in universities on a scale that should not be ignored. Many of America's best technical universities, such as Cal Tech and Carnegie Mellon, are setting up campuses in East Asia and elsewhere. "You have to go to where the market is," said the head of a distinguished private college in New England that recently opened a campus in Singapore.* But it is in terms of inventiveness, risk capital, research money, and quality of government that America is falling down.

For more than a century America has been the world's biggest magnet for people of talent. From Andrew Carnegie, who was born in Scotland, to Andy Grove of Intel from Hungary, or Sergey Brin of Google from Russia, foreign-born entrepreneurs are as American as pizza and bagels. Almost one in two start-ups in Silicon Valley is created by people born elsewhere, mostly India and China. So, too, are foreign-born scientists. From Albert Einstein to a large portion of the scientists working on the Manhattan Project that developed the atom bomb and to the university and corporate research teams in today's America, foreign scientists are as American as Hollywood special effects. More than 70 percent of U.S. PhDs in physics are awarded to foreign students. Just over half of U.S. patents are now issued to foreigners.

Study after study shows that immigrants are far greater risk takers than the native-born in any society. That pioneering spirit

---

*Having the best universities is not on its own enough to stop decline if so many of its brightest graduates go home. According to the QS-World University rankings, the United States has thirteen of the world's top twenty universities, while the UK comes in second place with four. Since the United States has 311 million people to the UK's 61 million, a UK citizen is nearly twice as likely to attend a top university as an American. As American readers might know, if anything the UK faces even tougher economic challenges than the United States.

was unique to the rise of America for its first 150 years. And it was replenished in the 1960s, when Congress lifted the barriers to nonwhite immigration. Yet in the decade since the September 11 terrorist attacks, the United States has ceded much of its attraction as a destination. The vast majority of foreign students, including Chinese and Indians, are required to return home. A small number get H1B visas in the lottery for the annual quota for foreign skilled workers (which had dwindled to 68,000 by 2011). Given the rise of opportunities at home, many foreign students would have returned anyway, even if green cards had been stapled to their degrees.

Take Ajeet Rohatgi, who is America's leading photovoltaic scientist and head of the school of electrical and computer engineering at Georgia Tech. To be accepted by Rohatgi as your PhD supervisor is to enter a camp near the summit of global science. There are perhaps only two other solar scientists in the world who belong in Rohatgi's category—Martin Green in Australia and Stefan Glunz in Germany. Now in his early sixties, Rohatgi is a latent entrepreneur having licensed his university patents to Suniva, one of America's few remaining solar panel manufacturers. Rohatgi's labs, which are a warren of micro (and nano) testing devices, are situated in a nondescript redbrick portion of the university in downtown Atlanta. Nearby is the swimming pool built for the 1996 Atlanta Olympics, which is powered by Rohatgi's solar panel technology.

Rohatgi, who was born in India but, like so many of his peers, studied in the United States, said his doctoral students are mostly foreign. Of the twelve PhDs Rohatgi is supervising nine are foreigners. Unlike their predecessors in the 1990s, when Rohatgi started his lab, almost all will return home. When I met Rohatgi in his lab in 2011, he had recently bid farewell to three Korean students and two Indians. "The salaries in their home countries are shockingly competitive," said Rohatgi, who is a UP Brahmin (upper caste Indian from the northern state of Uttar Pradesh). He studied at Virginia Tech and Lehigh University after having completed his undergraduate degree at one of the renowned Indian Institutes of Technology. When he visited India as a student in the

1970s he went to a research lab in Delhi. The experience confirmed Rohatgi's decision to become an American. "It wasn't what you knew," said Rohatgi, "it was who you knew. There was no way I could work as a scientist in India."

Back in the United States, Rohatgi got a job in the research lab at Westinghouse. But as the 1980s wore on he realized that corporate R&D in the United States was turning into a routine and mostly incremental activity. "I hadn't reckoned on the impact of quarterly shareholder culture," he said. "We went from being research scientists to being fund-raisers." So he set up the lab at Georgia Tech with the sponsorship of the government's Department of Energy.

Even in the mid-1990s America remained the place to be. The United States still accounted for the bulk of global solar panel production and most of world demand (principally from California). Since then, America's share of global photovoltaic production and capacity has plummeted—in each case to below 10 percent.[42] The United States has gone from being the big fish in a small pond to a minnow in a growing lake. "We don't have a supply chain in the United States any more," Rohatgi said. "You can't even find an American silicon wafer supplier."

I was introduced to Suniva via the U.S. Department of Commerce at a dinner in Washington, D.C. The department wanted to showcase a company that was still manufacturing in the United States. In fact Suniva was already exploring whether to expand its operation outside of the country, probably to China. A few days later I arrived at Suniva's sleek plant about thirty miles south of Atlanta. Based on its "secret sauce" production methods, Suniva turns out a crystalline silicon cell every three seconds. It operates 365 days and nights a year. The plant is state of the art. Rohatgi's American partners are world class. Yet the company wants to grow elsewhere.

Bryan Ashley, a senior executive, explained to me that China, among several other countries, was offering high-quality facilities to Suniva at a cutthroat price. No such backing was available from Washington, D.C.—or from Atlanta. "Do you know how difficult it is to find a good process engineer in America nowadays?" asked Ashley. As Rohatgi keeps pointing out they are going home. A passionate American patriot, Rohatgi keeps a chart on his wall that shows how much more people with PhDs earn over a lifetime in the United States; it comes to almost $3 million. He drums that fact into American students.

Fewer and fewer are doing doctorates in science. There are twice as many Americans studying MBAs as the combined total of those studying engineering at postgraduate and undergraduate levels.[43] Until recently that didn't matter because so many foreign engineers stayed on after graduating. But now they are harder to persuade. "If you look at my generation, then the top solar scientists were mostly American," said Rohatgi. "The generation below me and the one below that are all outside of America." He mentioned the University of New South Wales in Sydney, whose booming photovoltaic department is virtually owned by China's Suntech, the world's largest solar company. "When you lose the market you lose the people," says Rohatgi. "Then you lose the innovation."

It is a point that often gets lost in Washington. Since they lack the lobbying power of their rivals in the coal, oil, and gas sectors, clean tech entrepreneurs have voted with their feet. One wafer company visited by Obama since he became president has shut up shop (Solyndra[44] in Silicon Valley) and another is now expanding in China (Cree in North Carolina). A third, Evergreen Partners, announced it was moving lock, stock, and barrel to China in spite of having been lavished with tax breaks by the state of Massachusetts. Later it filed for bankruptcy. "As far as our industry goes, the fossil fuel lobby owns Washington," said Ashley. He added that many legislators do not even understand the basics about solar power. "I had one senator ask me how he was supposed to boil water with a solar panel," said Ashley, who made me promise not to mention the politician's name.

The same trend threatens to obliterate what remains of U.S. production of light-emitting diodes (LED), the semiconductor-powered lighting of the future. East Asia has lured most of them away. The few that are still based in the United States confine their onshore work mostly to R&D. "Washington is steadily removing any good reason to manufacture here," said Bill Watkins, chief executive of Bridgelux, an LED company based in Livermore, which is across the San Francisco Bay from Silicon Valley. If Rohatgi is gently disapproving of America's self-inflicted wounds, Watkins is notably outraged. Much of Watkins's frustration boils down to the lack of qualified people. "I can go anywhere in the world and hire an MIT graduate or a Stanford graduate if I need to," said Watkins, whom I visited at his company's world-class LED research center in Livermore. "Even the government bureaucrats you deal with in Asia went to MIT."

Watkins, a former chief executive of Seagate International, the world's largest producer of disk hard drives, said he is trying to think of ways to keep Bridgelux's remaining operations in the United States. All of its manufacturing is outsourced to a contractor in Taiwan. The company is also thinking about opening a plant in India. It is very close to shifting its R&D center from Livermore to Singapore. On top of a generous subsidy, Bridgelux can recruit all the researchers it needs in the city-state.

"As an American, it is painful for me even to think of shifting jobs outside of the United States," said Watkins. "But I have to act in the company's interests." The company's R&D lab in Livermore is staffed almost entirely by foreigners; of Bridgelux's 250 researchers, almost three-quarters are from China and Taiwan. Most have PhDs. The starting salary is around $100,000 and can increase to a multiple of that. "Competition in Silicon Valley has pushed salaries through the roof," said Steve Lester, head of the lab at Bridgelux. "There aren't enough good ones to go around any more."

More of a headache than corporate rivals, however, was the constant battle to keep Bridgelux's employees from going home. Known jokingly as "serial kidnappers," Chinese recruiters are constantly in touch with Bridgelux's best scientists to offer them jobs in Chinese universities and state enterprises. "These guys get calls all the time," said Lester, waving at a group of Chinese scientists who were studying minute crystals through microscopes. Our conversation was somewhat surreal. Everyone was wearing protective face masks. Lester and I stood discussing how to stop China from poaching Bridgelux's employees within earshot of some of those it was trying to poach. "A lot of them will think twice about going back," said Lester. "The reality isn't always as good as recruiters make it sound."

Now fifty-eight, Bill Watkins has been in the high-tech industry since before China started to open up its economy in the late 1970s. At Seagate, Watkins was visited in the 1980s by a group of Chinese government officials who were on a trip to America to learn about computers. They had been shopping. Some of them were wearing dark suit pants with clashing stripy suit jackets. The shop labels were still attached. "We laughed and laughed afterward," said Watkins. "They were like country boys on their first trip to the big city."

When the Chinese returned a couple of years later, they had lost the labels. "Some of the suits were still mixed up," Watkins said. "But I remember thinking, these guys have learned a lot." Now Watkins gets visits from Indian government representatives. He showed me a card of an official from the office of Manmohan Singh, India's prime minister, who had visited the previous week. "There are a lot of very serious governments out there and America is training half of their economic talent," said Watkins. "The only government that doesn't seem to be serious is our own." And China is making most of the suits.

One such coordinated dresser has paid repeated visits to Ching-Hua Wang, an immunologist who heads the biotechnology department at California State University in Camarillo. Wang, who came from China in the early 1980s to do her PhD at Cornell, said China's overtures have become increasingly alluring. Her prospective kidnapper, Charlie King, who runs a "U.S.-China business council" in Los Angeles, did not return my calls. "He talks to me about all the support government is putting into science and education in China," said Wang. "When I compare what is happening in China to the budget cuts we're getting in California I feel really tempted."

According to Wang, King's outfit works on commission. Some of its earnings come from placing Chinese students in American universities. And some comes from persuading Chinese graduates to return home. Wang says she knows of a growing number who have taken the offer to go back. Her brother-in-law, who worked at Intel and has an MBA from Harvard, went back in 2002. The main thing that is stopping her is the fact that her husband, Nian-Sheng Huang, who is also a professor in California, teaches U.S. colonial history. "China is not the right place to research U.S. colonial history," she said with mild understatement. In addition, her children were born and remain in the United States.

When she was a child during China's cultural revolution, Wang was separated from her family and sent to Inner Mongolia for six years. Her husband was banished for ten years. "It was very tough but everyone went through it," she said. Coming to America in the 1980s was like emerging into the light after years of darkness. And now, in spite of all that happened to Wang and her family in China, she is tempted to return. According to a 2010 survey by Vivek Wadhwa, an immigration scholar at Duke University in North Carolina, fewer than 10 percent of Chinese students in the United States say they want to stay on permanently in the country. "Things have changed much more dramatically than I would have expected," said Wang.

Wang's wavering has little to do with homesickness— both she and her husband are happy in America and it is their children's only home. It is about the cold, hard reality of resources that governs the life of scientists. China seems to have a lot of resources. America apparently does not. Even more than the money, though, Wang talked of the very different time horizons between the two countries. In China, she said, people tend to think in the long term. Americans seemingly cannot see beyond the next electoral cycle. "When I was a child they had a slogan: 'Overtake the UK and catch up with the U.S.,'" said Wang. "China is halfway there and the goal hasn't changed."

In contrast, although Wang and her husband "treasure the U.S. political value system over China's"—a point she underscored—they can no longer figure out what America's goal is. She contrasted the foreign students she teaches with their America peers. The former work hard, she said. Most of her American students don't. "They don't seem to know that the world has changed," said Wang. "Most of them don't read the news. They are very provincial compared to the foreign students." I wondered if that was entirely fair. Almost by definition students studying outside their home country will be more cosmopolitan than their hosts. But Wang was sure of her ground. Everywhere Wang looked, it seems, America was stagnating. "I don't feel so confident about America any more," said Wang. "It seems to have lost its vision." It may also be losing its fabled appetite for risk.

If you go into the first building at Facebook's headquarters in Palo Alto, there is a wall near the large cafeteria. Unlike the one on your homepage, a question is scrawled across the top of this wall: "What would you do if you weren't afraid?" it asked. I spent a few minutes perusing the scrawled answers. One said, "Hug a lion." Another said, "Write graffiti on the wall." Then there was "Walk around naked" and "Find my dad." This being Silicon Valley, and this being its hottest company of the moment, the answer that grabbed my attention was "Fail harder." If two words could summarize how the people who live and work along Route 101 see themselves, "fail harder" might work. I once attended a pink slip party in Palo Alto in which hundreds of people who had lost their jobs after the dot-com bubble burst in late 2000 "came out" to each other as unemployed. They spent most of the evening swapping business cards and plotting their next failures.

Having been raised in Margaret Thatcher's Britain, which loved the word "entrepreneurialism" but which ultimately failed to California-ize the UK economy, I grew up immune to its underlying meaning. Spending a few months in Silicon Valley at the turn of the century helped to disabuse me of that. Since my sister-in-law Anuradha Basu and her husband, Shanker Trivedi, live down the road from Palo Alto in what seems to be the almost permanently blossoming Atherton, it is never a difficult decision to visit.

Nothing outward has changed about the valley since then. But it was only in 2010, when the big social media companies Facebook, Groupon, Twitter, and LinkedIn began the valuation process for their initial public offerings, that Silicon Valley reacquired some of the froth, and dubious valuations, of the dot-com era. This time around there was a great deal more media skepticism in the IPO pipeline. Even within Silicon Valley, and particularly among some of the big venture capitalists, there seemed to be a much flintier, and less romantic, idea of what the valley was about nowadays.

Top of the list of concerns was the changing nature of venture capital itself. If attracting the world's best brains is America's talent, marrying their ideas with cash is Silicon Valley's. Should the people with the money start to develop risk aversion, the alarm bells ought to go off. That is certainly the view of Steve Wozniak, the cofounder with Steve Jobs and Ronald Wayne of Apple. The Wizard of Apple, as Wozniak was known, because he was its technical genius, got his first venture capital funding in the mid-1970s when he had long hair and was working out of the back of Jobs's garage. Things have changed since then. Wozniak believes Apple would not be able to raise any money in today's Silicon Valley because it would lack the "proven track record" that most funds now require.

Many venture capitalists agree with Wozniak's view. "Of course they'd throw Jobs and Wozniak out—they'd see them as hippies," said Ed Penhoet, a partner at Alta Partners, a large fund based in downtown San Francisco. "Most of the VCs have been taken over by former investment bankers. They don't back ideas, they back management teams." The change might sound secondary. But in Penhoet's view it is killing the spirit of risk taking that made the valley into the world's most precious incubator. Penhoet's other view, which offers a panoramic take on the San Francisco Bay and the nearby Transamerica Pyramid, offers a reminder of how lucrative his line of work can be. Among the paintings on his office wall is a prized David Hockney called *The Scrabble Game* and also several paintings by the great abstract expressionist Sam Francis.

The fruits of earlier investments aside, Penhoet also has a strong public interest in the future of Silicon Valley. Not only is he on the committee of scientists that advises President Obama, he was also the former dean of Berkeley's school of public health and is a trustee of the Gordon and Betty Moore Foundation, endowed by the legendary founder of Moore's Law. But his immediate concern, like most other VCs who specialize in biotechnology, is his own sector's very weak outlook. "A lot of biotech VCs are going to go out of business in the next two or three years," he said. "The IPO market is as good as dead."

Barring the social media, which will make some investors, notably Goldman Sachs and its clients, very wealthy indeed, that outlook was approximately true for the rest of Silicon Valley, renewable energy technology included, Penhoet said. The numbers back up his diagnosis to an almost startling degree. In 2000 Silicon Valley raised $200 billion. Then the bubble burst, leaving a lot of badly burned investors. Dotmania led to a prolonged stopover at hangover.com from which some investors believe the valley has never fully recovered.

Since 2000 the largest annual fund-raising in Silicon Valley touched $30 billion, less than a sixth of its peak. It has not once exceeded $20 billion since the financial meltdown—a number that is smaller than Wall Street's annual bonuses. More worryingly, the number of funds seeking to raise money has continually shrunk. There were 233 VC fund-raisers in 2006. That had fallen to just 76 by 2011.[45] More than a decade after the Nasdaq crash money continues to lose interest in the valley. "The fact that the number of firms raising money successfully remains at such low levels confirms an ongoing contraction of the venture capital industry," said Mark Heesen, president of the National Venture Capital Association.

More puzzling is the contrast between Silicon Valley and Wall Street, which appear to have wholly delinked from each other since

2000. If the role of the capital markets is to allocate investment to where it will get the highest returns, then either Silicon Valley is no longer offering decent returns, or Wall Street has found much more lucrative ones elsewhere. Nor is the drought confined to venture funds. Since 2008 risk aversion seems to have paralyzed the banking sector from lending to small businesses. The rate of American business start-ups in 2010 fell to a historic low, according to McKinsey, having already been on the decline before the meltdown.

Groups such as the Kauffman Foundation, which promotes entrepreneurialism in the United States, blame much of this drought in risk capital on the "financialization" of the U.S. economy, by which is meant Wall Street. "Using debt to fund asset purchases that themselves generate collateral for further asset purchases is not a productive way of allocating capital [for an economy as a whole],"[46] Kauffman has stated. The foundation pointed to the generous tax breaks that Wall Street continues to garner on debt-financed investment, in addition to the massive implicit subsidy enjoyed by the thirteen or so financial institutions that are considered "too big to fail."

For different reasons, perhaps the banks too should embrace the motto "fail harder." After the 1929 Wall Street crash the great economist John Maynard Keynes wrote: "When the capital development of a country becomes the by-product of the activities of a casino, the job is not likely to be well done." That critique remains as trenchant now as it was before the 2008 meltdown.

Naturally, Wall Street's alleged partner in crime, from the VC point of view, is Washington, D.C. Given that there is no lobby for entrepreneurs as a group, aspiring risk takers have only a hypothetical voice at Mancur Olson's* table. And since larger, established companies are increasingly visible and well armed in Washington, that gap is likely only to grow.

---

*Set out in his two classics *The Rise and Decline of Nations* and *The Logic of Collective Action,* Olson brilliantly depicted why special interest groups would maintain an ever tighter grip on the distribution of resources in stable societies. (We will come across Olson in more detail later in the book.)

Always on the lookout to raise money, politicians are rarely swayed by counterfactuals. "Pointing to start-ups that don't happen is not a very convincing argument," said Bill Watkins, himself a former entrepreneur. "When I make all the obvious points in Washington about American competitiveness, they say, 'Sure Bill, I totally agree.' Then the next time I hear from them it's 'Hi Bill, How are you? I wonder if you'd like to contribute . . .'"

Investors also have a more specific gripe against Washington—the 2002 Sarbanes-Oxley Act that was passed in the wake of the scandals that felled Enron, WorldCom, Tyco International, Adelphia, and their auditors. The bill, which critics subsequently lampooned as "the Full Employment for Accountants Act," imposed stringent reporting requirements on U.S.-listed companies. Larger companies have been able to absorb the cost of all the new paperwork, even of the notorious Section 404, which requires executives and their auditors to personally sign off on every internal control.

The bill has hit smaller companies hard, though. Those with revenues of under $100 million a year pay up to $3 million a year in compliance costs, according to one study. Since only listed companies are required to comply with "Sarbox," the law has prompted an exodus of small cap firms from the stock exchanges and led to a shriveling of the flow of new IPOs. Since Sarbox was passed the overall number of all companies listed on American stock exchanges has fallen by almost half to 4,048,[47] the steepest drop by far in modern U.S. history. That means there are 3,500 fewer American companies in which to invest. But that number also understates the decline, since it cannot account for all the counterfactuals that never went public. "After Sarbox, most start-ups have had no intention of going public," said Penhoet. "Why would you go through all that pain?"

It also means that the action is moving east. In 2010, according to Dealogic, Chinese companies introduced 391 global IPOs (mostly in Shanghai and Hong Kong). America managed barely a quarter of that. At $89 billion, the value of the Chinese offerings was more than five times the size of their American counterparts.

For Penhoet, this is a measure of the damage America has inflicted on its entrepreneurs. It also tells the tale of what has happened to Silicon Valley's start-up culture. Since the IPO exit has been largely shut off, most VCs now plan on the "acquisition exit"—selling the start-up to a larger company.

Sometimes an entrepreneur with a good idea and friends in the business can get money from a small circle of private "angel" investors. More often, though, the start-up is treated as an elaborate goose, which investors fatten up for purchase. Others have labeled them "quack companies." It has transformed the approach to investing. "It is impossible to run a company like a real company if your whole purpose is to be acquired. The psychology changes," said Floyd Kvamme who, as a "partner emeritus" at Kleiner Perkins, Silicon Valley's largest VC company, was present (and active) at the creation of many of the valley's biggest companies. "If your job is to dress things up for the near term you are never going to produce disruptive technologies."

Investors in the ailing biotech sector, which in the early part of the "naughties" had generated such buzz, talk about getting new businesses ready for the "boa constrictor"—their description of the large pharma companies in search of new ideas. In spite of their generous R&D budgets, the pipeline of new drugs from big pharma has dwindled in the past few years. They swallow whatever innovations they can find. Often their aim is simply to acquire the patents owned by the start up, which is then promptly disbanded. "This isn't the way to make big advances in science and medicine," said Penhoet, who spends a lot of his time trying to hammer this message home in Washington. "We are literally killing innovation and nobody in Washington seems to be able to do anything about it."

Often, when I ask interviewees why Washington does not respond with greater alacrity to America's declining competitiveness, they cite that old cliché about the frog in boiling water: America's political classes appear to be acclimatizing to their country's steadily weakening position. In the absence of a shock, each development is put in the in tray to be addressed at a calmer time. Such a moment continues to remain elusive. Meanwhile, inch by inch and quarter by quarter the United States is ceding ground. Silicon Valley is no exception.

"Americans are very smart, I still have faith they will eventually figure this out," said Naren Gupta, another big venture capitalist and also India-born.* "At some point we will get to the point where necessity will be the mother of invention." Until then, however, people like Gupta, who is the founder of Nexus Venture Partners, a fund dedicated entirely to Indian start-ups, are putting their money elsewhere.

Although Gupta, who is another "IIT-an," used to invest entirely in U.S. start-ups, now he puts nothing in. Nor is he a big exception. Much of the already shrunken $15 billion to $25 billion in annual Silicon Valley fund-raising goes to Asia. Sequoia, one of the valley's largest funds, now has eight offices, of which only one is in the United States.[48] The rest are in Bangalore, Israel, Shanghai, and elsewhere.

I wanted to talk to Gupta because he is something of a lodestar for many young entrepreneurs. We met a couple of times at Gupta's low-key offices on Sand Hill Road, the rolling green stretch above Palo Alto on which most of Silicon Valley's money is headquartered. Gupta's story is an extraordinary illustration of how much has changed in America. In 1980, after he had graduated from nearby Stanford University in engineering, he set up a company, Integrated Systems, which designed embedded software (principally to run cars and planes).

One of Gupta's biggest customers said that it could not do business with him after it was discovered he was not a U.S. citizen. Gupta drove in a panic to the passport office in San Francisco. This was make or break. "I need a passport in less than four weeks," he told the officer, who replied, "That shouldn't be a problem, sir."

---

*Readers suspecting an India tilt by the author should look down the staff lists at any big Valley company or venture capital fund. They are replete with Singhs, Mukherjees, and Subramanians.

Gupta got the passport. He went on to make his fortune from his company's IPO in 1990.

Such a story is now very hard to imagine. I could write a chapter on the tales I have picked up from friends around the world who have been denied visas to attend academic conferences in the United States. It would include examples of foreign students who were blocked from returning to America after going home for the Christmas holidays. And it would cite entrepreneurs who have returned to their home countries to set up thriving companies they had otherwise hoped to establish in America. Gupta could write a book on it.

My main interest was in the changing nature of American risk capital, a subject on which Gupta is passionately informed. Also on the board of Caltech, which is home to the famous Jet Propulsion Laboratory that builds robots to explore the solar system, Gupta is an engineer's engineer. He believes that "hard innovation," as opposed to social media, is the bedrock of a strong economy. He is in despair about how little money, and how few ideas, are around nowadays.

Gupta listed for me the key figures of the 1970s and '80s, such as Don Valentine, the "grandfather of Silicon Valley VCs," whose money helped create the semiconductor industry, personal computers, software, and digital entertainment. Such investors were usually former entrepreneurs, said Gupta. Valentine founded National Semiconductor. The late Eugene Kleiner founded Fairchild Semiconductor, from which the breakaway Intel was founded. They understood science as well as the nuts and bolts of what it takes to set up a company. Their principal fascination was with new ideas. Money was secondary—although of course always welcomed. "Their aim was to build companies that would last for fifty years, which is what they did," said Gupta.

In contrast, today's typical investor is a "metrics person," more often than not a former banker and usually uninterested in ideas. "They think very differently from entrepreneurs," said Gupta. "They look backward at what has worked and put money into that. So you get a lot of me-too Facebook investments." The key difference is that they need to see their payback within a short horizon. "They don't believe in deferred gratification," he said. Again, the entrepreneurial investor thought differently. "They tried to imagine what the future will look like and find investments that can excite them," Gupta said.

The outcome of this metamorphosis in the typical VC—from "the believer to the mercenary," in Gupta's words—was that innovation was slowing. Like many others, Gupta was wary about the stratospheric numbers companies like Facebook were attracting. Between our first and second meeting in three months, the company's implied valuation had risen from $50 billion to $70 billion. Indeed, when Facebook did issue its IPO, it was valued closer to $100 billion. But he was more skeptical of whether the social media companies qualified as innovators. "We haven't produced anything really new in thirty years," said Gupta.★ "Everything you think is new comes from fundamental breakthroughs that were made a generation ago [including the Internet]. Now we're just picking the low-hanging fruit."

I had a similar conversation with Craig Barrett, the former chief executive of Intel, a few days earlier. Barrett said that the best measure of where innovation was happening could be found on the balance sheet of Intel Capital, the company's venture capital arm. Fifteen years ago, every dollar of Intel Capital's investment was in America. That number had fallen to just over half by 2011. "There is innovation happening all over the world and our job is to find it and support it," said Arvind Sodhani, head of Intel Capital, to whom I was introduced by Barrett.

Intel also needs to take a growing stake in its biggest markets, said Sodhani. More than 80 percent of Intel's semiconductors are shipped to non-American customers. Since America was losing much of its innovation infrastructure, Sodhani expected these trends to continue. To counter them, the United States needed to do

---

★Anyone wishing to explore the counterintuitive idea that innovation has slowed in the age of the Internet should read Tyler Cowen's thought-provoking *The Great Stagnation* (Penguin, 2011).

many things, among which include giving small companies "relief from Sarbox," making America's R&D tax credit permanent (and more generous), and, most important, lifting the quality of U.S. education. Unless America rebooted its ability to innovate, the troubling trends would continue. "In the past the whole world copied American technology," said Sodhani. "Now we are getting into the habit of copying others."

Much like Robert Solow, the Nobel economist, who estimated that innovation has accounted for up to 40 percent of America's economic growth, Barrett, Sodhani, and Gupta all argue that growth ultimately derives from innovation. All went out of their way to be dismissive of Wall Streeters. Much like Paul Volcker, the former chairman of the U.S. Federal Reserve, who said the only innovation Wall Street had produced in the past thirty years was the ATM machine, they described the U.S. financial system as a growing problem for America's competitiveness.

Some of their Wall Street critique is about taste—few in Silicon Valley aspire to be bankers. But there is a sharpness to what people say today that I had not picked up on before. One of the valley's guiding principles is "patient capital," that is, money that can bide its time. Some economists, including Larry Summers, point out that patient capital can also be "dumb capital." This is sometimes true. But when Gupta, for example, contrasts America's budgetary trends with the hundreds of billions of dollars Asian governments, universities, and investors are putting into green energy, military technology, and scientific research, it is a cause for deep concern.

When we see how quickly an impatient Wall Street regained its precrash remuneration levels (albeit to taper off somewhat when the markets turned down in 2011) that concern only intensifies. Gupta mentioned a string of relatives who work on Wall Street, including a nephew who, in 1992, landed his first job at Lehman Brothers. His starting salary was higher than Gupta's was, as the chief executive of a public company. Another nephew works at Barclays. Gupta said that he did not enjoy the job but the money was big. Gupta's daughter, on the other hand, recently joined a start-up. "I told her that if your main aim in life is money, then you will end up hating it," he said. "We need to get back to doing exciting things in America. We have more than enough bankers and accountants to go around."

Every now and then, Ernst Rothkopf drives past Bell Labs, the greatest private research operation America has ever produced. Nowadays the New Jersey operation is owned by Alcatel-Lucent, one of the "Baby Bell" descendants of AT&T, the former monopoly telephone provider, which was broken up twenty years ago. "The parking lot is usually empty," said Rothkopf. "Nothing much going on in there." An octogenarian who still teaches occasionally at Columbia University, Rothkopf spent most of his career at Bell Labs. As had so many of America's postwar scientists, he came to America as a refugee from the turmoil in Europe. Rothkopf and his family, Jews from Vienna, arrived in late 1939 when he was a young teenager. He said they were lucky to escape the Nazis.

Still containing accented traces of his Viennese upbringing, Rothkopf described what it was like to work at the research lab that produced the fax, the laser, the transistor, voice-recognition technology, the cellular network, and the first photovoltaic cell. Bell Labs employed about twelve thousand people during the 1950s and '60s, of which about twelve hundred worked on basic scientific research. Rothkopf was in charge of learning and instruction. In the next-door office someone dabbled in musical composition and computers. Another nearby colleague investigated standing wave tubes. And directly above Rothkopf was a scientist who had won the Nobel Prize in physics for having detected thermal noise in the universe.

It sounded a bit intimidating to me. But to Rothkopf, who met colleagues from different fields for tea every day, it offered the ideal cross-pollinating environment for ideas to flourish. "Someone from a completely different field would drop by my office and say, What's up?" Rothkopf said. "That's the kind of setup that produces unexpected ideas." He contrasted it with the atmosphere at Columbia University, where colleagues concentrate in more specialized clusters and are often in competition with one another for funds and recognition. "When I sat in my office at Columbia nobody would wander in," Rothkopf said. "What nonscientists often don't understand is that competition is bad for innovation. Scientists work best when they are collaborating."

Given how schooled we are in the benefits of competition, Rothkopf's statement was unorthodox. He quickly clarified that his point did not apply to other kinds of innovation, such as applied research or in business models. Yet evidence of Rothkopf's observation can be found at the heart of the story of modern American science—from Bell Labs, which was owned by a monopoly with handsome, state-regulated profit margins, to its government-owned counterparts at DARPA and elsewhere.

It can also be found by examining the R&D budgets of America's corporations. In 2010 the U.S. private sector spent $330 billion on R&D, but only 5 percent of that went to basic research.[49] Corporate R&D executives spend a lot of their time explaining to envious scientist friends at universities that life as a corporate researcher is not the lavish ticket the numbers would imply. "I would love to tell you that we spent all our time doing fundamental research," said Roger Perlmutter, who works at Amgen, one of America's largest biotech companies, which spends $2 billion a year on R&D. "But only a fraction of our time and budget is spent on that. Mostly we're dealing with the FDA, doing clinical trials, or doing after-market research, which are very different things."

Indeed, the field in which U.S. commercial innovation is probably strongest is in semiconductors, which is unusual for an industry in being highly collaborative on R&D, and which works closely with both universities and federal research agencies. In most of corporate America, however, R&D budgets are subjected to constant scrutiny by the big equity funds, which have as little time for patient research as they do for patient capital. In the words of William Baumol, one of America's leading economists of innovation: "Corporate R&D

is not the realm of unexpected but rather a bureaucratized activity of memorandums, rigid cost controls, and standardized procedures that are the hallmark of trained management."

It is a description with which Rothkopf would agree, as would Ajeet Rohatgi, the Georgia Tech solar scientist who quit corporate R&D for academia. For most of its existence, Bell Labs' budget was protected from shareholder pressure by an elaborate ownership structure that gave it autonomy. Money was rarely an issue. Most of Rothkopf's colleagues were paid a decent salary. There was no performance-related pay. But research budget requests were almost never turned down. Rothkopf remembered a colleague asking for a vast laboratory to research solid-state physics, which he promptly received. "If we wanted to fly down to Brazil, say, to do some research, they would put you on coach but you'd always get there," he recalled.

The overall result, in Rothkopf's words, was a "monastic" environment in which chance could work its magic on discovery. "Serendipity is the secret to scientific breakthrough," said Rothkopf. "Setting two-year targets is not." It may no longer be reasonable to expect serendipity from the hypercompetitive private sector. After several consecutive quarters of company-wide losses, Alcatel-Lucent in 2008 said Bell Labs was pulling out of basic research in order to focus on more direct goals for its bottom line.

After eighty-three years and seven Nobel Prizes, Bell Labs was finally turned into a corporate lab. "We decided that the team was going to have a hard time integrating its research into product development," said Gee Rittenhouse, head of Bell Labs. A company spokesman added, "In the new innovation model, research needs to keep addressing the need of the mother company."[50] The "normalization" of Bell Labs attracted only a modicum of comment. Alcatel-Lucent was merely confirming what had already happened in practice.

More significant by far was the decision in 2010 by Applied Materials, the big Silicon Valley equipment maker, to shift its chief technology officer Mark Pinto to China. The company, which makes highly innovative equipment for the semiconductor, flat panel, and solar industries, and which is in the Fortune 300, had just completed building the world's largest solar power R&D facility in the Chinese city of Xian. The decision to move Pinto to Xian may have heralded the start of the reversal of an established trend—the flow of Chinese talent to America. In addition to being situated near Xian's famous Terracotta Army, the world's largest solar power research center would now sit opposite the world's leading research institute for clean coal, a Chinese state-owned concern. Interestingly, Pinto had started his career at Bell Labs.

Some people attacked Mike Splinter, the chief executive of Applied Materials, as being unpatriotic. "You wouldn't believe some of the letters I got," he told me. But in truth Splinter had little choice. In the 1990s Applied Materials sold most of its products in the United States. Now America accounted for just 10 percent of its sales. I went to see Splinter at his company's headquarters in Santa Clara, in Silicon Valley. Splinter's office is a curious mixture of Americana and chinoiserie. Amid the team scarves and cups was the model of a terracotta soldier on his desk. Splinter, who was dressed in a thick sweater in spite of the warm spring day outside, said the company had to shift to where its customers were. Most of the world's new investment in solar power is happening in China. "Our equipment is heavy—we can't just put it on a plane from California," he said. "Nothing would give me more pleasure than setting up a manufacturing plant in the United States. But who in their right mind in my industry would do that nowadays?"

Naturally, China sweetened Applied Materials' path to Xian. Quite the opposite was happening in Washington, D.C. As part of the Capitol Hill deal in December 2010 to extend the modest middle-class tax cuts Obama had pushed through the previous year, the White House agreed to Republican demands that the president renew the larger Bush-era tax cuts for wealthier Americans. In the process the bill eliminated the obscure-sounding—and short-lived—Section 1603 grant that provided U.S. manufacturers an incentive to install clean electricity, either by retrofitting buildings or by constructing energy-efficient ones.

Its $2.3 billion cost paled against the $858 billion ten-year price of extending the tax cuts. The newly victorious Tea Party Republicans insisted on its removal. Since the item was a grant it qualified as public spending. That act terminated one of the few fiscal subsidies the renewable technology industry could claim. And it would cost at least fifteen thousand American jobs, according to some estimates. "The rest of the world is fighting tooth and nail to attract high-quality jobs and we're not even turning up to the fight," said Splinter. "What the hell were they [Congress] thinking?" The truth, of course, was that there wasn't much thinking involved.

The deal coincided with a National Journal "Heartlands" Poll in which a majority of Americans for the first time agreed that the United States lagged behind China as the strongest economy in the world (a decade ahead of the most pessimistic forecast). In addition, almost two-thirds of respondents agreed that Washington should help the U.S. manufacturing sector with more tax credits, even if they added to the fiscal deficit.

Still, Splinter and others in the industry say the tides will continue to move eastward unless the government in Washington takes more drastic steps to change U.S. public policy. "The clean energy sector is America's best chance to get a slice of the biggest twenty-first-century growth area in high-end manufacturing," said Splinter, who did little to conceal his disdain whenever he heard the letter D followed by a C. "Washington is still stuck in the mind-set of twenty years ago when we didn't have to play the game."

Splinter was talking more about resignation than hope. Any prospect the United States would shift decisively from fossil fuels to clean energy was dashed in 2009 with the failure of the Waxman-Markey cap and trade bill in the Senate. In killing the bill, Washington not only put paid to hopes of a meaningful result to the Copenhagen global warming summit later that year, it also marked a victory for the big fossil fuel suppliers, notably oil and coal. It meant that the United States had abandoned its last opportunity to gain the first mover advantage in the creation of a new industry. According to a report by the Breakthrough Institute, the United States will be outspent three to one by East Asia on clean energy between 2010 and 2015.[51] This includes spending on high-speed rail, batteries, and nuclear power as well as other renewable technologies.

By ceding the advantage on clean energy, it also meant that the Silicon Valley–style clusters of the future were emerging in places like "Electricity Valley" in Baoding, China, and around Seoul as part of South Korea's "Green New Deal" rather than in California, which had all the initial advantages. These clusters would be built around "dense networks of relationships" that would offer a magnet to others with capital and ideas. In other words, Splinter's game was already half over before Washington even realized what was happening. Even then, it has been unable to act with much clarity. "I still don't think it's too late," said Splinter. "America remains a very innovative country. But we're steadily giving away that lead."

Some investors hope that Washington lawmakers can be short-circuited by finding a radical "black swan" technology that will enable the United States to leapfrog everyone else. Of these, Vinod Khosla, the cofounder of Sun Microsystems and one of the valley's biggest names, is perhaps the best known. Khosla's contempt for linear thinking—those who extrapolate from the past to predict the future—is legendary. On a recent visit to Silicon Valley, Angela Merkel, Germany's chancellor, asked Khosla how Germany could stimulate more entrepreneurialism. Khosla offended Merkel's entourage by pointing to the German chief executives she had brought with her and saying, "You should stop listening to these guys."

Khosla has also drawn the ire of American environmentalists by dismissing most of their projects as Lilliputian. Wind power, electric cars, and solar cells will get them nowhere, he said. What we need is something that can "scale" rapidly. "We need something the linear thinkers would never think of," he said. Partly in response to how many environmentalists he had offended, Khosla in 2010 hired Tony Blair to join the board of Khosla Partners and help to provide it with a diplomatic face. Most of Khosla's investments are in clean technology. Each of his "clean dozen" investments sounded incredibly unlikely (they included quantum batteries and carbon-negative cement). Yet if any one of them worked, they could change the world, he said. "If Obama keeps listening to the chief executives of Fortune 500 companies, we are doomed," said Khosla. "They never did anything original in their lives."

Khosla's view is quintessential Silicon Valley—it sees the story of the world as a series of disruptive technologies that were dreamed up by the bold and brainy. The future is not set. It belongs to those with the bravest imaginations. As a Berkeley study once showed, experts have a worse record at predicting the future than a monkey throwing arrows at a dartboard. "The opposite of linear thinking is to imagine the future as you want it to be and never to be afraid of failing," said Khosla. "If just one of my investments makes it, then they will outweigh all the failures many times over."

Khosla offers an exciting vision. If it captured the whole picture, we could stop fretting about big corporations, gridlocked governments, and the predictable mind-sets of scholars and experts. Let the entrepreneur loose and the future will be bright. But it is also a flattering self-image. If Silicon Valley thrives on the future, it is perhaps understandable it pays little attention to the past. Amnesia is surely a price worth paying for creativity. Yet if he were to give a full account of Silicon Valley's success, Khosla would also mention the big, and indispensable, helping hand it got from the U.S. government. Intel did not invent the integrated circuit board. It came from the U.S. military. Entrepeneurs did not come up with the transistor, which was produced by Bell Labs. Google did not invent the Internet. DARPA did.

As the Breakthrough Institute report shows with regard to clean energy, and as the Pentagon demonstrated with the Internet, the private sector rarely builds platforms—or "public goods." Apart from the prohibitive cost, no single investor could have created the Internet. Most of the gains would have been captured by others. The same applies to renewable energy. It would make no more sense for a single company to lay down a smart electricity grid than it would for Khosla to rain his billion-dollar fund in cash from a helicopter. To describe the full ingredients of Silicon Valley's success, government has to be there.

Nor would its role be confined to R&D. Not only did Washington supply many of the ideas that were picked up by entrepreneurs, it then followed up with large orders. Without public procurement IBM, which is credited with inventing the computer, may never have survived as a company. During the 1950s more than half of its data processing revenues came from the B52 bomber's so-called SAGE—Simulation Air and Ground Engagements.[52] More than half of IBM's research budget also came from the federal government. Without that IBM may never have developed "system 360," which catapulted computing into a new age. Indeed, without public science, Khosla's own Sun Microsystems would have been unable to build its transformative computer workstations.

It is a story both Silicon Valley's believers and its mercenaries appear to have forgotten. So, too, has Washington, D.C. Yet governments elsewhere in the world evidently studied and dissected it in great detail, even if they sometimes left the price tag hanging from their suits. A large part of America's century of scientific and technological domination was spurred by necessity. It was born neither from government nor by the private sector but from a collaboration of the two. Fear and pragmatism were its parents and imagination was its currency. Amnesia seems to be its price.

I knew nothing about Ted Wheeler before I met him. After having done so, I made a mental note to keep an eye on his career from then on. Oregon's state treasurer is unusual for an elected politician. Not only does he have scholarly breadth—he graduated in different disciplines from Stanford, Harvard, and Columbia—he is also something of a sporting prodigy.

As far as I can tell, no other American politician has climbed Everest, as Wheeler has done. No other completed the Kona

Ironman, the world's toughest triathlon. It starts with a 2.4-mile swim, followed by a 112-mile bike ride, and is finally rounded off with a pleasant 26.2-mile run (the marathon). And I am certain no other politician walked to the North Pole on his honeymoon. All of which Wheeler, who is widely tipped as a future governor of Oregon, can claim.

I was visiting Wheeler to hear about what Oregon is doing to boost its competitiveness, not about how to cope with foot blisters. By the end of our talk it struck me that it might be easier to do the Kona Ironman. If the United States is unable at the federal level to compete with other governments for global jobs and investment, America's fifty state capitals have no such legal constraints. Some, such as California, appear to be paralyzed from doing anything to unravel the red tape in which the state is wrapped. Others, such as Texas, which has zero corporate taxes chiefly because of generous oil and gas revenues, have used what fiscal muscle they have to attract investments—among them Facebook, Google, and other doyens of Silicon Valley.

For Oregon the job is at once more difficult and easier. This is the easy bit: Portland, the state's main city, is a very pleasant place to live, which means it attracts a lot of educated young people. Graduates from across America often move to Portland without having first secured a job offer. Many seem happy to work at Starbucks by day and sample one of the city's reputed microbreweries by night. It helps explain why Oregon's unemployment rate is above the national average.[53] But it also means prospective investors can pick and choose from a highly educated pool of applicants. Nor would it be a tough decision for investors to relocate here.

Unlike most American cities, Portland banned urban sprawl in the 1970s when it put a limit on its city boundaries. The city streetcars and its tree-lined boulevards give the Pacific city a European character. It is at once small and international. As the bumper sticker says, "Think Globally, Act Locally." Portland's community college offers two-year associate degrees in viticulture (wine) and wind turbine engineering. Vestas, the Danish wind turbine maker, which is the largest in the world, placed its U.S. headquarters here. "Portland is probably the most aspiring city in America," said Wheeler, whose family fortune comes from the vast timber forests in the east of the state. "It is a small gem of urban, liberal America."

Here are the difficult bits: no matter how hard Oregon tries, most of the promised investment isn't coming. There are many reasons for this. But in Oregon's difficulties can be found America's biggest challenge writ small: what can be done to lift competitiveness? The first problem is politics. The state, which is the same geographic size as Britain, is bitterly divided between a depressed eastern portion, which has yet to recover from a long-term decline in its timber industry, and a relatively prosperous coastal—and near coastal—strip, which is home to the cities of Portland, Eugene, and Corvallis. This very stark red state–blue state bifurcation often ties Oregon's legislature up in knots.

"People in east Oregon think everything would be fine if those urban liberals stopped trying to interfere," said Wheeler, who is a Democrat. "In their view the only thing liberals care about is the spotted owl [which is on the endangered species list]." Like California, Oregon also has a ballot initiative, the results of which cannot be overridden by lawmakers. Because of referendums, Oregon spends more on prisons than it does on schools. Oregon's lawmakers are almost equally constrained in their fiscal room to maneuver, as is California (which we will look at in more detail in chapter 5). According to one notorious rule, the state has to return to the taxpayer any revenues more than 2 percent higher than the official projections made two years earlier. Like many "citizen legislatures" in the United States the state has a biennial budget.

This so-called budget kicker deprives Oregon of most of its leeway to make capital investments. There are many other self-binding constraints. Trying to navigate Oregon's budgetary complexity—and dodge the minute fiscal rules that tie it down—presents Wheeler with a permanent headache. Once the line items have exacted their toll, there are precious few resources left over to upgrade the state's deteriorating infrastructure or to improve its education. The state has also bogged itself down with an infamously heavy burden of environmental and construction regulations, many of which even liberals concede are superfluous. "It takes us thirty years to deepen our port channel by a couple of feet," said Wheeler. "China can build a whole new port in half that time."

Speaking to Wheeler, and to several investors that I met in Portland, it became clear just how colossally China looms on the West Coast's economic radar, both as an opportunity and as a threat. When Madame Liu Yandong, a politburo member, stopped off in Portland en route back to China from Washington in April 2011 the Confucius Institute remarked that the state had developed "Chinese fever." The previous year, Oregon had become the first American state to offer Mandarin classes to any child who wished to learn it. Liu was there to open twelve "Confucius classrooms." At a banquet in her honor, Madame Liu said, "You are leading the United States and the world in terms of the teaching of the Chinese language."

As a potential investor in Oregon, and as a growing export market for its products, China has long since displaced Japan. Oregon has a century-old Japan-Oregon friendship society. Madame Liu's reception showed how clearly the state's eyes were now riveted on Beijing. Oregon took her presence very seriously; Madame Liu is the sixth most senior member of China's politburo. According to Tim McCabe, head of Oregon's business development department, two Chinese camera crews trailed Liu. "For Oregon this was a huge visit—I mean huge," said McCabe, who made it sound like he had had an audience with the pope. "Have you any idea how much money the Chinese spend?"

China's railways minister had also made a recent appearance in Oregon and talked about investing in a high-speed link between Eugene and Vancouver (the one in Washington State not the one in Canada). In spite of the crash in eastern China a few months later that killed thirty-nine people, and which exposed many short cuts in Beijing's dash to build a high-speed rail network, Oregon and many other U.S. states could look on China only with envy. As part of its 2009 fiscal package, China unveiled nearly $200 billion in spending on a national high-speed rail network. Beijing's largesse offered an increasingly familiar contrast with Washington, which had set aside a mere $8 billion in Obama's stimulus.

The newly elected Republican governors of Wisconsin, Ohio, and Florida nevertheless returned their portions of the federal government's rail stimulus money in early 2011. Their gestures proved highly popular with Tea Party activists to whom the entire concept of rail travel is unacceptably European. Rick Scott, Florida's controversial governor, who sent $2.4 billion back to Washington, wrote off the planned Tampa-Orlando rail line as a "boondoggle." Citing studies that even some Republican critics dismissed as biased, all three governors projected cost overruns and low passenger uptake. But their decisions almost certainly had more to do with cultural signaling: it is hard to imagine people arriving at a Nascar rally by train.

Oregonian liberals, who lose few opportunities to extol the subtleties of the state's pinot grigio and whose choice of vegan outlets mark them as some of the most macrobiotic people in America, could only splutter at the red states' ingratitude. McCabe mentioned that Japanese contractors, who had offered to help fund, build, and even operate California's Los Angeles–San Francisco project, had estimated it would cost $70 million a mile to lay down. China then said that it could do Oregon's much shorter journey at just $40 million a mile. The fact that Japan, which invented the bullet train in 1964, has never had a serious accident may have weighed more heavily on Oregonian minds after the crash in China a few months later.

As yet, though, and in spite of many years of effort, Oregon can point to very few investments from China, or from anywhere else. Apart from Nike, which has its headquarters in Oregon and still makes some of its equipment there, Intel also has a plant, and there are some small investors in solar power. Oregon has persuaded a few big Internet companies, including Facebook, to locate data centers in the forested western expanse of Oregon, among its worst-affected timber towns. Each has generated excitement, but they are too small scale and capital intensive to have a big impact on the state's economy.

For Wheeler, who points to the state's outdated infrastructure and weak education system, the biggest fear is that Oregon will become involved in "a race to the bottom" that will leave Oregonians less economically secure than before. The state's per capita income is still marginally below the American average. Many of Oregon's paper and pulp mills have closed. In spite of being a developed state in a highly industrialized county, Oregon exports a lot of timber to China and sometimes reimports the finished product as furniture. "This is madness," said Wheeler. "The only possible way we can compete with an economic juggernaut like China is if we are adding value."

Wheeler's frustrations were acute. He recently visited China with his school-age daughter and they caught a glimpse of some of the country's freshly built suspension bridges and deep-water ports. Not only was Oregon unable to avoid large cuts in education and infrastructure, the state's "kicker" rule might rob less austere budgets in the future of any chance to make up for it. He seemed pessimistic the rule could easily be overturned—voters love getting cash back in their pockets. "China can throw huge amounts of money around and it executes projects at a speed we can only dream about," Wheeler said. "They don't have to deal with a system of ballot initiatives and local democracy."

Portland's business establishment, which is led by Randy Miller, a successful entrepreneur, does its best to bring jobs to the city, which is home to so many overqualified waiters. Many are puzzled that Portland is not more of a success. In some ways the city is suffering from an "Egypt syndrome": lots of graduates and few jobs, except that its woes clearly don't stem from a lack of democracy. "We have such a high quality of life in Portland but our jobs market is still lackluster," said Miller, whom I met at a demo tasting kitchen in the offices of Tazo, a tea company now owned by Starbucks that started in a building he rents out to start-ups. It is not the kind of small business you find in Cairo, or in China for that matter. As one does, I was sipping a cup of African Red Bush tea (offering a flavorful hint of "tart hibiscus, lemon and a sprig of rosemary," according to the label).

Miller had taken delegations from Oregon to visit cities around the United States in search of tips on how to create jobs. But the model he liked best was that of Copenhagen, a city of trams and high-quality jobs. "We are surrounded by basket cases so it should be a pretty low bar for Oregon to succeed," Miller said, listing California, Arizona, and Nevada as states that in his view were politically in a much worse condition than Oregon. "But we also suffer from sclerosis. It can be really difficult to get things done."

America's states often face different challenges. Oregon may well be hampered by its acute divide between its interior and the coastal cities. They also have two things in common: a federal government that finds it hard to team up with them to win jobs and investment (not least because Washington would inevitably be accused of bias in favor of one state or another) and a fiscal outlook that looks bleak for a long time to come. It is not a good combination.

Wheeler, who in spite of turning fifty looks like he could be a young executive at Facebook, is passionate about making Oregon more competitive by building on its progressive values rather than by lowering the cost of labor. That would involve better education for those born in the state as well as more incentives to bring in good investors. It is unclear which comes first—good jobs or good education. Few economies have faced this problem before. It is also unclear where all the new infrastructure will come from, let alone how quickly. "After we have accounted for all the spending and tax priorities voters have given us through the ballot initiative we don't have the resources left over for economic development," said Wheeler. "It's very hard to escape that fact."

For America as a whole the picture is not that much different. Just after Obama took office, the American Society of Engineers issued a report card on the condition of the nation's infrastructure and awarded it an overall D grade. That year China spent 9 percent of its GDP on infrastructure. For Europe, the figure was 5 percent. For the United States it was just 2.3 percent. The number has fallen since then. The society concluded America would need to spend almost $450 billion a year for the next five years simply to maintain the existing quality of its infrastructure. It may as well have asked Washington to launch another race to the moon.

"If we act boldly we will emerge stronger and more prosperous than we were before," said Obama in defense of his 2009 fiscal package. The $787 billion two-year stimulus was passed. But much less than a third of it went to infrastructure and most of that went to "shovel-ready" projects that were selected for their speed rather than for their quality.★ Unlike the 1930s, which produced memorable projects such as the Tennessee Valley Authority, LaGuardia Airport, and the Hoover Dam, the stimulus left few durable signs that it had ever happened. Nor was its economic impact sufficient to make up for having missed a big opportunity to build up America's future productive capacity. By the time the stimulus petered out two years later America's economy was again slowing.

Any hope Obama had of pushing his idea to create a national infrastructure bank was dashed by the 2010 Republican midterm victory. America's bridges, roads, schools, electricity grid, waterways, rail system, air traffic network, and levees have already dropped to second world level. It remains to be seen how much more deterioration the American electorate will tolerate. To judge by America's investment rate, potential business investors, both foreign and American, are steadily losing their patience. "We have to find a way to compete without tying our hand behind our back," said Wheeler. "We need to succeed because of our values not in spite of them."

★And the speed element to many of the shovel-ready projects was overstated. Anyone living near Eighteenth Street in Washington's Northwest, as this writer does, would attest to its opposite. At the time of writing, the stimulus-funded project, which extends just over a mile's worth of road, was well into its third year. At no time were more than twenty workers visible. The project combines the worst of the developing and developed worlds: it progresses with inconvenient lassitude, yet it employs hardly anyone.

After seeing Wheeler, I met his colleague Brad Avakian, who is Oregon's labor commissioner, for a beer in one of Portland's Irish bars. Avakian told me he was doing what he could with what little resources he had to boost workforce training in the high jobless blue-collar communities in Oregon. The fact that this small state had nine different workforce development agencies, each competing for the same resources, often duplicating the efforts of others, made his task more difficult. Having flown in from Washington, it all sounded very familiar to me.

But it was something else Avakian told me that stuck in my mind. A few months earlier, he had been on an official visit to Taiwan. One evening his hosts took him out for a drink. They began to unwind. The conversation turned to America. "These guys were literally laughing at America," Avakian said. "They couldn't understand the game we were playing. 'Please keep sending us all the jobs, everything else will follow,'" Avakian remembered them saying. Now contending to be the Democratic nominee for an Oregon district in the U.S. Congress, Avakian said he was still agitated by memories of that evening. "I realized when they let their guard down that they saw America as a joke," he said. "It was a real shock to me."

At a New York dinner in 2010 Amar Goel had an epiphany, although not of the kind he wanted. Goel, who was born and bred in Sunnyvale, Silicon Valley, was meeting with a group of Harvard classmates he had not seen for a long time. Everyone was updating his or her life story. Many were working on Wall Street. Goel, who started up his first business at nineteen during his first undergraduate year at Columbia University and who now owns three, had recently moved to Mumbai with his wife, who is also Indian-American. The Harvard classmates wanted to know how long they planned to stay in India. Goel is now twenty-five and one of his businesses handles all of Facebook's sales and advertising in India. He said they had no plans to return to America soon. There was a revolution happening in Asia, he said. It was like America in the late nineteenth century.

That observation sparked a heated debate, with Goel on one side and everyone else on the other. In essence, Goel's classmates insisted that America would remain the center of the world. An incredulous Goel felt he needed to educate his friends about the changing world around them. "They said, 'There isn't a child in India that wouldn't come to America given half the chance,'" Goel recalled. "America was still number one in everything. Everybody in the world still wanted to be American." Goel was not sure how many of his friends he had convinced. "It was really frustrating," he said. "We could have been having this conversation in 1990. It was like nothing has changed."

In many contexts, I have observed how complex the relationship can be between Americans and the land from which their forebears came. Everyone has a different story and it is absurd to generalize. But I have picked up a fierce pride among Indian-Americans about India's sharp rebound in the past twenty years. Unlike so many first- or second-generation Americans from Asia—particularly Chinese-Americans—Indian-Americans almost all came to the United States in search of economic opportunity. None were fleeing tyranny. "My father couldn't get here fast enough," said Goel. He came in 1971 to study chemical engineering at the University of Notre Dame. He then moved to Silicon Valley to work for Dell. "If someone had an engineering degree in India and they weren't trying to get to America, friends would ask, What is the matter with you?"

That was the narrative that Goel's Harvard friends had remembered. Many had seen the movie *The Namesake,* based on a poignant story by Jhumpa Lahiri, the New York–based novelist, about a young Indian couple who moved to America in the 1970s. Goel, whose Mumbai business, Komli, employs almost four hundred people and whose ambition is for it to become "Asia's premier platform for digital advertising," had more contemporary stories to share with his classmates.

Goel had recently lost his best intern in his Mumbai office to higher education. The young man was exceptional. Goel offered to promote his studies in the United States. The intern said he could see no reason to be educated away from home. He chose to go to the Hyderabad School of Business. The decision was practical. The young Indian wanted to start a business at home and said it would make far more sense to network with Indians than with Americans. Goel had other such examples from other parts of Asia. Komli also has offices in Hong Kong and Sydney. "What I realized was that America is no longer automatically number one in the minds of the new generation in India," Goel said. "They have been raised in a different world."

Goel's moment of shock came when his Harvard classmates refused to accept this story at face value. Goel would never sever his ties to the United States, and he will probably return to Silicon Valley at some stage. "Both our parents still live in America," Goel said. "I don't want to get a phone call in the middle of the night." He still loves the land of his birth. But he is worried that the United States has entered what he called "an age of denial and narcissism" that will hinder it from confronting its challenges. When Goel was setting up his two U.S.-based businesses— one of which, Chipshot.com, delivers customized golf equipment from Silicon Valley—American investors often asked if he had an international strategy. "What is this international strategy?" Goel said. "*International* doesn't mean anything. There are a lot of big and growing countries out there that are very different from each other."

Goel is acutely aware of the systemic corruption and the extreme poverty that still exist in the country of his forebears. But the country is on the move. "It is incredibly exciting to be looking at all these sectors that are doubling every ten years," he said. "You are in a world that is transforming." Meanwhile, America seems to have stalled. I mentioned the phrase "American exceptionalism." Goel took this as a cue to unload. If a country believed in its heart that it was destined to prevail, he said, then it would not need to do very much to help things along. America was suffering from a form of denial that precluded it from taking remedial steps. "If Americans were thinking differently, I'd be much less worried," Goel said. "To overcome a problem, you must first recognize it exists."

4

Gulliver's Travails

WHY BUREAUCRACY IS HARMING AMERICA'S COMPETITIVENESS

There is something good and motherly about Washington, the grand old benevolent National Asylum for the helpless.

Mark Twain, *The Gilded Age*

IT IS NOT often that you are offered a glass of fine wine at ten a.m.—let alone a vintage Nobile di Montepulciano. But Vint Cerf, who is Google's "Internet evangelist," plays by his own rules. Unlike Al Gore, the former vice president, Cerf can say with a straight face that he invented the Internet. Along with Robert Kahn, with whom he wrote the first Internet protocols in the early 1970s, and their boss Larry Roberts, Cerf is co-parent to the most revolutionary innovation of our times. Now sixty-nine, Cerf works for a company that in online terms is a distant descendant of what he helped to create. "Sergey [Brin] and Larry [Page] said to me, 'Why don't we call you Archduke?'" Cerf recalled of Google's twenty-something cofounders. "I thought chief Internet evangelist sounded better."

The legendary Pentagon scientist is certainly a persuasive talker. With his groomed blue-silver beard, boating jacket, and silk breast pocket handkerchief, Cerf might almost be called debonair. Words, aphorisms, and asides tumble out of him in no strict order. What he lacks in sequence he makes up for in perspicacity. Cerf spends three-quarters of his time on the road talking at universities, international conferences, and meeting with investors and officials around the world. Sometimes he is to be found in Washington, D.C., which is just a stone's throw away from where he lives in northern Virginia (in a small mansion with a legendary wine cellar).

In Washington Cerf often finds that his evangelism deserts him. He mentions the names of several Republican lawmakers who have developed a following by mocking science and tarring nonmilitary research as a liberal boondoggle. Several lawmakers had recently ridiculed a line item funding research into honeybees, which are mysteriously dying out all over the world. "Do they know how important bees are to human survival?" asked Cerf. Most notorious was James Inhofe, a senator from Alaska, who built a PR-stunt igloo on Capitol Hill during Washington's five-day "snowmageddon" in 2010. Inhofe believed the snowstorm disproved global warming. When Washington experienced unseasonably warm T-shirt weather in January 2012, there were no tanning beds put on display by Senator Inhofe.

"The Republicans have become a party of demagogues against science," says Cerf. "We didn't used to face this problem." In addition to blocking action to reduce carbon output, rising hostility toward science meant that Congress was unlikely to restore Washington's research and development budgets to anything like their former levels or, indeed, to the ratios of America's competitors today, he said. In spite of having invented the R&D tax credit, the United States now has only the eighteenth most generous in the world.[54] And it is still not permanent. Congress refuses to give up its right of annual renewal.

Dwindling tax incentives for corporate R&D was only a small part of the problem. In addition to the anti-science legislators, Cerf had some critical words for economists (Democrat and Republican), a profession that is largely silent about what causes innovation. In most economic models, innovation is treated as a "black box," something that mysteriously emerges from the private sector. Most economists are not enthusiasts for big federal research budgets. For these reasons, they were also a problem, Cerf said. "Do they think Google would exist without public research?"

Combine Luddite politicians with indifferent economists and you get stagnant science budgets. If you throw in fiscal austerity the outlook gets bleaker. Add in a final ingredient—the increased bureaucratization of the U.S. federal government and the hyperregulation of public science grants—and the story starts to look sobering. It is not hard to see why Cerf is yearning for the past. "I grew up in the golden era of public science," said Cerf. "People understood that we needed time and money to make big breakthroughs. You didn't spend your whole life justifying your existence."

If a budding scientist could choose one time and place in history to be in high school it would have been alongside Cerf in Connecticut (and later Stanford) in the late 1950s. The Soviet launch of Sputnik in 1957 sent shudders through Washington, D.C. The ability to launch satellites into space could give the Soviets a decisive nuclear advantage over the United States. It meant the Stalinists could be winning the Cold War. Washington's response, which put a man on the moon twelve years later, came with purpose and alacrity. One of Eisenhower's most important steps was to drastically boost funding in public education. Science, engineering, and calculus were big beneficiaries. As was Cerf. "It was the perfect time to be at school," he said. "When the Soviets launched Sputnik they launched my future."

Another big step was the creation of the Defense Advanced Research Projects Agency (the legendary DARPA), which was lavished with funding and strong backing from both parties. Cerf made his name there in the 1970s. A huge proportion of today's most critical technologies were born at DARPA, among them the global positioning system, the Internet, stealth technology, and the computer mouse. Some economists may doubt that nations compete. Perhaps fortunately for the U.S. economy, and particularly for Silicon Valley, DARPA worked on a different assumption during the Cold War.

Both Cerf and Robert Kahn, whom I also visited at his office a few miles away (Kahn runs his own research group), were adamant about one thing. Without the long-term support of the

Pentagon the Internet would not exist. Much like Eisenhower's interstate highways program, ARPANET, the forerunner of the Internet, was designed to help the United States survive a nuclear war. ARPANET would ensure the military's ability to maintain communications in the event of a nuclear attack. Even after it was created, DARPA kept pouring more money into it. Scientists, rather than officials, drove the budgeting requests.

"If DARPA had withdrawn support in 1980 we would have had no Internet," said Cerf. Kahn agreed, saying, "The private sector would not have had the patience or firepower to fill DARPA's shoes." Both freely admitted that the quality of public research has declined. They pointed to the culture of risk aversion among bureaucrats and scientists, whose main focus is on upgrading existing technologies rather than aiming for that eureka moment. In today's Washington, it is unlikely that federal R&D budgets would produce the breakthroughs that were so common in their prime. "Sputnik put the fear of God into us," said Cerf. "There just isn't the same commitment to public science today."

One example was the so-called Valley of Death—by which public innovations often remain beyond the commercial reach of private companies. In much the same way that DARPA's investment in the ARPANET enabled companies such as Netscape and Google to come into being, private investors need a platform to bridge the valley between fundamental research and commercial application, such as a smart grid that could transmit and store renewable energy. "Creating the infrastructure is very different from picking winners," said Cerf. "You are building an arena in which the winners can compete."

In the absence of galvanizing panic, scientists complain that the machinery of U.S. government has become less ambitious over time. Positions that were once highly prized, such as the head of the National Aeronautics and Space Administration, are difficult to fill. According to two administration sources, seven people refused Barack Obama's offer to head NASA in 2009 before Charles Bolden, a former astronaut, finally agreed. NASA may be a specific case, since Obama had announced the end of its forty-year run of manned space flights.

Beneath the heads of the big public science agencies, it is also harder to recruit high-caliber scientists. The pay is poor. And the conditions attached to research grants are often stifling. The standard contract specifies very precisely the goal of the research and usually limits funding to one or two years. "Most breakthroughs come by accident," said Cerf. "If you prevent scientists from exploring what has been thrown their way then you will get timid, predictable science."

Along with the declining budgets comes waning ambition. Many scientists were outraged when Washington in 1993 refused to put up the cash for the supercollider particle accelerator project, which was already under construction in Texas. Instead, the vast project, which aims to answer some of the biggest questions in physics, is run from Geneva by the Europeans. "Thirty years ago, there would have been no question that we would have funded a supercollider," said Greg Tassey, chief economist at the National Institute of Standards and Technology, which was set up to be the civilian counterpart to DARPA.

Harold Varmus, the Nobel Prize–winning former head of the National Institutes of Health who now runs the National Cancer Institute, says researchers need freedom and yearn to be able to make progress. But the spigots in today's Washington are unreliable. In 2011 Washington went through its third consecutive year of "continuing resolutions"—measures to keep budgets going at the previous year's level when Congress fails to agree on a new one. Most public science agencies have little confidence as to what their budgets will be next year, or the year after. "In research you need security of funding," said Varmus. "You can't make progress if you spend all your time raising money."

The same difficulties apply to the U.S. Patent and Trademark Office, which takes three years to process an application (roughly twice the average time it takes in most of East Asia, for example). Attracting and retaining scientists is an uphill task. Like other agencies, the USPTO, which was set up directly by the U.S. Constitution, lives from hand to mouth under continuing budget resolutions. Unlike its counterparts in South Korea, Canada, Mexico, Japan, and German, the USPTO cannot run itself like a business. Although the U.S. Patents Office is self-funding—it takes fees from applicants —Congress often takes the surplus and spends it elsewhere.

"It is a tax on U.S. innovation," says Jon Dudas,[55] who was head of the patents office until 2009. "We cannot match the investments other countries are making." They also find it hard to recruit U.S.-born scientists. A few years ago the USPTO asked its sixteen hundred scientists to complete a questionnaire. Many could not answer the questions. "I thought it was the typical reticence that you get from engineers," said Dudas. In fact, it was because so many of them had a poor command of English. That same congressional tendency to drain self-funding agencies of their budgets has frequently hobbled the Securities and Exchange Commission, which remains light-years behind the algorithmic software of the players it is supposed to regulate.

Then there are ethics regulations. Varmus, who was previously head of Sloan-Kettering, the world-class cancer hospital in New York, says that public scientists are stifled by increasingly pedantic rules. In 2011 Varmus was invited to give the prestigious annual Rede Lecture at Cambridge University in the UK. The federal ethics officer told him that he could not stay with the university vice chancellor, whom he had known for years. Even to meet me for a tandoori meal in Washington Varmus needed clearance. Varmus is seventy-three and a world-renowned scientist. But he did not have the authority to agree that either he or I would pick up the $45 bill. We split it carefully. "This way of doing things isn't good for morale," said Varmus. "It puts good people off from working in government."

American politics has almost always divided itself between those who believe in less government and those who believe in more. In the past three decades or so the former have been getting the upper hand. Ronald Reagan famously said that the nine most frightening words in the English government were, "I am from the government and I am here to help you." By the time Bill Clinton was president the Democrats had conceded most of the argument. "The era of big government is over," said Clinton. But as every president since Reagan has found out, the White House's ability to change how the federal system works is tightly limited.

In a report on nanotechnology for the Obama White House,[56] a group of scientists pointed out that the government's research dollars were scattered across twenty-five federal agencies. There was no single person in charge of research into this critical technology of the future. "It is shockingly difficult for the president to do anything about the agencies," said Ed Penhoet, the Silicon Valley entrepreneur, who also sits on the White House's science advisory board. Common sense suggests Obama should at least appoint someone to coordinate all the nanotechnology spending across Washington. But this would be hard to achieve in practice.

Each agency, whether the National Science Foundation, the Department of Energy, the Pentagon, or NASA, is jealously overseen by its own appropriations committee on Capitol Hill. Each also interacts with a key constituency, or lobby group, that seeks to influence its behavior. The congressional appropriators, in turn, raise campaign funds from the special interests. Much like the three-way relationship between the congressional agriculture committees, the U.S. Department of Agriculture, and large agribusinesses, they work together closely in an "iron triangle."

Breaking it up would not be easy. Penhoet, who works on a Silicon Valley schedule, was obviously stunned by the discovery about how rigidly Washington's iron triangles are set in place. "Difficult stuff isn't even worth trying," he said. "Let's say the president wanted to combine all research money into one agency—he wouldn't stand a chance." The easiest step would be to set up a new agency, which would then compete with all the others for funds and authority. The net result would be more complexity.

The same stories repeat themselves across Washington. None of these problems are about the size of the U.S. government but rather its suppleness. As Jonathan Rauch, a highly reputed journalist and follower of Mancur Olson, puts it, in the U.S. federal government "the rate of calcification outstrips the rate of adaptation."[57] The right argues for shrinkage, the left for maintaining (rather than expanding) its size. Both are missing the bigger picture. The government may be fat and sclerotic or thin and sclerotic. What matters is that it lacks agility. "The size of government is not the real problem," says Rauch. "It is its flexibility and responsiveness."

When Dwight Eisenhower took over the White House from Harry S. Truman, the latter worried about his successor's ability to cope with politics. "Poor Ike," said Truman. "It won't be like the army at all. He will say 'do this' and 'do that,' and nothing will happen." Truman proved too pessimistic. With the help of the Soviets, America's most famous Republican soldier prodded Washington's deliberately slow-moving system into feats that arguably it has not achieved before or since.

Today America faces a challenge of similar magnitude but far greater complexity. Capital and power are draining steadily—and perhaps inexorably—from West to East. The threat may manifest itself in terms of credit rating downgrades rather than visions of nuclear Armageddon. But it is just as real. "If you stick the words *national security* in front of things, then Republicans are suddenly in favor of strong government action," says Vint Cerf. "God knows we need to find a sense of urgency again."

From Germany to China, governments have teamed up with domestic businesses and continue to siphon investment, jobs, and technology from the United States. In the late 1990s the United States had a $30 billion annual surplus in advanced manufactured goods, the high-tech products that enabled the nation to dominate the global economy. Now it has a $40 billion deficit. As recently as 2000, the United States was ranked first in the world in terms of its ability to innovate, according to the Information Technology and Innovation Foundation, a group that monitors U.S. competitiveness. By 2010 it had moved down to sixth. In the first decade of this century, the United States came last out of forty countries in improvements to its climate for innovation.

America's leading companies have responded rapidly to these changing signals. In the past decade some of America's most impressive companies shifted large chunks of their corporate brains offshore. In 2003 IBM had 6,000 employees in India and 135,000 in the United States. Now it has 110,000 employees in India, which has overtaken the company's U.S. workforce. GE, which is America's largest manufacturer, has five global R&D centers, of which only one is in the United States (near Albany, New York). The other four are in Bangalore, Shanghai, Rio de Janeiro, and Munich. Fewer than a tenth of GE's full-time "technologists" are based in the United States.

"The difference between America and all its competitors is that they are working with their governments," said Rob Atkinson, who heads the ITIF. "It is not GM versus Toyota. It is GM versus Toyota and the government of Japan. It is Google versus Baidu and the People's Republic of China." Atkinson spends his life arguing that point with Washington's policy makers. He says it is like "wading through molasses." Yet there are some corners of the U.S. government that agree with him, not least at DARPA and NIST (its civilian counterpart).

Greg Tassey, the NIST economist, ascribes Washington's inertia to "installed wisdom" (which, in turn, defends the "installed base"). Washington conventional wisdom tells us governments can do little or nothing to affect productivity, the most important measure of an economy's potency. In the standard model, when a company moves production overseas, it reinvests the savings at home. Consumers will use what they save from cheaper imported goods to buy more domestic products or boost their personal savings. Everybody gains.

America's experience increasingly belies that theory, Tassey argues. In a world where the biggest economic actors are global but where the focus of governments is domestic, "success for any economy will be determined by the competitiveness policies of that country's government."[58] Should the U.S. consumer's purchasing power continue to decline, U.S.-based companies will be reluctant to invest revenues back home. The center of gravity will shift from the American middle class to its counterparts in the East. It is a good description of what has happened to America in recent decades.

Tassey is one discordant voice. Another is Regina Dugan, the director of DARPA. Nowadays the scientists at the agency have a much more modest mission than in the days of Vint Cerf and Robert Kahn. A change in the law in the 1980s directed that DARPA should confine itself strictly to military innovation. That would rule out many of the applications it came up with during its heyday in the 1960s and '70s. DARPA also devotes a much larger share of its budgets to applied, rather than fundamental, research—to improve existing technologies. This lowers its chances of coming up with disruptive breakthroughs.

"You're not going to change the world like that," said Cerf. Yet DARPA still sees itself as an agency with a mission. In testimony to Capitol Hill in 2010 Dugan described it as "the nation's elite army of futuristic technogeeks." Their job was not as straightforward as it used to be, she said. Americans were consuming more goods made overseas than ever before. But they were less likely to be in a manufacturing job than at any time in the previous century. "We believe that this decline impacts the nation's ability to innovate," said Dugan. "Quite simply, to innovate, we must make."

Dugan's testimony was another reminder to lawmakers of the changing world around them. But her words had little impact on their behavior. A year later the U.S. Senate cut 5 percent from DARPA's budget, which took it to below $3 billion, a fraction, in real terms, of what it used to spend and much less than what America's competitors are spending today. After years of cuts and micromanagement by Congress, those at DARPA had little choice but to conclude that it would probably face many more years of the same. "Everyone else is now innovating or trying to innovate," said Cerf, whose evangelical tendencies remain unblunted. "But Washington seems to be losing its appetite."

Washington's largesse may be dwindling, at least with regard to its ability to invest in America's future productive capacity. So, too, are its ambitions. But the ability to hold the federal government to account keeps getting more difficult. Thirty years after Ronald Reagan launched what has become an unbroken mission to streamline government, it is safe to say that the project remains a failure.

In spite of his rhetoric, Reagan left government larger than he found it. He managed to shut down only four programs—general revenue sharing, urban development action grants, the synthetic fuels program, and the Clinch River Breeder Reactor.[59] Reagan's most famous attempt to simplify government came in 1986 when he reformed the tax code. Within five years Congress had made 5,400 changes to it. It is now more than five times larger than it was under Richard Nixon.[60] Even Douglas Shulman, the head of the IRS, farms his taxes out to an accountant.[61]

Whichever party is in control, the federal government keeps getting murkier. The tax code is a good barometer of its complexity. Another would be the Federal Register of regulations, which is about the same length as the tax code at 70,000 pages (perhaps unsurprisingly since discrete tax breaks often correspond to discrete regulatory changes). A third is what the Pentagon calls "brass creep," which in civilian terms means adding one layer of management on another, each a self-defeating attempt to cope with the complexity created by the previous one.

During George W. Bush's administration the number of executive titles rose from fifty-one to sixty-four.[62] In much the same way that almost everyone at Citicorp appears to be a vice president, anyone who wants to be someone in Washington has a chief of staff. That particular title inflation began in 1987 when the first deputy chief of staff position was created for a cabinet secretary. By 1991 there was a chief of staff to a deputy secretary. Then it started to cascade. Suddenly everyone wanted one. My favorite is chief of staff to the associate deputy assistant secretary. "Without a chief of staff you are nobody in Washington," says Paul Light, the government scholar. "It would be like a gentleman without a valet."

Today Democrats are alone in arguing for government reform. Many Republicans say they want to starve it. In the words of Grover

Norquist, the antitax crusader, they aim to shrink government "to a size where we can drown it in a bathtub." Yet the last time Republicans had control of the first two branches of government (for most of the time between 2001 and 2007), the federal government continued to bulge. With the creation of the Department of Homeland Security after the September 11 attacks, Bush created the most confused agency in Washington, which is overseen by twenty-two congressional committees. Congress has resisted any suggestion of slimming that down.*

Republican Congresses have as bad a record as Democrats do in specifying in detail what agencies can and cannot do. When Bush created the Transportation Security Authority to handle airport security after 9/11, Congress said its pay and personnel should be managed by the private sector. Accenture, the private consultancy, got the $224 million annual contract. Congress even stipulated the detail of the uniforms that TSA officers should wear. Some people say the TSA stands for "Thousands Standing Around." Others believe its officers are too ready to frisk their "junk." Either way, the president has little authority to interfere even with the smallest of details.

Al Gore, Clinton's deputy, offered the last sustained attempt to reform federal bureaucracy with his plan of "reinventing" government. Slimmer government did not necessarily make it smarter, as Gore and others had intended. "Reinventing government is sitting in some cyber cemetery at the University of Texas," says Paul Light, perhaps the leading scholar on the U.S. federal government. "It has been dumped and forgotten along with all the reform efforts in the last thirty years." Nor did it necessarily amount to smaller government. Many of the 250,000 jobs eliminated in Gore's effort reappeared almost instantly as outside contractors.

Indeed, the growing use of outside contractors has morphed into a kind of hidden workforce that is often beyond any reach of

---

*When I spoke to the military officers at the National Defense University, I asked them which of all the dramatic reforms they proposed for Washington would be most difficult to achieve. "Reducing the number of congressional committees," was their reply.

accountability. According to a *New York Times* investigation fewer than half of all government contracts were awarded through open bidding in the time of its survey (2004).[63] Effectively that meant that more than $200 billion in contracts were handed out to friends of the administration. Most, such as those during the Bush years that went to Halliburton in Iraq or to the defense companies General Dynamics, Raytheon, and Lockheed Martin, were sole bidders.

The arrangement suits both Democrats and Republicans— Democrats because they can expand government without appearing to and Republicans because they can make use of government without appearing to. Defense and security companies were the largest recipients of government contracts during the Bush era and were large donors to Republicans in turn. Since 1951, when it imposed an informal cap of 2 million on the size of the federal civilian workforce, Congress has virtually guaranteed the expansion of a hidden federal workforce. At that stage America's population was half what it is today. Since then, Washington's shadow army of contractors and people who receive federal grants has grown from almost nowhere to 10.5 million people, in other words, more than five times the size of the official workforce.[64]

According to Light, there is virtually no chance Congress will remove that 2 million ceiling given the benefits it reaps. In 2005 alone, the five largest defense contractors spent more than $100 million on lobbying.[65] The system is sustained because of "pure political incentives," he says. Efficient government has nothing to do with it. "They [contractors] not only lobby Congress and the president for larger contracts, they provide campaign contributions to friendly incumbents," he wrote.

When presidents become frustrated with how little control Congress has left them over the civilian bureaucracy, they create White House policy czars to try and knock heads together. In this regard, and this alone, Obama is very much a czarist. Obama has a czar for ethics, information, cars, Mideast peace, Sudan, green jobs, the Great Lakes, food, climate, drugs, AIDS, and, of course, government transparency. In all, he has thirty-seven czars. Bush had thirty-three. Clinton had eight. Bush Senior had just two. The growth of czarism is a good yardstick of Washington's growing complexity.

Critics of rampant czarism, particularly on Capitol Hill, say the White House uses these ad hoc appointments to hoard power for itself; czars, unlike formal nominees, do not have to be confirmed by Congress. In reality, such czarism is a measure of a president's impotence. None has authority over the budgets or decisions made by the departments that they shadow. A czar's power is measured almost solely by his or her personal access to the president. Inevitably, a large number of czars, particularly in Obama's White House, rarely see the inside of the Oval Office. Often they spend their time projecting whatever influence they have onto their cabinet doppelgängers. This rarely turns out well.

From interviews with administration officials, it is clear very few of Obama's czars have had regular access to the president, and a large share have met him on only a handful of occasions. It is also apparent that most of Obama's cabinet secretaries, like their predecessors in the Bush administration, respond to czarist intrusions by falling prey to departmentalism. The czar and cabinet secretary both battle for the ear of Obama, which they rarely get (events having kept him in almost continual emergency mode). The demands of a reelection campaign have only eaten further into Obama's schedule.

By creating a new czar, a president aims to slice through the bureaucracy. But it usually complicates lines of communication. In practice, as was seen during the attempt to pass the cap and trade bill in 2009, the czar (in that case Carol Browner) and the White House staff manage the public message and relations with Capitol Hill. Meanwhile, the relevant cabinet secretaries (in this case, Stephen Chu at Energy and Lisa Jackson at the EPA) retreat into routine departmental work. For the latter, most interactions with the media must be cleared through the White House. Since they work in the White House, young press officers often have the upper hand over seasoned agency heads.

"I had these twenty-five-year-olds from the White House on the phone telling me what I could and could not say in public about science," said the chief of a major regulatory agency after the tsunami hit Fukushima in early 2011. The agency wanted to reassure the public there would be no radiation fallout in the United States from the Japanese nuclear shutdown. Sensing political danger in any premature reassurance, the White House applied a gag. For several days nervous consumers on the West Coast rushed to buy potassium iodide. "When the White House is in panic mode even the tiniest public communication has to be cleared with them," said the agency head. "At this stage in my career it is just humiliating."

In that instance, as in numerous others, the White House contravened Obama's pledge to "Let scientists speak," which was meant to undo the damage done by Bush junior who banned scientists from referring to global warming. In others, however, the White House simply cuts out the cabinet secretary altogether. Barring the pro forma cabinet meetings Gary Locke, Obama's secretary of commerce, had almost no genuine meetings with Obama during his two and a half years in the job. On one occasion in early 2010, Valerie Jarrett, Obama's senior business adviser, invited business leaders for a meeting at the White House. She forgot to invite the key cabinet principal. Obama had to appease Locke by inviting him to lunch a few days later.[66]

The White House's fondness for czars makes the president look like a control freak. In reality, though, czarism has flourished in response to Capitol Hill's tendency to micromanage the bureaucracy. In its unending tussle with Capitol Hill to control the rest of the executive branch, the White House is usually on the losing side. "The Obama administration has the most centralized White House in modern history and that is now true of each succeeding one," says the head of a large Washington think tank and a former senior official under Clinton. "Yet each White House has a little bit less control over the bureaucracy than its predecessor."

Capitol Hill's favorite tool of control is to block or delay the president's appointees, which add up to roughly three thousand people, of whom about a third require Senate confirmation. Again, it is getting steadily worse. John F. Kennedy's appointees were confirmed within ten weeks of his taking office in 1961. By Reagan's time it took twenty weeks. Obama had to wait ten months before all his nominees were in their jobs.[67] That also understates the problem. In case after case, Obama has been unable to put his preferred candidate forward in the knowledge that Republicans would block them. Several agencies, including the board of the U.S. Federal Reserve, the Federal Housing Finance Agency, and the Federal Elections Commission, were depleted through most of Obama's first term.

Then there is the toll on individuals of a process that Terry Sullivan, a Brookings scholar, describes as "fabulous, formless darkness."[68] Going through the humiliation of all the background checks is deterrent enough. The financial disclosure form, for example, has twelve pages of instructions. Depending on the form, the nominee must provide a history of which foreign countries he or she has visited in the previous fifteen years and when (including day trips to Canada and Mexico). They must also provide a history of all prescription drugs taken, every psychiatrist, social worker, and marriage therapist seen, and any traffic fine paid over $150.

That's before even getting to the finances. Likewise, the national security form is substantially unchanged since the McCarthy witch hunts of the 1950s. One of its questions is: "Do you know of anyone or any organization that might take any steps, overtly or covertly, fairly or unfairly, to criticize your appointment, including any news organization?" As the Washington saying has it, "Innocent until nominated." The form leaves unclear whether mothers-in-law would count.

As we saw, Obama found someone to head up NASA only on his eighth attempt. To varying degrees the same was true of dozens of other positions that were his (supposed) gift. "I very nearly pulled out twice," said an official who was confirmed in a senior position at a major department. The Senate committee had asked him for receipts for $1,200 worth of furniture that he had donated to charity in 1998 and entered on his tax form as a deduction (entirely legitimately). The effort kept him in paperwork for three months. His accountant charged north of $20,000. "By the time I was nominated I was in a state of nervous exhaustion," he added.

Another midlevel nominee pulled out after Republican Senate staffers began inquiring about his wife's sex life at college. Then there are the many who failed to clear the initial checks because at one time or another they had paid cleaners, gardeners, or nannies in cash. Unsurprisingly, many talented people will not even consider accepting a job. "I have turned down more government jobs that you can probably guess," says Rey Ramsey, head of TechNet, which represents Silicon Valley's biggest companies in Washington. "Life is too short for that."

Admirers of the United States are often shocked at the inefficiency of its bureaucracy. It is easy to forget that the U.S. Constitution intentionally designed the confusion—if not the paralysis. As James Madison said, "Ambition must be made to counteract ambition." Much like the people of Lilliput on coming across Gulliver, lawmakers lash new ropes to the giant whenever it twitches. It is no surprise then that the American public disdains government even if those same sentiments prove self-fulfilling. Politicians get high grades when they attack the bureaucracy. Yet in demonizing those who work under them, they breed sullen resistance among the people whose help they need to improve the system.

Some White Houses trumpet plans to eliminate malfeasance, others to bring "sunshine" to the bureaucracy, still others to instill managerial autonomy or even to reinvent government. Each wave adds "a sediment of bureaucratic confusion," says Light. Obama, like his predecessors, has focused on eliminating waste, fraud, and abuse. Naturally, this has done little to improve morale among federal employees. Like virtually every president before him, Obama has also frozen the salaries of federal employees. Much like Obama's attempts to eliminate waste, fraud, and abuse, which is the fiscal equivalent of rummaging for coins under the sofa, a federal salary freeze sounds good. What it saves barely amounts to a budgetary rounding error.

In private many Democrats, and even some Republicans, agree that politics often unfairly hounds bureaucrats for obeying the constraints politics itself has imposed on them. Only a handful would declare this publicly. Elizabeth Warren, Obama's adviser on consumer financial affairs, is unusually blunt, a rare trait in a town where players weigh words with systematic caution. By the time I saw Warren she was toying with the idea of entering politics as the Democratic candidate for the late Ted Kennedy's Senate seat in Massachusetts, which she later did. Her views echoed those of many Democrats frustrated with Obama's readiness to cede tactical ground to the burgeoning "drown in a bathtub" wing of the Republican Party by dwelling on waste, fraud, and abuse.

That, in turn, makes it much harder for Obama, or any president, to make the case for government when it is needed, such as during hurricanes, natural or financial. Warren parodied the attitude with this metaphor: "Here we have an old man with syphilis and a drug problem. Now, after we've cleaned up his syphilis we want him to help you because he is your friend," she said. "Call me pedantic, but I'm not sure that's the best way to build up the government's legitimacy in the eyes of the people. Will someone, please, make the positive case for government?"

Obama did make a bold and eloquent case to reform Washington during his 2008 campaign. It has barely been heard of since. Perhaps he was wise to sidestep a battle he was very unlikely to win. Government may be getting worse at what it does, including R&D. It may also be ever harder to reform. This matters greatly for America's competitiveness, a concern that two of America's most important industries, the semiconductor and pharmaceutical sectors, raise with growing urgency. We turn to them in the next section.

When Obama gave his "Winning the Future" address to Congress in January 2011, he raised his biggest laugh when he talked about Washington's spiderweb of regulatory agencies. He used salmon as his illustration. "The Interior Department is in charge of salmon while they're in fresh water, but the Commerce Department handles them when they're in saltwater," he said. "I hear it gets even more complicated once they're smoked." Sure enough, Obama followed up with another, slightly more labored, one liner in his 2012 State of the Union address when he said he had scrapped a regulation that classified milk as oil, which had forced dairy producers to prove to regulators that they could contain a spill. "With a rule like that, I guess it was worth crying over spilled milk," he said. What the president gained in small business votes was probably outweighed by his losses among late night comedy viewers.

In fact, that was only half the story. Depending on whether they are farmed or caught, salmon also come under the regulatory purview of the Department of Agriculture or the Environmental Protection Agency. Once the salmon reach the shops the Food and Drug Administration takes over. The FDA regulates all fish that are sold to consumers. Except for catfish. They belong to the USDA. The latter regulates farmed chickens. The former regulates chick feed. And so on. Who would want to deal with this if they could avoid it?

If there is one thriving industry in the United States that has always tried to keep clear of Washington it is the semiconductor industry. The founders of Intel, which remains America's most cutting-edge chip maker, believed the government was either irrelevant to their fortunes or potentially a menace. Unlike their friends in the oil, defense, real estate, health care, and government contracting businesses, and many others, the chip makers stayed aloof from campaign donations and aggressive K Street lobbying. It worked pretty well for thirty or so years. "We didn't play the political games others play," said George Scalise,[69] who headed the Semiconductor Industry Association at the time. "We didn't think Washington was relevant to us."

That changed in the 1980s when Japan began to vacuum market share from U.S. chipmakers. Japan was dumping large quantities of chips at artificially low prices in the United States and blocking American imports from their domestic market. Japanese companies also practiced aggressive intellectual property theft. Realizing its survival was in the balance, the U.S. industry reluctantly approached Reagan for help. Senior Reagan officials, in turn, recognized that the computer chip was perhaps the most important strategic technology in the world. America could not afford to lose its leadership.

Out of that was born a partnership that was to roll back Japanese protectionism and restore companies such as Intel, Texas Instruments, and Micron Technology to the driving seat. They even set up a public-private company, Sematech, to share the results of R&D. Semiconductors are now the country's largest single export and the jewel in America's reputation for technological innovation. "Reagan was the last time an administration entered into a strategic partnership with business," said Scalise, who is celebrated within the industry as one of its saviors. "During the Cold War Washington was a lot more pragmatic about these things."

In 2010 the SIA moved its headquarters from Silicon Valley to Washington, D.C. "We recognized that Washington was unavoidable," said Brian Toohey, who succeeded Scalise as its head. The industry even set up a political action committee to raise money for campaigns. "If you want to do business in Washington, you have to play by its rules," said Toohey.[70]

The SIA had also become increasingly concerned about Washington's ignorance of semiconductors, a fact that continues to shock senior executives. At a meeting with Harry Reid, the Senate majority leader, and twenty semiconductor chief executives before the SIA's move, Reid started off by asking, "So what's a semiconductor?" according to one of the executives present. After having had it politely explained, Reid kept referring to the "supercollider," which has as little to do with computer chips as french fries.

Today, America's chip companies face a very different challenge than they did in the Reagan era. In spite of advances by South Korea's Samsung and Taiwan's TSMC, both of which are increasingly innovative and benefit from strong government backing, America's biggest chip companies remain at least eighteen months ahead of their rivals, that is, a full generation in the life of a chip. But they are finding it increasingly expensive to manufacture in the United States. Unchecked, that trend could jeopardize America's intellectual leadership. Terms such as "innovate in China" and "designed in Mexico" are becoming commonplace at Intel and elsewhere.

That pressure is likely to intensify as the primary sources of demand continue to move eastward. More than 80 percent of U.S. chip production is for export.[71] And most companies like to be near their customers. Televisions, laptops, and cell phones may all be produced in Asia nowadays, but the much more cutting edge chip technology that powers them is still likelier to be made in the USA. On average U.S. chip companies pay their employees $100,000 a year, more than twice that of most manufacturers.[72]

People in the industry believe that keeping those jobs, and the design roles that go alongside them, is far more critical to America's strategic interests than the fortunes of the social media sector that has recently captured all the attention. "We need to sort this out before it's too late." says Toohey. "Once companies start to move production elsewhere, then design usually follows." It is a drum his industry keeps banging in Washington, D.C. It is still surprisingly tough to get heard.

Whether they are autocratic like China, authoritarian like Singapore, or democratic like Japan, South Korea, and Taiwan, governments around the world are configured differently than Washington. Even in Germany, France, and elsewhere in Europe, Washington's ways stand out. Put crudely, other governments are paying whatever inducements will work to persuade American high-tech companies to shift operations abroad. In Singapore the government is aggressively pursuing high-tech corporate R&D centers. Taiwan is promoting the so-called chip foundries, which make other people's designs. In China it is both and on a scale no one has previously seen.

According to Intel, if you add up the standard incentives offered by Beijing to set up an $8 billion plant in China, it saves the company a billion dollars in taxes, capital costs, and land over the following decade. That is a billion dollars it would lose if it sited the plant in America. The price of labor in China has almost nothing to do with it. Wages amount to less than 10 percent of the overheads for a semiconductor plant. "People should get it out of their heads that we are being undercut on wages—this is not the textile industry," says Craig Barrett,[73] former chief executive of Intel. "America is being outbribed."

Theory tells Washington's lawmakers this is not a zero-sum game. If China wants to waste foreign exchange reserves on subsidies for foreign companies, then the American consumer will benefit through cheaper prices. The United States should not squander taxpayer dollars on a race to the bottom with China. It is a reasonable argument, particularly in an age of fiscal scarcity.

Yet there are many low-cost steps Washington could take that it is still reluctant to pursue. The most consistent complaint from chip producers, which is echoed in many other American industries, is that there is nobody in the capital with whom they can talk. "It is the equivalent of Henry Kissinger's telephone problem with Europe," said Scalise. "Who do you call when you need a grown-up conversation?"

In Singapore there is the Economic Development Board, whose representatives greet you at the airport and do all your paperwork. Likewise Germany, China, Taiwan, and others have similar one-stop shops for potential investors. In Washington, by contrast, there is the Department of Commerce, the Treasury, the U.S. Trade Representative, the National Economic Council, the Council of Economic Advisers, and so on. None of these agencies are paid to fight to keep jobs in America, either by talking to domestic producers or by attracting foreign investors. That is the role of the market, in their view.

In other countries, it might be the job of the Commerce Department. But in Washington that department has neither the authority nor the budget to make much of an impact. When U.S. industry groups meet with Commerce officials, they sometimes suspect indifference. Foreign investors rarely bother to stop by. It is perhaps best known in the city for the enchanting aquarium in its basement. "You know that saying 'Asia can produce the best semiconductors, but America has the best orchestra conductors'?" said Clyde Prestowitz, a former Reagan trade official who served on the board of Intel. "I sometimes feel they think that at Commerce."

Some officials at Commerce are trying to make their contribution more relevant to American business and to potential foreign investors. But they lack the influence in the White House to make their case. When Obama announced plans to double U.S. exports within five years in 2009, Commerce was given the budget to send a handful more officers to embassies around the world. They can look only with envy on Germany, which has thirty economic officials based in Shanghai alone. Berlin spends about a billion dollars a year on trade fairs. The U.S. Commerce Department has a trade fair budget of about $30 million. "The things we could do if we had Germany's resources," said a senior official at Commerce. "But it's a tough sell in this town."

When Obama's senior economic officials do hear the case, it is usually with a skeptical ear. Larry Summers is famously dismissive of offering public incentives that could distort private investment decisions, even if other countries are doing so. That skepticism also extends to more modest requests. However, proponents of an overhaul were buoyed in early 2012 when Obama proposed to merge the U.S. Trade Representatives office and other agencies with Commerce to make it look something more like a Department of U.S. Competitiveness. Other agencies, like the U.S. Census and the National Oceanic and Atmospheric Administration, which had nothing to do with commerce or trade, would move elsewhere. Whether or when the proposed reshuffle would ever pass Congress is another matter. More than seventy congressional committees oversee different aspects of the affected agencies. "We live in a twenty-first century economy, but we still have a government organized for the twentieth century," Francisco Sanchez, undersecretary of Commerce told me. "The president's plan to consolidate all the trade-related entities into one department is the right move. This means one phone number and one Web site, making government more efficient and effective for the businesses we serve."

Austan Goolsbee, the Chicago economist who headed Obama's Council of Economic Advisers until August 2011 and is the economist who has known Obama the longest, said U.S. businesses were dreaming if they thought Washington could emulate Singapore. "It is every business person's fantasy that they can have something like the Economic Development Board in Washington," Goolsbee told me in an interview shortly before he returned to Chicago. "They should forget it—this is Washington. It isn't going to happen." Goolsbee argued that U.S. businesses were too ready to swallow China's public relations. He predicted that people would point to China ten years from now and wonder how it could have wasted so much money. "How many of these airports and high-speed trains are warranted by consumer demand?" he asked. "How much overcapacity are they building? My guess is that we'll look back on a lot of these programs as boondoggles we were fortunate to avoid in America."

President Obama often meets Paul Otellini, the chief executive of Intel, who also sits on the White House advisory board on U.S. competitiveness. Yet Obama's ability to respond to the industry's demands is limited. In particular, chip makers have been fighting two running battles with Washington's bureaucracy. The White House has had marginal influence on either. The first is with the Environmental Protection Agency, which is possibly the least liked regulator in town. Defenders point to the huge importance of having a regulator that enforces minimum standards on pollution. Detractors say the EPA uses its legal powers as a bludgeon. It is dominated by lawyers rather than policy makers.

There is truth to both views. But when discretion is needed, U.S. government lawyers are the last people you want on the other side of a negotiating table. After Obama's cap and trade bill collapsed in 2009, the EPA said it would take the lead to reduce carbon emissions through regulatory action. Chip makers count for only 0.12 percent of America's global warming emissions, and they had voluntarily slashed their emissions in the first decade of the twenty-first century. They also installed the world's most sophisticated carbon emission monitoring systems in their plants. The industry said it would be happy to comply with the EPA's new regulators. Then it saw what the EPA had proposed. "The EPA's plan could have shut us down as an industry in America," said a senior executive.

What followed over months of tortuous negotiations would have made Franz Kafka blush. The EPA directive said chip plants would need a separate permit every time they deployed a new tool or piece of equipment. Although chip production is probably the fastest evolving industry in the world, the cost of complying would have been manageable. The killer blow came when the EPA said it would take one to two years for it to evaluate each permit. Under Moore's Law, which dictates that the price of a microprocessor will halve every two years while its power will double, this EPA regulation would have killed the U.S. chip industry's domestic production in its tracks.*

The EPA seemed unfazed by that prospect. No matter how hard chip officials tried they could not convince EPA's lawyers that the real-world impact of their opinion should play a part in their consideration. They even set up an Oval Office meeting with President Obama to press their case. They stressed to Obama that they had no dispute with the goal of reducing emissions. They merely wanted to reduce the time it takes to get a permit. "Seeing the president helped a little bit, but not as much as you would think," said the industry executive. "We were surprised by how little happened, frankly."[74] Eventually, the EPA began very slowly to cede ground, paragraph by paragraph, subclause by subclause. Even then, its lawyers did not swing fully around.

For the chip industry it offered an unnerving taste of how little flexibility exists in Washington, even when it comes to the viability of America's most strategic industry. At the EPA they

---

*Written by Gordon Moore, one of the eight cofounders of Intel in 1957, it is one of the most accurate predictions in the history of science. Under the inconspicuous heading "Cramming more components onto integrated circuits," Moore foresaw the exponential growth rate in computer power that holds true nearly fifty years later.

even encountered hostility. "We certainly agree that industry should never be too cozy with regulators," said one semiconductor executive. "But EPA represents the other extreme where you have activists who see every industry as the enemy. That leads to this unbelievable situation where we have had to spend countless hours and millions of dollars trying to unwind a ruling that never needed to be issued in the first place." This was the part that threw the chip makers: the EPA's rule was irrelevant to its own stated goals.

Then there was the altogether more comic battle with the Department of Homeland Security. If the EPA saw itself as Julia Roberts in an anticorporate B movie, the DHS appeared to be inspired by Monty Python's dead parrot. In short, lawyers at the DHS and at Treasury in 2008 abruptly altered their advice on what customs officers could do to prevent counterfeit chips from entering America, mostly from China. Roughly 15 percent of all chips in the United States are fake. Some have found their way into Pentagon military hardware. Others have contaminated the supply chain. Alarmingly little is known about how much potential damage these chips could do to U.S. national security.

By redacting the serial numbers on the photographs of each chip, the DHS stopped the semiconductor industry from being able to say which was counterfeit and which was not. There was no other way of telling. Again, the real-world argument had little bearing on the lawyers' decisions. They were seeking to shield port officers from any liability for disclosing confidential information. Each time a chip is suspected as counterfeit its picture is sent to the relevant company to be checked. Given the smooth operation of the system over many years, that risk was not even mildly realistic in the SIA's view.

Again, the lawyers were unbending. In this instance, the SIA managed to get Capitol Hill's attention. "How can you possibly identify if something is counterfeit when they have taken off all the code numbers?" asked an incredulous Mike McCaul, the Republican committee chairman. Brian Toohey, who was testifying for the industry, said it would be impossible. "So as a result of this legal policy we probably have God knows how many counterfeit chips coming into this country?" Yes, said Toohey. "And we're excluding the private sector from being able to assist DHS in identifying counterfeit chips coming into the country, is that correct?"

Toohey replied, "We're desperate to help, Mr. Chairman. We've been begging Treasury and DHS to let us help stop these dangerous chips that are coming in." Again, it was to no avail. In the name of removing a minuscule threat to their employees, federal lawyers were prepared to jeopardize U.S. national security. "I don't know whether to laugh or cry," said Toohey to me later. At the time of writing, the three-year standoff was unresolved. "If there was a person we could talk to who could cut through all this, we have yet to find out who that is," he added.

Compared to what pharmaceutical executives say about Washington, the chip industry sounds almost mild. Nor are these complainants trivial: semiconductors and bioscience are two of the fields in which America still leads the world. Both are facing ever tougher competitors. Once seen as the gold standard of American (and global) regulation, the Food and Drug Administration is held up by many of its industry critics as a paragon of what has gone wrong with the federal government.

To be fair to the FDA, no agency could possibly respond to all the complaints that are leveled at it. Former employees describe it as "fundamentally broken"[75]; venture capitalists say the FDA has had a "devastating" impact on U.S. innovation[76]; Big Pharma companies say it is routinely slow on drug approvals; and liberal groups say it is in bed with big business. To cap it, conservatives have called the FDA "godless" after it approved an anti-pregnancy drug in 2000.

As a result, the FDA has drastically slowed the process of drug approvals; it now takes an average of fifteen years. Things started to go really wrong in 1999 when the FDA approved Vioxx, the antiarthritis drug. Mounting controversy about the drug's side effects, including the increased risk of heart attacks, forced Merck to withdraw the drug from the market in 2004. After that sustained public beating, the FDA's already lengthy approvals process got even longer. Once bitten, twice shy, the agency has become the scapegoat of choice for a cacophony of critics.

You have to feel sorry for the FDA. It gets beaten up for approving drugs and then they get beaten up for not approving drugs. Whatever they do, they get beaten up. The impact has been nearly paralyzing. In the past ten years, the U.S. pharmaceutical and biosciences sector has seen a sharp slowdown in its rate of innovation. Many believed that the Human Genome Project, which mapped all 3 billion DNA pairs in the human body, would unleash a new golden age of innovation in medicine. That may still happen, over time, as scientists come to grips with the most complex data set in human history.

In the meantime, the industry is taking out much of its frustration on the FDA, and with some reason. In a 2011 report on the slowing innovation in biosciences, a group of investors laid the blame squarely on the FDA's slow approval process. Four U.S. medical start-up companies had recently closed or moved country. "The FDA has a strong predisposition toward more studies, more subjects, more arduous conditions, all under the name of patient safety—with no regard for the burden placed on the company," it said.[77]

If you did a blind tasting of the FDA and the European Medicines Agency, its London-based counterpart, you might think the FDA was the bureaucratic offspring of the European Union. Because of the EMA's insulation from politics, it has a clear advantage over its American counterpart, say industry executives. Scientists, rather than lawyers, control the process. Many American companies prefer to deal with the EMA.

In contrast, pharmaceutical executives are openly disdainful of the mind-set they encounter at the FDA. After years of budget cuts it has become hard for the agency to recruit top-flight scientists. In the first decade of this century it lost 1,300 staff and $300 million in budget cuts. "In Europe we get a predictable timeline that we can anticipate and plan for," says Roger Perlmutter,[78] head of

R&D at Amgen, one of America's largest bioscience companies. "At the FDA we often get stuck in regulatory hell. Nobody knows what is going to happen next." Perlmutter's views were mild in comparison to what some in the industry say.

It follows therefore that no sane person would agree to head up such a beleaguered outfit. Yet Peggy Hamburg, the very able former health commissioner for New York, says she knew exactly what she was getting into when she took over in 2009. "I had no illusions," she said. "Many of the criticisms of the FDA have been valid. It has become too slow, too unpredictable, and too bureaucratic. And we are doing everything we can to try to fix that." Even critics concede Hamburg has approached her Himalayan task with skill. That has not stopped Congress from making her job much tougher. "It's all about doing more with less," said Hamburg wearily. "Isn't that true of everyone nowadays?"

As is often the case, Congress has proved a perfect outlet for society's conflicting impulses. In early 2011 it passed a bill requiring the FDA to sharply increase its rate of inspection of food and drug plants. Then it imposed a cut on the FDA's budget. The same fate has struck most of Washington's regulatory agencies in recent years. But the FDA has probably had it worst. Although imports of both drugs and food have soared, the FDA's capacity to inspect shipments was cut by about a third during the two Bush administrations. They are hunting for needles in a haystack. In 2008, the FDA managed to inspect just 100 of the 190,000 international food plants that export to the United States and just 30 of the more than 3,000 foreign drug plants.[79]

When Obama came to office some of the FDA's budget was restored. In 2010 it even managed to regain the head count it had in 1994. Yet the milestone was pyrrhic. Imports multiplied in those sixteen years. So, too, have public health scares. From outbreaks of E. coli and salmonella to contaminated pet foods and counterfeit prescription drugs from China, barely a month seems to pass without a new threat emerging to public health. Four-fifths of the chemical components used in U.S. drugs are now imported (mostly from China),[80] as is a growing share of America's food supply.

Yet in 2011 Congress removed even the small budget gains the FDA achieved in Obama's first two years. Whenever the next health scandal strikes, Congress will doubtless be loudest in its condemnation. To rub salt into the FDA's many open wounds Congress keeps loading new requirements onto it. While cutting the agency's budget since 1994, it passed laws that added more than one hundred new areas of responsibility. It has also started to second-guess the FDA; in 2011 the House passed a bill to stop it from approving genetically modified salmon (Obama's salmon tale scratched the surface). The FDA had been evaluating GM salmon for years.

Even the administration's biggest critics realize the impossible is being asked of it. With a staff of barely eleven thousand people, the FDA employs just double the number of people who play in U.S. military bands. Yet it is supposed to regulate one quarter of everything that is bought by the nation's consumers. "If Congress would just take a holiday from demanding new things of the FDA that would be a plus," said Kevin Sharer,[81] chief executive of Amgen, which blames a lot of the slowdown in drug innovation on the agency "If it would provide decent budgets so they can do their jobs, that would also be a plus. Without these the FDA will continue to have a negative impact on our industry in the coming years."

Thomas Jefferson once said that people get the governments they deserve. He might have directed that remark at regulators. As a high-caliber scientist with years of government experience, Hamburg could be leading a good life in the private sector and earning quadruple the salary. She devotes most of her time trying to find ways of doing more with less. In mid-2011 Hamburg came out with a proposal to share the FDA's burden with its counterparts in other countries. If Australia's regulator had inspected a Chinese laboratory, the FDA should not have to. And vice versa. The proposal struck most people as sensible.

"We now live in a world where there are global supply chains for drugs and food and many more points where they can be contaminated," she said. "We need to create a new paradigm for a very different world." The FDA should stop thinking in terms of defending America's borders and instead export its expertise to build up regulators in places like China. "Our budget prospects are getting slimmer and we are being asked to do more and more," she said.

Whether Hamburg's proposals get past Congress is an open question. Some Tea Party Republicans raised concerns about pooling regulatory sovereignty with other countries. Much might depend on public opinion. Hamburg said she was frustrated with Washington's failure to debate the future of food and drug regulation given how much the world has changed since the administration was set up (in 1930). But in U.S. politics the urgent keeps driving out the important. "The administration is looking for an opportunity to hold a national conversation about this," Hamburg said. She is still waiting.

The same point applied to the U.S. media, a subject that nearly caused Hamburg to lose her poise. Since Congress often reflects, rather than counters, public misperceptions, the media's voice is critical. Unhappily it is usually negative, said Hamburg. One factor driving the FDA's hypercaution on drugs approval is the growth of risk aversion in public opinion. Most people have a weak grasp of probability. They happily eat hamburgers and fries every day but are intolerant of a one in ten thousand risk there may be side effects from a drug. They fear flying in airplanes but will readily jump in a car.

Educating the public about the risk-benefit trade-offs from a drug approval process is hard enough on its own. It becomes impossible if the media are on the other side. Hamburg cited widespread myths that had been stoked by the media, such as the link between inoculations and learning disabilities. Once entrenched, such fears can be impossible to dislodge. "More often than not, the media are not our allies in public science," says Hamburg. "They turn myth into fact and they rarely correct it."

The same, of course, could be said for Congress. From the EPA to the FDA, America's federal regulatory agencies are suffering a crisis of legitimacy. Each time they fail, or overreach, Congress binds their hands tighter. Each new constraint breeds a deeper sense of hypercaution. From the private sector's point of view, the net outcome is a federal government that increasingly stifles the innovation America needs to regain its economic mojo.

Among the more thoughtful private sector leaders there is also a keen appreciation that an incompetent regulatory system is bad for America's competitiveness. "If foreign companies no longer see U.S. regulatory approval as the gold standard, America will start to lose control of the global commons [public standards]," said Amgen's Sharer. "That is in nobody's interests, including Washington's." Sharer would doubtless agree that it is easier to destroy a reputation for competence than it is to rebuild it.

Over three decades Washington's think tanks have issued periodic alarms about the future of U.S. competitiveness, with titles such as "Nation at Risk," "Before it's Too Late," and "The Gathering Storm." Since the capital's pearly monuments are still standing, such warnings have for the most part been filed away. Washington has also got in the habit of ignoring reports by its chief government watchdog, the General Accounting Office, which chronicles the government's decomposition in merciless detail. Each comes with a roll call of proposed steps to set things right. Each follow-up report lists how few were put into practice.

Gene Dodaro, head of the GAO and a lifelong employee, says the worst offenders are within America's national security apparatus, the Pentagon and Homeland Security in particular. It is one thing to point to bureaucratic malpractice in the postal service or at Commerce. It is another to come across it in the heart of America's military-industrial complex. "The Pentagon has more than twenty-three hundred different IT systems," said Dodaro when I interviewed him at the GAO's Washington headquarters. "It's a big place but it still seems a little high." The Pentagon spends more than $10 billion a year sustaining a kind of electronic Tower of Babel. Most of its software systems are incompatible.

Dodaro sounded matter-of-fact when I asked how this could be so. "They haven't yet followed our recommendations," he said. According to his agency, such confusion has material consequences on the battlefield. Since 2002 the U.S. government has spent $16 billion on civilian aid to Afghanistan, of which its road-building program is one of the largest.[82] Given that the United States is pursuing a counterinsurgency strategy, America's legitimacy in the eyes of Afghans is its most important weapon. Yet neither the Pentagon nor USAID (the aid agency) would tell each other what they were doing.

In spite of what the GAO had urged, there was still no central database in which the two agencies could check in which parts of Afghanistan the other one was building roads. The Pentagon was unaware even of where it had laid its own roads. "[Pentagon] staff said that because of missing documentation and frequent staff rotation they did not know where some of their roads were built," said the 2011 report. In its levelheaded language, the GAO patiently recommended that the two agencies should set up a centralized database so they could "leverage each other's resources more effectively." In English that would be: "Stop treating each other as though you were the Taliban."

In a potentially more lethal example, the GAO found that the Pentagon had dozens of separate units that were developing ways of countering IEDs, the improvised explosive devices that have killed more U.S. soldiers in Afghanistan and Iraq than have bullets. After much prodding, the Pentagon had set up an expensive "technology matrix" that would allow all the units to pool their results. Even this didn't work. No one was required to use it. So they didn't. The GAO's advice was ignored.

America's homeland security is equally affected by a chronic inability to coordinate. The GAO had urged the White House to get a grip on public spending on defense against biological attacks, a nightmarish potential future tool of terrorism. The money was scattered across the usual alphabet soup of agencies and few knew what the others were up to. In the GAO's understated way, it pointed out that the White House homeland security council "did not respond" to its advice.

Sitting listening to Dodaro in his dark suit giving his low, mono-tonic responses it felt almost as if I were dealing with an undertaker—a friendly and very professional one but funereal nonetheless. Dodaro, a lifelong staffer at an agency that everyone loves to ignore, said it was hard to explain why so much confusion could be so widely tolerated for so long. "Government is getting more and more complex," he said. Yet its inadequacies were staring his agency in the face.

That was only half the story. For more than twenty years the Pentagon has resisted taking steps that would enable the GAO to carry out a financial audit on it. Primarily because of the Pentagon's reluctance (or inability) to comply, the agency had been unable to issue a financial statement on the U.S. government as a whole, Dodaro said. Unsure I had heard correctly, I asked Dodaro to re-peat himself. "We cannot give a financial statement on the federal government," he repeated. "We don't know enough about it."

The agency has amassed enough evidence about each nook and cranny of the federal government to know the degree to which Congress is to blame for what has gone wrong. Almost every problem it finds bears some fingerprints from Capitol Hill. Almost every remedy requires legislative action. In isolation, many of the programs mandated by Congress look necessary. In the ag-gregate they often lose coherence. Perhaps understandably, because the GAO relies on Congress for its annual budgets, Dodaro was reluctant to draw big conclusions about what Capitol Hill might do, and what it might avoid doing, if it were to become part of the solution. "Congress can provide a good oversight role," was all Dodaro would say after prodding.

Just as Washington often immobilizes regulatory agencies from doing their jobs, Congress also presides over the most sprawling and most self-defeating program of economic mobility in the rich world. Since the republic was born, equality of opportunity has been at the core of the American way. The government is now actively undermining that ideal. Every year it spends $746 billion on economic mobility (at 2010 levels),[83] which is more than the total annual budgets of most industrialized countries. But the United

States distributes its spending very differently than do most of its peers. Two-thirds of Washington's subsidies go to the wealthiest 40 percent of Americans. Less than 4 percent goes to the poorest fifth.[84]

Too many numbers can sometimes bring on migraines. In the case of America's spending on economic mobility, they are sprinkled with Alice in Wonderland glitter. They tell a tale of large federal programs that are designed to level the playing field but which have the perverse effect of tilting it even further toward the privileged. What is bad for mobility is also bad for U.S. competitiveness. No economy can hope to get richer indefinitely when the bulk of its labor force is not. The GAO breaks down how the money is misdirected. Pew's Economic Mobility Project best explains the pattern behind it.*

The bias of public spending toward the wealthy is very much an American exception compared to other developed countries. So skewed have Washington's budgets become over the past generation that the United States has fallen to the lowest rate of income mobility in the industrialized world. America is now level with Britain for lack of income (and class) mobility. If you are born poor in Canada, you are more than twice as likely to move up to a wealthier income bracket in your lifetime than if you are born American, according to Pew. And for Germany it is twice as likely.

"This is not the America heralded in lore and experienced in reality by millions of our predecessors," reported Pew. Not only has America's escalator come to a halt. But the federal government appears to be ensuring that it remains jammed. Since most of Washington's spending on economic mobility comes through tax expenditure—subsidies that individual filers claim via their IRS returns—there is clearly foreknowledge of the outcome. The poor do not file tax returns. The rich have accountants. "Washington's policies actively reinforce the polarization in the economy," says Paul Romer, the Stanford University economist.

---

*It is worth emphasizing that Pew's breakdown is uncontested. The project is funded by four think tanks, two of which—the Heritage Foundation and the American Enterprise Institute—are conservative.

The most egregious item is Washington's mortgage interest relief subsidy, which is available for second, and even third, homes and which has no upper limit. Inevitably, the wealthiest fifth of Americans capture more than four-fifths of Washington's home ownership subsidy. Meanwhile, not even 4 percent of the subsidy finds its way to the "bottom sixty percent of Americans."[85] Even Alice in Wonderland might care to peruse that number. But that understates the negative impact it has on the poor. By helping to inflate home prices, this remarkably generous subsidy pushes housing beyond the reach of many in the middle class. Instead of promoting the American Dream, Washington helps to lift it out of the price range of average Americans.

The second largest subsidy goes to work-related tax benefits, such as health care insurance and retirement saving, which, again, are overwhelmingly directed at the richest fifth of Americans (roughly, households with annual incomes above $100,000). A large chunk of subsidies for higher education are also captured by the wealthiest Americans, which helps to explain why three-quarters of those who graduate from America's top 146 universities are from the richest quarter of American households.[86] Although they are born fortunate, these graduates get another helping hand from Washington. As Larry Summers is often fond of pointing out, "If you are dumb and rich in America you have a higher chance of graduating than if you are smart and poor."

Economists remain divided about the ultimate cause of U.S. income stagnation. Most agree on the diagnosis, but they diverge on the causes. Many on the left blame the great stagnation on globalization. Their prototype is the assembly line worker in Shenzhen who makes iPads and iPhones for $10 a day. Another singles out the explosion of new technology. Think of the back office person who, much like those shoemakers in the fairy tale, now stitches your accounts in Bangalore while you sleep. Then there are those who blame it on the politics, notably the impact of the conservative backlash on the state since 1980.

With or without a conservative backlash, Washington remains a central and evolving part of the explanation. By designing subsidies that Pew states are "actively harming" America's poor and middle classes, the U.S. federal government reinforces nature's bifurcations. Most of the roughly $200 billion in annual spending that does reach the poor, such as unemployment insurance and food stamps, is money well spent. It helps keep the wolf from the door of tens of millions of Americans.

There are also dozens of programs—according to the GAO—that are aimed at improving the skills of poor and middle-income America. These include worker training and job placement, financial literacy drives, and programs to raise the quality of teaching in schools. In fact, there are more than dozens of such examples. Washington runs fifty-six separate programs to promote financial literacy. It maintains eighty-two "distinct projects" to improve teacher quality. And there are fifty-one "entirely duplicative" schemes for worker assistance and job placement training.[87]

So divided is the money and so scattered are the projects (worker training spans eleven federal agencies and departments) that much is wasted. All told, spending on worker training amounts to a fifth of what is spent on mortgage relief. And the sums for each such program are often "too small on their own to have a material impact." Some, such as social housing, "lack a reporting mechanism to capture how funds are used." In others, such as teacher training, "it is unlikely that improved coordination alone can fully mitigate the effects of the fragmented and overlapping effort."

With a weary familiarity, the GAO concludes each assessment with a plea to "improve coordination." Much like Obama's inability to control the government's nanotechnology budgets, the GAO rarely goes so far as to propose putting one person in charge of each gaggle or assembling each under one roof. That would be unrealistic. Coordination, rather than consolidation, is the watchword. Yet even that modest goal is usually a bridge too far. Here is a typical GAO follow up: "Recommended coordinating mechanisms have not yet been put into place."

I asked Dodaro whether it was self-defeating to suggest so many new coordinating committees in Washington (I had stopped counting at fifty). In the unlikely event the GAO's advice was followed, wouldn't half the town be spending half its time coordinating rather than doing? "Coordination is very important," Dodaro explained patiently. "If you coordinate well then you will save time and money." At some point, the suspicion arises that the GAO oddly epitomizes the problem it keeps trying to identify: the collapse of ambition in American government. Rather than insisting on excellence, it politely calls for bare minimum competence. Instead of blowing the whistle, it understates its complaints. At the risk of shooting the messenger (and mixing my metaphors), the GAO does not seem to want to shake things up.

Yet that is probably unfair. The GAO is a meticulous messenger. And Washington's problems are beyond easy repair. Indeed, many argue that it may already be too late for America's capital to regain the once stellar reputation it had for competence. It may also be too difficult. There is no shortage of scholarly ideas for how to reform the U.S. federal bureaucracy and even Congress. But imagination gets hazy when picturing the scenario in which they would come about.

Who will cut through the jungle to find a path out? Some, like Dodaro, may be too close to the trees to see the canopy. Others may be too far away to appreciate the difficulty. Students of Washington often fall into the arms of Mancur Olson. Even a generation ago Olson feared it would be difficult to unpick the multiple vested interests that enmesh Washington in such constricting webs. Only countries that were defeated in war, or overturned in revolution, got the chance to do that.

"In Germany and Japan, the fierce cataclysm cleared away the detritus of stability," he wrote. In stable countries, argument would have to substitute for catastrophe. "Ideas certainly do make a difference," said Olson. "This is what I expect, at least when I am searching for a happy ending."

5

Against Itself

WHY AMERICA IS BECOMING LESS GOVERNABLE

America has been spared class conflict in order to have moral convulsions.
Samuel Huntington

I F GEORGE W. BUSH believed democracy might spring from the barrel of a gun, David Price hopes it can take root through patient example. The moderate Democrat from North Carolina is ideally qualified to tutor budding foreign parliamentarians about the pros and cons of democracy, a role he performs frequently, including with Iraqis. "It is one of the things I care about the most," he said of the House Democracy Assistance Commission, of which he is cochair and a founding member.

Having been in the House since 1987—barring a two-year hiatus during the Gingrich revolution—Price is one of the few remaining white Democrats to represent a southern state (his district includes much of the high-tech research triangle around the relatively liberal pockets of Raleigh and Durham). Unusually for a chamber dominated by lawyers and businesspeople, Price is also a scholar. He taught political science at Duke University before deciding he would get more of a kick out of practice than theory. "Getting elected to Congress was like a long field trip," he said.

Nowadays, however, it seems the cons of being in Washington are competing with the pros, even to one for whom Congress has been a lifelong passion. On this occasion, in the midst of yet another Washington round of fiscal Russian roulette, Price was speaking to a group of fourteen foreign lawmakers who were visiting America's capital to get a sense of how things worked. Price told me beforehand he was conscious things did not look too good in Washington. But he did not want to discourage these fledgling parliamentarians.

In the event, one or two of his guests, who were from Iraq, Indonesia, Afghanistan, and several African and Latin American republics, were more concerned about their afternoon schedule. "Do we get any shopping time?" asked an Iraqi woman in a bright yellow head scarf. We were sitting in a grand meeting room at the back of the underground U.S. Capitol visitor's center beneath the east plaza entrance to Congress. "Let me from the outset say that I am not here to lecture you about how you should do democracy," said Price, as several of his guests put on their headphones for translation. "We are not holding the American system up as a model—far from it. But there are things we can learn from each other."

In his gentle southern cadence Price then treated his guests to a description of the committee system, his area of specialism as a scholar and the most precious feature of America's first branch of government, in his view. The United States was unique in having an arrangement that divided lawmakers between those who appropriate money and those who authorize the bills. Each of the twelve appropriations subcommittees exists in parallel to its authorizing counterpart. Was everyone following? They nodded.

In recent years, Price continued, the U.S. committee system had started to deteriorate to a point where it was no longer providing effective oversight of the executive branch. Committee chairs used to be independent figures who could command the attention of the White House with a terse request or a phone call. Nowadays, however, they were mostly creatures of the party leaderships, which had been getting stronger and more centralized over time. Indeed, so bad had things become that Capitol Hill was starting to look— dare he say it?—*parliamentary.*

Price reassured his guests there was nothing wrong with parliamentary systems per se. But if you married the U.S. separation of powers with a system of rigid party discipline you were courting paralysis. "It is just not how the U.S. system was supposed to function," said Price. It was an apt observation on a day when it was apparent that Congress would fail to pass a budget for the third year running. It also came in the midst of the rolling high drama over the U.S. national debt ceiling. Having promised to change Washington, Obama had become its victim, unable even to secure what had once been routine permission to issue Treasury bonds. Price felt obliged to apologize for the current state of the nation's democracy.

"The way that we have been wrangling over the budget, well, it's terrible legislating," he told the parliamentarians, with an almost pained expression. "I am simply not in a position to make great claims about our democratic system right now." Then it was time for questions. It may have been a problem with the translation service. But one or two of the guests appeared to have misunderstood what Price had been trying to say. A lawmaker from Afghanistan asked, "So is it the White House that passes the budget?" In its dreams, one imagines.

What Price meant by "parliamentary" is different from how many people nowadays think of the term. Americans used to look at Ottawa, or London, and feel relieved that they had a separation of powers. The U.S. system may work more slowly, they said, but it was more surefooted. When big bills were enacted, such as Social Security in the 1930s, or Medicare in the 1960s, they required broad coalitions of Democrats and Republicans. No Congress can bind the actions of a future Congress. But successor Congresses have rarely tried to undo the landmark reforms of their predecessors.

In today's Washington that no longer holds true. From health care reform to Wall Street regulation, Obama watched helplessly as the Republican-controlled 112th Congress tried to unpick almost everything he passed in the 111th Congress. No one, least of all in the private sector, could feel confident Obama's reforms would stick. As a result of what others call stasis, some American legislators confess to suffering from "parliament envy"—the yearning for a more decisive system of majority government. They mean it mostly as a joke.

Almost nobody expects the United States to hold another constitutional convention, which is what it would take to make material changes to the political system. Any change to the Constitution requires ratification by two-thirds of each chamber and three-quarters of all states. Some conservatives and liberals still want to hold a convention. Almost everyone else dismisses it as a fantasy. "The catch-22 [of American politics] is that the only viable and defensible route to fixing our broken system lies through our broken system," writes Jacob Hacker in his book *Winner-Take-All Politics*.

Mark Warner, a Democratic senator from Virginia, counts himself among those with parliament envy. As a former governor of Virginia and a private telecoms executive, Warner admitted he was destined to be impatient with the workings of any legislature. But he had not expected Capitol Hill to be this bad. "We can't even fantasize about doing half of the stuff other countries are doing," he said, pointing, a little improbably, at the beleagured coalition government in the UK. "Literally and figuratively we have ground to a halt."

The thought reminded Warner of the famous, and possibly apocryphal, conversation between George Washington and Thomas Jefferson, in which Washington urged his colleague to be patient with the slow workings of the Senate. The Senate was there to temper the democratic passions of the House, much like you would pour tea into a saucer to cool it, he said. Warner reeled off a list of pragmatic steps the Senate could be taking to revitalize the U.S. economy but was unable to because it was so consumed by fiscal trench warfare. "I mean the stuff that this body [the Senate] wastes its time on . . ." said Warner, trailing off, as if wondering whether to say how he really felt. "Let's put it this way," he said. "We are no longer cooling tea in a saucer. We are freezing it."

Scholars have a large menu from which to choose in isolating why Congress has turned into "the broken branch" over a single generation. Some highlight the breakdown of its codes of behavior.

They focus on the growing use of supermajority tactics in the Senate, where the constant struggle to muster the required numbers to shut off debate is now a permanent block to getting anything done. The last of the legendary filibusters took place in 1964 when southern Democrats tried to block civil rights legislation. It took fifty-seven days. "I vividly remember watching Roger Mudd [the CBS correspondent] starting his coverage in the snow on the steps of the Capitol and ending it when the bill passed during the blazing summer," says Don Ritchie, the Senate's official historian.

After the marathon filibusters of the 1960s, the Senate decided to reform itself. It reduced the number of votes it needed for cloture from sixty-seven to sixty. Things only got worse. In the 1960s, 8 percent of bills were subjected to a filibuster. By 2008 it blanketed 70 percent of legislation.[88] Instead of serving as a tool of the majority, it has become the minority's weapon of paralysis. "The proliferation of the filibuster is probably the best measure there is of what has gone wrong with the Senate in the last ten to twenty years," says Chuck Hagel, a former Republican senator from Nebraska who stood down in 2008. Ultimately, though, it remains more of a symptom rather than a cause.

Other scholars emphasize the fact that the two parties barely socialize any more. Gone are the days when most lawmakers kept a home in Washington, D.C. Now they rent single rooms or even sleep in their congressional offices and shower at the House gym, a notable practice among Tea Party Republicans. Then on Thursday evenings or Friday mornings they fly back to their districts or their states to attend to the real business of preempting any challenges to their incumbency. They do not usually return to D.C. until late the following Monday. The legendary Washington salon is also a thing of the past. "Over time, the Washington weekend has just disappeared," says Tom Daschle, a former Democratic Senate minority and majority leader. "You could blame it on the airplane, I suppose. But the real reason is that lawmakers need more and more to be in their districts."

Nor is weekday socializing any longer much in evidence. Don Riegle, the former Michigan senator, took me to the Senate dining room one lunch hour. In spite of being one of the most exquisite historic hideaways in the Capitol, nobody uses it any more. There are two main tables—one for each party—that are placed so intimately you would dine there only if you wanted to chat with opponents. "Not very long ago, you would walk in here and find someone like Daniel Patrick Moynihan [the New York Democratic senator] in conversation with someone like Bob Dole [Republican, Kansas]," said Riegle. "It was popular then for the same reason it is empty today—you got to speak to people from the other party."

Another reason lawmakers socialize less is because they are too busy raising money, the galloping cost of elections being a leading culprit among scholars explaining the decline in the quality of American politics. Most lawmakers now spend about a third of their time raising cash, whether in the dreaded "dial-a-dollar" cubbyholes (rented in buildings just far enough from the Capitol to be technically off campus) or by attending back-to-back events in the evenings at the archipelago of hotels, clubs, and steak houses around Congress.

"I would guess that fund-raising now takes up about a third of the time for ordinary lawmakers and about half the time for leaders," said Dick Gephardt, former Democratic majority leader in the House. When Gephardt first ran for the House in 1976 he had to raise $70,000. It did not take him long. Now each race costs between $2 million and $5 million. "Whatever you are doing, money is never far from your mind," he said.

Money has also warped the system of seniority on Capitol Hill. Important assignments are now allocated on the basis of how much money a lawmaker raises for his or her party, rather than how effective or knowledgeable they might be. "I'm not going to name names but you've got some low-caliber people now running some of the big committees only because they're good at raising money," said an old-style Republican lawmaker in the House who wanted his name withheld. "What the committee does is an afterthought."

Few make much pretense about it. Rahm Emanuel, the former number two in the Democratic House leadership, who was widely credited as the chief architect of the Democratic 2006 midterm victory, told his staffers, "The first third of your campaign is money, money, money. The second third is money, money, money. The final third is votes, press, and money."[89] In 2011 Jeff Bingaman, the senator from New Mexico, became the latest in a long line of senators to announce retirement much earlier than expected. Others included Jim Webb, from Virginia, who had served only one term in the Senate.

Relinquishing a Senate seat did not used to come so easily. Bingaman, who had been on the Hill since 1986, said he was tired of the lifestyle. For the typical lawmaker, each day is minutely divided up by staff into fifteen- or thirty-minute increments, of which fundraising is among the most continually intrusive. Bingaman said that even those in safe seats now had to show they had swollen bank accounts, otherwise they might be seen as vulnerable. In turn that would invite a primary challenge or a tougher opponent for the general election. Money is the truest measure of your worth. "It is vastly more important than it was when I arrived," said Bingaman. "Most of us do not enjoy the money side of the job at all. But there are some in this body [the Senate] who take to it like a duck to water."

Then there is media. As in other democracies, the decision to televise proceedings in the 1980s changed behavior on Capitol Hill. I watched David Price give an address to an empty chamber. The cameras are not allowed to pan in order to show the empty pews. Lawmakers speak in order to get into the congressional record rather than in the hope of changing anyone's minds. That seems like an almost chivalrous concept nowadays. "I guess you get used to it," said Price. "Some of my colleagues have become very good at pretending they are talking to a large crowd of people." Indeed,

Newt Gingrich, the former speaker, partly came to public attention as a backbencher by his skill at giving rousing talks to an empty chamber while appearing to be speaking to a large gathering.

Since the only real media attention for most lawmakers comes from their home districts or states, those are the audiences to which they cater. "Everyone is just trying to show the folks back home what they have done, or how much contempt they have for Washington," says Hagel. As the public's appetite for political news declines, politicians have to resort to ever more cartoonish ways to grab attention. In 1960, the average sound bite for a presidential candidate on the major evening networks was forty seconds. By 2008 it had fallen to nine.[90] Studies show that the presidential address is now pitched at the English proficiency of a seventh grader. In the 1960s presidents spoke to the twelfth grade.[91]

The attention span has become much shorter in the age of Twitter, Facebook, and other online tools of rebuttal and prebuttal. Most senators now have separate staff for social media in their press offices, which continue to swell in size. "My motto is 'Speed kills,'" said the spokesman for a senior Democratic senator. "A lot of the media need to get things out fast, rather than accurately, and so we spend a lot of our time doing damage control. Journalists don't get punished for getting it wrong. They will be congratulated for beating the others."*

Self-preservation stops politicians from blaming the U.S. public, which, if truth be told, is richly deserving of it. The average voter spends less and less time on the news. Just under half of Americans (49 percent) believe that the U.S. president has the authority to suspend the U.S. constitution, an extraordinary misreading of his actual powers.[92] When asked which is the only country in the world to have used nuclear weapons, a majority polled were unaware the correct answer is America.[93] Most Americans cannot name their representative to Congress. Likewise, most are unable

---

*American readers probably know that however bad their media have become, it is not a patch on the situation in Britain (the *Financial Times,* and a few others, very much excluded).

to say which party controls Congress (a knowledge gap that helps explain why it is in the minority party's interests to ensure nothing happens in Washington).

According to one exhaustive study, Americans know less than they did fifty years ago about their political system even though graduation rates have more than doubled since then.[94] "America's ignorance about the outside world is so great as to constitute a threat to national security," said a report by the Strategic Task Force on Education in 2003. A year later the National Endowment for the Arts found that the number of eighteen- to twenty-four-year olds who read books had dropped by more than a third since 1980 (on a very low threshold of one book a year). Since then, the habit of book reading is likely to have fallen much further. There is only so much that can be blamed on the politicians. "We have met the enemy and it is us," joked Norm Ornstein, one of Washington's leading scholars on the U.S. Congress.

The depth of apathy in America's heartlands is matched only by the growing intensity among activists on the left and right. According to a study by the Annenberg Center on Public Policy, Rush Limbaugh's 20 million listeners are far better informed than the average American. Which is worse, believing Limbaugh or not knowing anything? Ornstein says that the public shares more of the blame than the media for the spread of the two blights—apathy and fanaticism. Both are rooted in consumer demand. "Let's say Fox News decided to be really nice to President Obama every day," he said. "How long do you think it would retain its audience? Within days Wolf News would be launched and we'd be back to business as usual."

Occasionally, one can find a politician who will blame at least some of the people some of the time, even their own supporters. Barney Frank, the outgoing Democratic congressman from Massachusetts and coauthor of the 2010 Wall Street reform bill, blames the partisans for what he calls the "dialogue of the deaf." Conservatives and liberals "inhabit entirely separate realities," he said. They hang out only with like-minded people and consume reaffirming media.

"Liberals who supported the public option [to include a government insurance plan in Obama's health care reform] couldn't believe it when the final bill didn't include it," says Frank. " 'Everyone I know supports a public option so how could that possibly happen?' Well then, I told them, maybe you should get out more often." Frank is also dismissive of the moderates who complain that both parties—but particularly the Republicans—have been taken over by extremists. "If it concerns people so much, why don't they vote in the [party] primaries?" said Frank. In politics, as in life, you get back what you put in.

It has been fashionable to complain about government since the birth of the republic. "There is no distinctively native American criminal class except Congress," said Mark Twain. It has also been fashionable to poke fun at the ignorance of the people who elect it. Opprobrium, too, has long been attached to the role played by special interests and lobby groups, a subject that is closely related to campaign finance and to which we will shortly return. But there is nothing in the modern era that compares to the low disregard with which Washington is held today. For that you would have to go back to Twain's Gilded Age in the late nineteenth century, before polling began.

The American public's trust in federal government has fallen steadily over the previous generation to below 20 percent today, according to Gallup.[95] During the postwar decades it consistently exceeded 60 percent. Although a majority of Americans do not know which party is in charge, they reserve especial blame for Congress. In late 2011 Congress fell to a historic low of just 9 percent approval.[96] In other words, the decline in public trust for Washington closely tracks the rise in ignorance about what it does. "You could say that ignorance and distrust walk hand in hand," says Ornstein.

Ignorance and distrust—it does not sound like a recipe for change. Yet on a bad day it offers a fair snapshot of the mirror that Congress holds up to America. On a good day, though, something positive occasionally happens. Before he quit Congress in 2010 Bart Gordon, a long-standing legislator from Tennessee who took the seat vacated by Al Gore in 1986, experienced both types of day. His valedictory effort as a legislator—the America Competes bill, which he had championed for years—offered a modest advance on the larger reforms Gordon and many others said would be needed to restore America's fraying lead in innovation.

Gordon and his colleagues were taking their cue from a group of America's leading scientists in a 2005 report called "Rising Above the Gathering Storm," which was updated in 2011 with the new title "Approaching Category 5." The report raised the alarm about America's declining competitiveness. It said America spends more on potato chips every year than on research and development. More than half of U.S. patents were now awarded to non-U.S. companies. And there were now almost as many people (770,000) working in the country's corrections industry, mostly as prison guards, as there were employed in the auto sector. "Gathering Storm" offered a powerful but nonideological plea for America to get serious about its challenges.

Gordon and others were confident they could win over the Republicans, as well as their Democratic colleagues, to the bill, which took steps to raise the number of qualified science and math teachers in the United States and to boost spending on clean energy research. But Gordon had not reckoned on his opposite number, Ralph Hall, one of the last of the old-style Texan "blue dog" Democrats who had defected to the Republican Party in 2004. Like many of his colleagues, Hall had often been hostile to public science. Now eighty-seven, and therefore the oldest member in either congressional chamber, he was also a noted skeptic on global warming.

Nevertheless, Hall told Gordon he was behind the bill. "We thought we were all set," said Gordon. In fact Hall had a different plan. A few days earlier, some employees had been caught looking at pornography at the National Science Foundation, a beneficiary of the bill. They were suspended. Hall deployed a maneuver called the "motion to recommit," which would kill Gordon's bill by sending it back to committee. He then inserted a clause into the motion saying that all federal employees who were caught looking at porn should be fired. Democrats were loath to be seen voting against the motion, which would mean they were opposed to firing people who watch porn. It is the kind of vote that could lose you an election.

"After all these years I felt my anger rising," said Gordon. "I mean to have it end like this." He had worked on the bill, and its predecessor, for five years. Although Gordon suffers from dyslexia and often feels tongue-tied, he addressed the House in a torrent of indignation. "Oh, I see, we're going to gut this bill for this little bit," said Gordon, his voice rising. "Nobody seriously thinks that we don't want to deal with pornography here for God's sake. So everybody that's for pornography raise your hand. Come on. Raise your hand. Nobody? Nobody is for pornography? Well, I'm shocked. So I guess we need this little bitty provision that means nothing, that's going to gut the entire bill. This is an embarrassment, and if you vote for this, you should be embarrassed."

Gordon's outburst failed to shame his colleagues. More than half of the Democratic caucus joined the Republicans in throttling the bill. In the event, Gordon managed to squeeze it through the House just before Christmas in the lame-duck Congress after the midterm elections. Hall stood down this time. It was Gordon's last act as a legislator. Following the Republican victory Hall took over as chairman of the science committee and made it clear that his interests lay elsewhere. "You have to wonder why it takes so much effort to achieve something so obvious," says Gordon, who now works as a lobbyist for clean energy firms. "Asia is rising and yet we're still playing clowns here in D.C."

Whether it is the colonization of a legislator's life by money, the capricious impact of instant media, or the sheer exhaustion of spending so much time trying to outflank activists in your party's base, people like Gordon are quitting politics. So, too, are people like Tom Davis, the widely admired Republican from Virginia, who threw in the towel in 2008 after grumbling from conservatives about his moderate stance on social issues. In their place, more often than not, come ideologues elected on a promise to disable Washington. When pressed to think about it, most of the rest of America would prefer Washington to reboot itself. But then again.

"Thinking? You're kidding, right?" says Davis. "Americans vote for people who look like them, and who talk like them, and that's mostly what it's all about." He mentioned a typical small town in which the Democrats get less than a quarter of the vote, or the slums of Chicago, where Republicans sometimes don't clear double digits. "Is it a surprise that Americans get the politicians they deserve?" he said. Like Gordon, Davis is passionate about America's competitiveness. An increasingly rare Republican in the pragmatic mold, Davis had little interest in the social and cultural dividers that can be used to carve up the electoral map. So he retired.

There was a time, Davis said, when everybody watched newsman Walter Cronkite and his words carried weight. "Now we can't even agree on the same set of facts," he said. "Instead of looking at the problems we have in common we spend our lives arguing about whether Obama is a Muslim." As a congressman, Davis attended two or three fund-raising events on most weekday evenings and then eight to ten events in his district on the weekends. "I barely had time to think," he said. These days he does a five-day-a-week job for a lot more money and gives up some of his spare time to try to push the Republican Party back to the mainstream. He now has time to think. Dialing for dollars has become a thing of the past for him. "Every Saturday, I wake up, do the crossword, and take the dog for a walk," said Davis. "Was I relieved to quit Congress? That would be an understatement."

The woman standing before us seemed very much an exception. Not only was she blonde, slim, and sassily dressed, she was also below the age of seventy. In every respect, barring one, Becka Rom, who must have been in her late twenties, struck a contrast with the audience to whom she was speaking. About fifty people had come to hear her at the local courthouse in Williamstown, Kentucky. Most were wearing sandals, hot pants or shorts, and a pink T-shirt. They were dotted in small murmuring clusters among the pews in the hearing room.

Rom, whose outfit, American Values, tours the country offering identikit presentations, launched into an energetic talk. The audience remained grim. Apart from their skin color, they had one important thing in common: their pink T-shirts all said "Restore America's Honor." Everyone was there to take America back. "I have a brother who serves in the U.S. military," said Rom. "Every morning, he gets up, salutes the flag, and he goes to work to defend America against her enemies both foreign and domestic." Some people nodded approvingly; Rom had their attention. "Tonight," she said, "I would like to talk to you about what you all can do to help him."

Since 1957, when the town was bypassed by the new interstate highway (I-75), Williamstown has been an economic backwater. Every now and then a train used to whistle through its dilapidated station on the old Cincinnati railroad. Now that is closed. Most of the economic activity begins about ten miles away, in Dry Ridge, which straddles a busy intersection on the I-75. "They've got the Walmart and they've got a McDonald's," an elderly lady said to me. "We haven't got anything like that in Williamstown." Now, at least, they had a Tea Party.

There was much conjecture over the Tea Party's true motivations when it started to mushroom in the spring of 2009. Many refused to accept at face value that it was a protest movement against Washington's fiscal recklessness. After all, there were only muted complaints from conservatives when George W. Bush converted the (ten-year) $5.6 trillion projected surplus he inherited into a $3 trillion federal deficit.

Some, therefore, saw it as the old Christian right masquerading in green eyeshades. Others saw it as a subliminal racist backlash against the election of Barack Obama. Still others saw it as a kind of American fundamentalist reaction against the uncertainties of modern life, with the familiar goal of restoring the values of the U.S. constitution. Much was rightly made of the antitax billionaires, such as the Koch brothers, who were funneling money to various Tea Party groups.[97]

In practice, given the movement's organizational diversity, the Tea Party exhibited all of these traits. And they don't necessarily clash. Each strand belonged in a larger tapestry. At its heart, like Rom's gathering, it is a movement of overwhelmingly white, Christian, middle-class, and middle-aged (and older) Americans who bitterly oppose spending federal money on people who don't fit that description. The symbols may be patriotic. But the underlying agenda is more targeted. Some call it "white panic" in an echo of the white flight to the suburbs that followed the riots of the 1960s and '70s. A Hispanic professor I interviewed called it "the last gasp of the Anglos." Nowadays, you could call it the soul of the Republican Party.

It was Rush Limbaugh, the most enduring cheerleader of modern American conservatism, who gave the best summary of the Tea Party's motivations long before it was even born. Limbaugh, whose radio show nets 20 million listeners a week—more than twice the combined audience of CNN, MSNBC, the *New York Times,* and the *Washington Post*—was as influential then as he remains now. "You are the ones who obey the law, pay the taxes, raise your children to be moral and productive citizens," Limbaugh wrote in 1993 just before Newt Gingrich's Republicans gave Bill Clinton his stinging midterm defeat.[98] "And you are doing it all with the help of God and your family, never once whining about the lack of federal funding, or burning down your neighborhood because the government is 'neglecting' you."

White panic, or otherwise, Limbaugh's shock troops seized control of Congress again in late 2010 and rendered America at least temporarily ungovernable. Where had all these people sprung from? According to its own history, the Tea Party was born the day Congress voted through a $700 billion bailout package for Wall Street, October 3, 2008, a vertiginous interlude that upended the presidential race and left the Republican candidate John McCain looking panicked. In contrast, Obama used the moment to radiate what David Axelrod, his campaign guru, described as his "inner serenity." Axelrod added, "We won the election in those nine days."[99]

With hindsight, it seems clear the Tea Party was conceived, if not born, precisely a month earlier, in Minneapolis, and three weeks before anyone had any idea there was going to be a financial meltdown. It was the day that Sarah Palin gave her acceptance speech to the Republican convention. Palin, who, as an indifferent first-term governor of Alaska, had been plucked from obscurity to be McCain's running mate, gave a drippingly sarcastic address.

Campaign consultants use the term "dog whistle" to describe thinly coded messages. Palin was using a normal one. Interrupted by chants of "USA, USA," she presented herself and McCain as the only true Americans in the race—people who did not look down on ordinary folk. Palin then alluded to Michelle Obama, who a few months earlier had rashly stated that for the first time in her life she felt proud of her country (having witnessed America's enthusiasm for an African-American candidate).

Describing the values of small town Americans, Palin said, "I grew up with those people. They are the ones who do some of the hardest work in America who grow our food, run our factories and fight our wars. They love their country, in good times and bad, and they're always proud of America." Then, in reference to leaked remarks by Obama on why blue-collar Americans voted Republican in such large numbers, Palin added, "In small towns, we don't quite know what to make of a candidate who lavishes praise on working people when they are listening, and then talks about how bitterly they cling to their religion and guns when they aren't."

Wherever Palin spoke on the campaign trail after that she was joined by ever growing crowds of supporters yelling "USA, USA." The Obamas had long since taken to wearing flag pins and covering every TV backdrop with the stars and stripes. Watching the pugilistic mood at the convention, and then attending dozens of rallies on both sides, it seemed clear to most observers, including me, that America was very divided, not so much in its surface politics (although there the contrast was clear) but in how different each side looked.

On the one, there were the educated, urban, white, brown, black, Jewish, and Asian Americans, amid a swelling army of volunteer students. It looked like tomorrow's America. On the other side were the angry, almost always Caucasian, blue- and white-collar middle class who, as William F. Buckley had once urged, were standing athwart history yelling "Stop!" At the time they seemed like a shrinking minority. To judge by events since then, people may have been underestimating their potency.

The Wall Street bailout accelerated the Tea Party's pregnancy. But its birth came only weeks after Obama had moved into the White House, when Rick Santelli, the CNBC presenter, erupted into his famous "live rant" on television. It was not the bailout of Wall Street bankers that prompted his outburst but an announcement by Obama that day of an otherwise minor—and ineffectual—plan to stem the flood tide of U.S. home foreclosures.

For Santelli it was another wasteful boondoggle for the undeserving. Crucially, however, these undeserving were poor. "This is America!" Santelli began. "How many people want to pay for your neighbor's mortgages that has an extra bathroom and can't pay their bills? Raise their hand! President Obama, are you listening? . . . It's time for another tea party! What we are doing in this country will make Thomas Jefferson and Benjamin Franklin roll over in their graves."

Thus, on the eve of the midterm election almost two years later, I found myself listening to Becka Rom's three-hour lecture on how to put Santelli's words into practice. By this point it looked like Rom and her friends were about to catch a break from history. In the 2010 elections, the Tea Party spearheaded the largest midterm swing in the House of Representatives (sixty-three seats) since the Great Depression.

To understand how to "take back America," Rom's audience needed to know what it was exactly they were trying to take back. Rom gave a potted version of what had happened to America since it was founded. Her account began with the timeless verities of the 1787 Constitution, to which was added the important Bill of Rights, including the critical Tenth Amendment in 1791, which enshrined the powers of state governments against Washington. Some Tea Partiers even refer to themselves "Tenthers."

Rom omitted to say that the Constitution had defined the black slave as three-fifths of a human being as represented in the confederation, which, by giving the outnumbered southern states more seats in Congress, had helped persuade them to ratify it. Nor did she mention the American civil war, and the resulting Fourteenth and Fifteenth Amendments, which formally ended slavery in the 1860s. "For most of our first 120 years, things went as they should have," said Rom. "Federal spending was only a fraction of the economy and private businesses flourished."

America had started to go astray, said Rom, only in the early 1900s, when the Progressive movement took off. Among its many sins was the Sixteenth Amendment of 1913, which gave the federal government the power to levy income taxes. Others included the creation of the Federal Reserve, also in 1913, and the direct election of senators, which reduced states' rights by depriving individual states of the power to appoint their senators to Washington. Now a century later, and with equal disregard for the intent of the Founding Fathers, Obama too was thumbing his nose at the gift that divine providence had given America.

Rom's millenarian forebodings were strikingly similar to what Newt Gingrich, the former Republican Speaker, had said a few weeks earlier when he described Obama as the greatest threat to American liberty since the 1850s, greater even than that posed by Hitler, Stalin, or the Progressives. Rom continued, "Obama wants to take even more of your hard-earned money so that he can spend even more on his pet projects and his friends. Now, is this what our founders had in mind when they said, 'We, the people . . .'? Do you think this is what they meant?" She paused theatrically amid a ripple of approving murmurs. "No? I didn't think so."

Rom's dog whistle seemed pretty obvious. Yet I was intrigued about whom precisely she meant by "We, the people." Most of her leading culprits were white Americans—"elitists" and "utopian statists" and "intellectuals" and anybody who apologized for their country. Moreover, her tent was open to people who "honored the Founding Fathers." This could include African-Americans and Hispanics.* Many Tea Partiers, including Rom, had reacted angrily when Jimmy Carter said the movement was created by "animosity toward President Barack Obama based on the fact that he is a black man." As the last Democratic president to win the South, Carter's words carried some weight. But outside of the former slave states, this seemed at best to be an incomplete description of what was driving the Tea Party.

A few weeks before the 2010 election I attended a better-heeled Tea Party meeting in the verdant outskirts of Springsboro, a small town about sixty miles north of Cincinnati in the Ohio valley. Since it was the group's inaugural meeting, Chris Littleton, head of the Cincinnati Tea Party, was there to help get it started. The gathering, which took place in a farmhouse next to a large horse paddock, consisted of fifteen people around the kitchen table discussing how to sell the Tea Party to their fellow citizens. The walls were crowded with mounted deer antlers, a fake moose head, and cuckoo clocks. Around the table were a Protestant pastor, an accountant, a package engineer, and several small business owners.

People glanced occasionally toward my notebook. Yet they spoke candidly of their frustrations at having to stick to the Tea Party's "fiscal script." God was nowhere to be found, they complained. Littleton tried to persuade them that it was in the Tea Party's interests to attract as many supporters as possible, including libertarians. Small-government fiscal conservatives hated taxes as much as anyone, he said. But some also held liberal views on abortion

---

*Whenever an African-American turns up at a Tea Party rally he or she invariably seems to be directed toward the podium where the cameras are.

and gay marriage. With an election around the corner, their support was needed. The group was skeptical. "How can you expect a morally bankrupt country to be fiscally conservative?" asked one.

Littleton patiently explained that a round of deep budget cutting in Washington resulting in the abolition, say, of the Federal Housing Finance Agency or the National Endowment for the Arts would serve both their moral and their fiscal purposes. "We want to go back to states' rights [Tenth Amendment], don't we?" People started to inch toward Littleton's viewpoint. Another wondered whether it wouldn't be out of place to say a prayer at the start of their meetings. "If God isn't the author of American liberty, then who is?" People agreed with the questioner. Littleton thought about it. "We sometimes read the Federalist Papers at our meetings," he said. "So God is already spoken." That seemed to settle the matter.

Littleton's quip could have opened up a whole new debate about what the Founding Fathers did and did not write. But when it comes to the U.S. Constitution, believing is often seeing. The word "God," for example, does not once appear in the 4,500-word document. When Benjamin Franklin suggested there should at least be a prayer at the start of the convention, Alexander Hamilton joked that America did not need more "foreign aid." When asked later why God had been omitted from the document, Hamilton said, "We forgot."[100] It was an odd oversight by a group of drafters whose attention to language is rivaled by few others in history.

Contrasting what the historical Founding Fathers said with what has been attributed to them is a time honored American parlor game. The first was a group of highly educated men who appeared in the flesh. The second are Old Testament lawgivers served up in marble. But anticipating how long, and with what effect, America's latest conservative challenge will persist is altogether more difficult.

The late Samuel Huntington said that America was prone to moral convulsions roughly every sixty years. The previous one, he said, was in the 1960s when the movement against the Vietnam War merged with counterculture protests to render America almost ungovernable. The conservative reaction to the street chaos of the 1960s, as well as to the extension of civil and voting rights to blacks in the South, helped to bring thirty-five years of liberal ascendancy to a close.

If, as seems true, the backlash against "out of control spending" since 2009 has been spurred at least partially by white panic over the changing face of America, then this latest moral convulsion could sputter on and off for a long time. According to the latest U.S. Census, whites will become a minority in America by 2040. The decennial census also revealed that 46.5 percent of Americans under the age of eighteen were nonwhite in 2010, up from 39 percent in 2000. Between those years the number of white children actually decreased by 4 million, while the number of American children of all colors grew by 6 million. This was due largely to the growth in the Hispanic population.

Election studies show that wealthier whites living in large minority states, such as Mississippi, Texas, and Arizona, are more likely to vote Republican than are wealthy whites who live in states with fewer nonwhites, such as Massachusetts, Oregon, and Vermont. Their surroundings make them more racially conscious. As America gets steadily browner in the years ahead, that trend may only deepen. In which case, Americans may continue to sort themselves into two opposing camps: lily white Republicans and the rainbow Democrats. Richard Hofstadter, the great American political scientist, once famously said, "It has been our fate as a nation not to have ideologies but to be one." His observation makes better sense during periods when there is broad consensus on what it means to be an American.

Blaming America's polarization on what's wrong in Washington is a popular pursuit. Some pin the problem on the growth in gerrymandering. By putting so many congressional districts beyond the reach of the other party, it has resulted in the entrenched power of party bases. This almost invariably produces candidates who successfully appeal to the most activist wings of their parties rather than to the electoral middle ground. This has been particularly well-exploited by Tea Party activists, who, in spite of their muted impact on the 2012 GOP presidential nomination, appear to retain as tight a grip as ever over key congressional and senatorial primaries around the country.

Yet to blame America's polarization on gerrymandering alone would be to let the electorate off the hook too easily. The fact that the U.S. Senate is now almost as partisan as the House indicates that America's growing divisions are rooted in society. Senators are elected statewide. State boundaries cannot be gerrymandered. In the rest of this chapter we will look at American polarization through its two largest states, Texas and California. Both offer a telling glimpse of America's demographic future. Both may also offer, alas, a foretaste of its national politics.

Trey Martinez Fisher is a liberal, a Democrat, and a Mexican-American. He also greatly misses George W. Bush. Just forty-one, Martinez Fisher is already a veteran of the Texas House of Representatives and is head of the Mexican American Legislative Caucus, the oldest as well as the most rapidly growing such grouping in the United States. Hispanics accounted for just under 90 percent of Texas's population growth between 2000 and 2010, according to the U.S. Census. In 2011 Hispanic children crossed the halfway mark to become the majority in Texan schools. Within the next decade Anglos (slang for non-Hispanic whites) will be outnumbered by Hispanics among all Texan age groups.

Martinez Fisher, whose office is dominated by a prominent large replica of the Texan Lone Star flag, exudes the confidence of a politician with demography on his side. "First it was the food. Now it's the politics," he said. "We're going Tex Mex." Bush Junior had only months left to serve as governor of Texas when Martinez Fisher was first elected to the state legislature in Austin, the Texas capital, in March 2000. So the young legislator, who is a career criminal attorney from San Antonio, had little interaction with the future president. By then Bush was spending most of his time on the campaign trail. But Martinez Fisher got enough of a flavor of the next president to feel nostalgic for what it was like to be in Austin when he was governor.

"Something happened to Bush after he got to the White House—a lot of people around here didn't recognize him any more," says Martinez Fisher. "The Bush we knew liked Democrats." Bush had even asked Bob Bullock, the Democratic lieutenant governor of Texas, to introduce him to the American public. More to the point, as governor—and as president—Bush expressed warmth toward Hispanic Americans, including ones who crossed the border illegally. When he was still running Texas, which has the longest border with Mexico of any U.S. state, Bush said, "Hell, if they can make it around the Rio bend we want 'em!"

Today, the state's Republicans are not quite so cheerful. The Texas Republican platform, a long and very unfriendly wish list, is the most nativist of any such declaration in the United States. It calls for citizenship to be revoked for the American-born children of illegal aliens, which would mean scrapping the U.S. Constitution's Fourteenth Amendment. Day labor centers should be closed and there should be tougher sanctions on anyone employing an "illegal alien." In addition, the government should do all it can to protect American heritage, including making American English the sole official language. Naturally, the platform is not very popular with the state's coming majority. "The Texas Republican Party has a 'minorities not welcome' sign hanging up on its front door," says Martinez Fisher. "Sometimes I think they should be called the Anglo Party of Texas."

Having been the Washington bureau chief of the *Financial Times* during Bush's last two years in the White House and having lived in the United States for the duration of the 2000 election that ended with Florida's "hanging chads" debacle, I found it difficult to recollect the "Dubya" who had run Texas. It took just three days talking to legislators in the resplendent Texas Capitol building (with its dramatic dome that exceeds in height the federal Capitol building) to realize that most Texas Republicans nowadays have come close to disowning America's forty-third president.

"I'm not really a Bush Republican. You won't find too many of those around here," said Leo Berman, a darling of the Texas Tea Party, which now dominates the state's Republicans. "He did nothing about the U.S.-Mexico border when he was president. He even tried to declare an amnesty."

Like almost all of his colleagues Berman, who is seventy-seven, says he is a proud Reagan Republican. We were sitting in his legislative office, which was covered in Texan memorabilia and hunting pictures. Pride of place went to a framed copy of a National Rifle Association article about Berman, who is a robust supporter of the right to carry concealed firearms into just about any building you can think of, from chapels to bars. The article was autographed in the cold, dead hand of Charlton Heston, the late president of the NRA.

I found Berman's choice of Republican hero a little puzzling. As governor, Bush gave Texans the right to wear concealed firearms in church. Meanwhile Reagan was the last American president to give an amnesty to illegal immigrants, a move that covered nearly 3 million, mostly Mexican-Americans. Bush did indeed try to overhaul U.S. immigration in 2006. But there was no mention of amnesty in that ill-fated bill.

All of which prompted me to question why Texan Republicans so disdained Bush. Berman looked at me indulgently. Although born Jewish, Berman somewhat unusually converted to Christianity and became both an ardent Episcopalian (Anglican) and a stalwart of the Christian Coalition in the Republican Party. Someone once joked that American Jews live like Episcopalians but vote like Puerto Ricans. In Berman's case the quip would require careful alteration. "Do you know the hospital in Dallas where they tried to save JFK?" Berman asked me. "Last year seventy percent of the babies delivered there were born to illegal immigrants."

I have conducted some eccentric interviews in my time. Berman comes high on the list. Our conversation toggled between his two obsessions: what Texas and America should do to preserve and strengthen America's heritage and why Rowan Williams, the Archbishop of Canterbury, should be replaced by someone with more spine. "Forgive me for being blunt, but the archbishop should go," said Berman with a Shakespearean glint in his eye. "It is not

the role of the Anglican Church to approve the Muslim sharia law."
Not, at that point, entirely sure what Williams had said about the
sharia (he had indeed been very polite about it), I was finding it
hard to keep pace with Berman.

The septuagenarian's principal narrative was more familiar: Texas
was being swamped by illegal aliens and its schools were being
colonized by Spanish speakers. Without a drastic change of course,
what was happening in Texas would happen to America. "I have
nothing against Mexicans whether they are legal or illegal," he
said. "But we should not be ashamed of being American. We need
to uphold the law of the land." A clear red line should be drawn
around the Texas public school system, he said. A third of Texas
now speaks a language other than English at home.

"If a student isn't speaking fluent English by third grade then
we have lost him—he never will," said Berman. By now he had
made that point and he flitted back to the General Synod of the
Anglican Church. "Nowhere in the scriptures does it tell us to
tolerate homosexuality," said Berman. The Republican Party's Texas
platform, to which Berman contributed, says homosexuality "tears
at the fabric of society." It also calls for a law that would give full
legal protection to anyone opposing homosexuality "out of faith,
conviction and belief in traditional values."

For Berman, as for the large cohorts of younger Tea Party
Republicans who dominate the Texas House of Representatives, culture is destined to play a large role in America's coming
political wars. Some of their agenda takes aim at the allegedly
growing influence of liberals in general, who are depicted as
neobarbarians within the gates of America. Other bits target the
Hispanics (large numbers of whom, ironically, are conservative
on social issues). They have forced entry inside of those gates.
Not all the state's Republicans are as hard-line as Berman. But
things are certainly drifting his way.

In contrast, things are pointing very much in Martinez Fisher's
direction within Texas as a whole and, indeed, America. The
young Mexican-American leader pointed out that Texas had

gained four more seats in the U.S. Congress, the largest decennial reapportionment since the post–Civil War era of Reconstruction. At least one of them would be Democratic. "The change isn't just happening, it's happening quickly," says Martinez Fisher. He mentioned the big cities of Texas, including its largest, Houston, which increasingly resemble Los Angeles. Anglos now account for under 30 percent of Houston's population. Pretty soon, three-quarters of the Texas Democratic Party will be either Hispanic or African-American.

In contrast, the Texas Republican Party, whose constituents are to be found mainly in the state's windswept and sun-baked small towns and in its sprawling retirement suburbs, looks conspicuously white. America's future may well be lurking in this stark topography. "What happens in Houston, then happens in Texas and what happens in Texas is the future of America," says Stephen Klineberg, a sociology professor at Rice University in Houston.[101] "America used to look like Europe and Africa, then we took in people from the Pacific. Now we're starting to look like the whole world and there isn't much that politicians can do about it."

Among demographers, at least, there is certainty about America's future. The same cannot be said for America's political scientists. Like California, where non-Hispanic whites became a minority more than a decade ago, Texas may offer clues as to how things will play out in Washington, D.C., in the coming years. Neither state gives much cause for optimism, although each is unhappy in its own way. "If California is any guide, the Texas Republican Party seems to be committing long-term suicide," says Manuel Pastor, a scholar at the University of Southern California in Los Angeles.[102] "You can't expect Hispanics to forget any of this in a hurry."

In both states the political divisions are largely ethnic. But the battle lines are increasingly generational. Most of their schools are nonwhite while most of the occupants of their retirement homes are white. Ron Brownstein, the highly renowned political director of the *National Journal,* memorably described this as the divide between "the gray and the brown." Politics will pivot more and more around how long a graying Smith can hold the line against a youthful Sanchez, particularly on fiscal policy.

"Like tectonic plates, these slow-moving but irreversible forces may generate enormous turbulence as they grind against each other in the years ahead," writes Brownstein.[103] "This struggle is likely to be between an aging white population that appears increasingly resistant to taxes and dubious of public spending, and a minority population that overwhelmingly views government . . . as the best ladder of opportunity for its children."

Down the corridor from Martinez Fisher's office sits Judith Zaffirini, a Democratic stalwart of the Texas Senate. As chairman of the Texas committee for higher education, she has been fighting a continual battle to preserve funding for public learning. In the biennial Texas budget that was finally passed in mid-2011 after a marathon five-month session, universities took a hit. The process, which was led by Rick Perry, George Bush's successor as governor and also a White House hopeful, somehow managed to bridge the state's large shortfall without touching taxes. Texas is rare among states in having no personal or corporate income tax. All of its proceeds come from a sales tax, and a levy on oil and gas, which it still produces in prodigious quantities. "The Texas budget defers payments, uses accounting tricks and discounts population growth in order to fully fund and balance the state budget," concluded an analysis by Wells Fargo Securities.

However, it was done mostly via spending cuts. For K-12 schools, the budget reductions were modest. Universities were cut by almost 10 percent. For Zaffirini, who represents the almost fully Hispanic border town of Laredo, which looks across the fence at the drug war–scarred Nuevo Laredo on the Mexican side, it was a fight between the future and the past. In this round, the past got the upper hand. She pointed to a proposal backed by Governor Perry to introduce a $10,000 degree, just over a third of what it currently costs. It was like the $100 laptop, or the $2,000 car, she said. It sounded great. But it was unrealistic. "It doesn't matter who you ask, it is impossible to offer a good four-year degree at that price," said Zaffirini.

Zaffirini's office was piled with files about the people behind the $10,000 degree. These included a number of Anglo ideologues, she said, who believed higher education should not be funded by taxpayers' dollars. Teaching could almost all be done online at a fraction of the price. Zaffirini and other opponents managed to confine the initiative to community colleges—four-year degrees continue to be protected. But the debate was one skirmish in a broader fiscal war that looks likely to dominate Austin's politics for some time. At the University of Texas, Zaffirini studied cognitive dissonance, which taught her that she has no choice but to deal with her opponents. "I try to keep an open mind," she said. "What I have learned from studying cognitive dissonance is that the higher the intellect the higher your ability to tolerate conflicting perspectives."

As for Perry, he was able to launch an ill-fated—and, at times, wince-makingly bad—2012 presidential bid on the back of a balanced budget and a record as governor of one of the few American states that was creating jobs at a time when the national machine had stalled. Perry's favorite line, and one that he repeated over the years with mounting plausibility, was that Texas was a better place to do business than California. The Golden State had throttled its businesses through regulation and high taxes, he said. In contrast, Texas had no taxes. "If you want to live in a state that has high taxes, high regulations—that is favorable to smoking marijuana and gay marriage—then move to California," said Perry on more than one occasion. "In Texas, we still believe in freedom. Freedom from overtaxation, overregulation, and overlitigation."

Most days Camarillo wakes up to azure skies and beautiful sunshine. Surrounded by some of the most fertile farmland in the world, California's newest public university sits in a valley that produces three crops a year. Its fruits are watered by the rain clouds that periodically blow through from the great canyons of Utah and Nevada and then into the Pacific. Like a Tuscan guard of honor, cypress trees flank the road that leads up to the campus.

On both sides are the rolling strawberry fields and lemon groves that have given California the apt name the Golden State. Any parent losing a child to higher education would be comforted by the knowledge they were living in Camarillo.

With its whitewashed Mission Revival architecture, it feels more like a seminary than a university. Charlie Parker, the great jazz musician, was once confined in Camarillo, which used to serve as a mental institution. It was here he wrote the well-known number "Relaxin' at Camarillo." Franklin Roosevelt's Works Progress Administration built the hospital in the midst of the Great Depression. It was closed in 1997 after a rolling scandal over staff abuse of the inmates, a variation of *One Flew Over the Cuckoo's Nest*.

Today, these gleaming buildings represent the best hope of escape for the offspring of the region's overwhelmingly Mexican fruit-picking population. But the university, which was created partly to meet the needs of a growing Hispanic population, was unlucky in its timing. Having launched in 2002, the college quickly sailed into the stormy waters of California's budget crisis.

Since 2007, the California State University Channel Islands—its official name—had been forced to turn away thousands of potential students because of a cap imposed by the fiscal authorities in the state's capital, Sacramento. Now, in the wake of the draconian 2011 Californian budget, which cut higher education by 23 percent, tuition fees will have to rise by nearly a similar amount. The faculty would need to be slimmed down.

"Here we are, all dressed up with nowhere to go," says Richard Rush, president of the university. "It is deeply frustrating." Even with these cuts, California's once globally renowned public university system would still be cheap compared to most states. But things have been getting a bit worse every year. In 1990, the state spent twice as much on its universities as its prisons. Now it spends almost twice as much on prisons.[104] "It tells you a lot about our changing priorities," said Rush.

In California, the yearly cost of housing a prisoner is roughly five times the annual tuition for a college degree.[105] Prisons keep taking up a larger share of the budget. Ventura, the town closest to the university, keeps expanding. For the next couple of years, at least, the university will have no new places to accommodate growth among the Hispanics in the area. "If you visit the high schools around here, there is a huge thirst for education and I am increasingly having to turn people away," said Rush. "If these kids take a different fork in the road, should we be comforted that there is still funding for the prisons?"

Like many American university administrators Rush is impatient with bureaucracy. Nowadays he spends most of his time courting sponsorship from local employers—with some success. Amgen, the pharmaceutical giant, is based down the road in Thousand Oaks. There is also a naval base nearby. But business partners prefer to sponsor customized postgraduate degrees in subjects such as bio-science and business. The general budget keeps falling. Rush has tried and failed to get three successive governors to visit Camarillo. The first two, Gray Davis and Arnold Schwarzenegger, showed no interest. He is hopeful that Jerry Brown, the veteran California Democrat, who was reelected in 2010 after a thirty-year interlude, will show more enthusiasm.

Rush has also tried and failed to enlist the help of Tom Mc-Clintock, the area's representative in Washington and a fervent Tea Party Republican. But Rush withholds his strongest frustrations for Sacramento, home to one of the least impressive democratic assembles in the Western world. If Washington is dysfunctional, Sacramento has ceased to function under any useful definition of what a legislature should do. Almost all of California's budget, which requires enactment by a supermajority of two-thirds in each chamber, is tied up in mandatory spending. Any, and all, tax increases must be submitted to public referendum (a quixotic enterprise that usually ends in a "No"). At times it seems as though Sacramento's role is to preside over a slow disintegration of the assets the state built up in the 1950s and '60s, the world-class infrastructure and public education that helped make California the place of the future.

For Rush and others whose job it is to nurture tomorrow's productive capacity, life is a constant battle to get the politicians to notice. "What business do we think we are in?" said Rush. "The blacksmiths and the people running the pony express and the stage coach all went bankrupt because they thought they were in the pony business." If they had realized they were in transportation they might have survived. The same applies to education, Rush said. "In education, we are in the tomorrow business, that is what we do," he said. "Sacramento is in the yesterday business. It has stopped investing in California's future."

Each of America's fifty states has seen at least a double-digit drop in revenues since 2007. Some, including California, have been hit much worse than that. But few are as hamstrung in their ability to cope as the Golden State, which has set up a fiscal system that drastically exaggerates the cuts it needs to make in a downturn. A few states, such as Colorado and Indiana, have been able to pull off something approaching the dual "cut and invest" agenda that all but the most ideological economists (on the left or the right) say is required—as, too, have Germany and Singapore.

Most American states, like Britain, have achieved only the cut portion of the twin approach. California, and in a different way also Texas, belongs in a third category of those that tend to "cut and disinvest." It makes no difference whether fiscal policy was consciously designed with disinvestment in mind. The outcome is the same. California now spends less than $8,000 per child in school, compared to $47,000 a year for each of its prisoners[106] (and that is in dangerously overcrowded conditions, according to the U.S. Supreme Court).

In the next few years, the ratio of teachers to pupils in California's elementary schools is set to rise from the present one teacher per twenty children to one per thirty or even one per thirty-five, according to Michael Kirst, who heads California's state board of education. "We'll need to find really creative ways of funding our schools in the future," said Kirst, who is also a professor of education at Stanford University. "The type of investments they are making in schools in Finland or Germany will be beyond California's reach for many years to come."

California's fiscal insanity originated with Proposition 13 in 1978, the ballot measure that electrified conservative America. Some political scientists date the rise of "movement conservatism" from that antitax ballot, which imposed the two-thirds rule on Sacramento that has so hobbled its fiscal room for maneuver. The proposition, which also put a tight cap on the annual assessment of California property values, the state's main source of revenue, issued the opening volley in a nationwide tax rebellion that has yet to play itself out. The election of Ronald Reagan, a former governor of California, to the White House followed two years later.

Like many states to the west of the Rockies, California has a "fourth branch of government": the ballot initiative. California's signature-based referendum system was designed in the early 1900s as a way of undermining the stranglehold the big railroad companies had over politics in Sacramento. Inspired by Switzerland, it was meant to be the people's answer to a legislature that had been hijacked by special interests. But in what became a significant example of the law of unintended consequences, the referendum has turned into their weapon of choice.

Given the high cost of gathering the half a million or so signatures needed to qualify for a ballot initiative, and the huge expense of advertising in the California media market, the referendum is no longer a check on corporate power. A few campaigns have cost more than $100 million from start to finish. In some cases, such as the notorious "three strikes and you're out" vote in 1994, which made lifers out of people whose third felony might be as trivial as shoplifting, the people agreed with the special interests behind it (lawyers and the prison guards union). Exactly half of America's states now have a three strikes rule.

In other instances, such as a vote to restore school funding, the Californian public approved a measure that clashed with what they had endorsed in Proposition 13. The result is a quagmire, in which the results of one ballot often contradict another but where both are by law superior to anything the Californian legislature might have to say. The people blame Sacramento. But since it is the people, and not their representatives, who have repeatedly chosen to cut taxes and boost spending, perhaps they should look in the mirror. As one reformer describes it, "California has become a Diet Coke civilization of consumer democracy, of services without taxes, like sweetness without calories."[107]

In 1949, when Carey McWilliams wrote his famous book *California: The Great Exception,* most people would have agreed with the saying that what happened in California was the future of America. That continues to be true of Silicon Valley, which remains the world's most fertile incubator of new technology. Americans should be praying the old maxim does not hold true with regard to either the state's politics or its broader economy.

Since 2000, California has ranked among America's slowest growing states, expanding by less than a fifth in the first decade of the century (Virginia and Maryland, both of which border Washington, D.C., and which both grew by more than a quarter, topped the rankings).[108] During the present recession California's jobless rate peaked at 12.4 percent—way above the national high. Nowadays the book of choice is 2010's *California Crackup,* a merciless chronicle of how the state turned into a political basket case. But the earlier book may still be relevant.

"California is not another American state," concluded McWilliams in his postwar history. "It is a revolution within the states." If the trends in Washington are a guide, can we still see America's future in California? I put that question to Paul Mandabach, who, as copartner of Winner & Mandabach, America's most successful referendum consultancy, is among the best-qualified people in America to answer it. What Mandabach said was intriguing.

We met in his sumptuous suite on the twentieth floor of the swankiest office building in Santa Monica with panoramic views that take in Beverly Hills, the old Pacific Coast Highway, and the

Getty Museum and which peers down at the Pacific Pallisades, where Mandabach is building his dream home. Mandabach, who generally tries to avoid publicity, (this was only the second interview he had given in fifteen years, he told me) is very good at what he does. He lives in a penthouse suite in the luxury residential tower at 1221 Ocean Avenue. Sometimes he bumps into Britney Spears in the elevator. A student and connoisseur of literature, Mandabach's office walls are stacked with rare items he has picked up in auctions and secondhand bookshops.

Among his firm's proudest successes is a 2004 initiative that converted California into the national center of stem cell research at a time when George W. Bush's administration had effectively declared America closed for business. Another, in 1998, enabled California's Native American reservations to set up casinos in the teeth of an opposing publicity blitz orchestrated in Las Vegas, which feared it would be undercut. "We portrayed Vegas as the cowboys and California as the Indians," said Mandabach.

Winner & Mandabach has achieved a 90 percent success rate on the 150 ballots it has launched around the United States. No other consultancy comes close. Its record means that corporations regularly beat a path to their door with ideas. It also means Winner & Mandabach can afford to be choosy. For example, the late John Walton, a member of the family that founded Walmart, wanted to sponsor an initiative that would launch a voucher system for California's public schools. "We advised them against it," says Mandabach. "They took our advice."

In contrast, T. Boone Pickens, the Texas oil king turned green energy proponent, ill-advisedly sponsored an initiative to promote the California gas market with a rival consultancy. It failed. Since ballot initiatives provide his bread and butter—and the finest wines from Napa Valley—Mandabach is reluctant to criticize their impact on America. But he conceded that the referendum had morphed into something it was not supposed to be. Any company, anywhere in America, can use its muscle to try to change California's laws, and even its constitution, he said. They often succeed.

Winner & Mandabach's skill at handling referendums—what Mandabach half jokingly refers to as the firm's "secret sauce"—tells us a great deal about how little attention the public usually pays to big issues. In truth, people can hardly be faulted for losing interest in a system that requires up to sixty or seventy decisions when Election Day comes around, from selecting the local school board to determining the next president, with ballot initiatives in between.

Unlike all the other boxes, where the voter can simply check the names of their preferred party, the referendum requires thought. Usually whatever thought voters can spare is last minute and highly volatile. Public opinion often swings 20 to 30 percent in the week leading up to the vote, way in excess of any swings in elections involving candidates. If normal elections are getting more volatile in the United States, "issue" votes are going haywire. "Very often we go late into the publicity, perhaps only a few days before Election Day, because most people aren't paying attention until then," said Mandabach.

Referendum publicity also frames choices very differently than do straight partisan commercials. Credible endorsers are key. On one referendum to close down a nuclear power station in Maine, in which Winner & Mandabach was acting on behalf of the nuclear company, the firm recruited a well-known local environmentalist to support keeping the plant open. "I will not accept acid-producing rain or oil tankers off our coast," said the environmentalist, against the backdrop of Maine's rugged shoreline. They won.

With just fifteen seconds to frame the issue, everything is in the message. "You need a good metaphor and a brief story line with a verb and a noun," says Mandabach. "It doesn't matter how much money you've got. Voters will lose interest after fifteen or thirty seconds." Language is critical. Readers can think of their own ways of reframing issues. "Clean coal" is my favorite.

Frank Luntz, the Republican consultant who is a near neighbor to Mandabach, is probably the most renowned political wordsmith of them all. "A car salesman doesn't sell secondhand cars," says Luntz. "He sells 'pre-owned vehicles.'" Never say drugs. Say "medication." And so on. The most well-known Luntz special was his substitution of "climate change" for "global warming." As one participant told him in a focus group on global warming, "climate change" sounded much less threatening, "like you're going from Pittsburgh to Fort Lauderdale."

Since the 1960s, and in myriad ways, America has grown steadily more democratic. As trust in politicians and public institutions has declined, voters' sway over what happens keeps rising. In the next chapter we will look at the "permanent campaign," in which the American presidency has gradually transformed itself by bringing campaign strategists into the bosom of government. Unlike the ballot initiative, which needs a public decision, the permanent campaign relies on a feverish and unending polling sample of what the public wants.

Much like the outcome of California's many successful propositions, what the public wants is not always consistent with what it can get. Americans want to reduce the deficit while protecting public services. They dislike big government but want Medicare and Social Security preserved at all costs. They want to be 100 percent safe in the air but hate intrusive pat downs at the airport. They want to tackle global warming but will vote out anyone who raises fuel taxes.

It is never hard to persuade people that America has strayed from the values of the Founding Fathers. "It's an easy answer to get," Ronald Dworkin, one of America's leading constitutional scholars, told me. "First you ask: Is the country on the right track or the wrong track. Next question: Has America departed from the Constitution?" Today it sounds quaint but in the Federalist Papers James Madison cautioned that a democracy needed an informed citizenry if it was to flourish. "A people who mean to be their own governors must arm themselves with the power knowledge gives," wrote Madison. Forty years later Tocqueville praised what the founders had created with its system of checks and balances that guarded against the "tyranny of the majority."

Alas, America is now subject to two simmering, and occasionally bewildering, tyrannies—the one posed by the rise of so-called Twitter democracy and the other by the powers of a deeply entrenched minority. Whether you observe the U.S. Senate in action, or the state assembly in Sacramento, rump minorities now wield permanent vetoes. In Washington, it shifts from Democratic to Republican and back again. In Sacramento, it looks to be permanently Republican.

Since 1992, when the Republican governor Pete Wilson sponsored a ballot initiative to deny any social services to illegal immigrants ("they just keep coming," he said in an infamous ad), Republicans as part of the population have been in long-term decline in California. More than 60 percent of the Golden State is now nonwhite.[109] Although Wilson's proposition was declared unconstitutional, it sent a chilling message to the state's rising Hispanic population. As Manuel Pastor said, the Republican Party was in effect committing electoral suicide.

Republicans may now have been reduced to only a third of the seats in the California legislature, but that is still enough to block anything meaningful from being enacted. The public, meanwhile, becomes steadily more frustrated and has voted for initiatives that further restrict Sacramento's leeway for action. These, in turn, make the politicians look even more fatuous. And so on in a vicious cycle that is steadily corroding whatever public trust remains. "In California, we have the tyranny of the minority," says Mandabach. "And if you think about it, the ballot initiative is the only way the public has of counteracting it."

Far too thoughtful to leave it at that, however, Mandabach permitted himself a little cognitive dissonance. "On the other hand, people forget that the Founding Fathers' main aim was to set up a republic, rather than a democracy," he said. "They were terrified of what the masses would do if left unchecked." After further reflection, Mandabach telephoned me a few days later. He enriched a story I have heard before.

America was dividing itself in disquieting ways, he said. By far the largest group was the amorphous majority of the electorate, which was becoming less knowledgeable about (and interested in) public affairs. Then there were the fanatics dominating the base of both parties (but particularly the Republicans) who, because of the Internet, had never before had access to anything like this much information or organizational reach. And they were making use of it.

Madison's citizenry were simultaneously too involved and too ignorant. Polarization and apathy—the unstoppable force and the easily movable object. It was an asymmetric equation that had turned politics into a running circus. W. B. Yeats said it: "The best lack all conviction, while the worst are full of passionate intensity."

For Mandabach, these twin afflictions pose a troubling dilemma to which he admitted he has no answer. On the one hand there were all these "looney tunes," as Larry Summers would put it, who were holding the nation hostage. On the other, there was the restless, apathetic, and alienated rest of America, which, when it isn't too bored or exhausted is looking for someone or something to blame. Washington usually tops the list. "I don't know which of the two is worse," said Mandabach. "But I know it's a bad combination."

6

Maybe We Can't

*Democracy is the theory that the common people know what they want and
deserve to get it good and hard.*

H. L. Mencken

THERE ARE TWO rules of social life in Washington, D.C. The
first, as Harry S. Truman famously advised, is that if you
need a friend get a dog. The second is that if Tony and Heather
Podesta invite you to a party you should accept. If the party
happens to be outside Washington, say in Denver, a few blocks
from the Invesco Field, where Barack Obama is about to get the
Democratic nomination for the White House, you should really
make sure to go.

This particular gathering, which the Podestas hosted in the ar-
boreal courtyard of a French restaurant, came with an ironic twist.
They called it a "Scarlett Letter" party after the eponymous Haw-
thorne novel in which an adulteress in Puritan-era Boston is forced
to stitch the letter "A" to her dress. Guests at the Podestas' event
were supposed to wear the letter "L," which stood for lobbyists.
Since they were playing the villains in Obama's electoral script, no
one needed the joke explained. "Will you accept a glass of champagne from a lobbyist?" said Tony Podesta, who, like Heather, owns
his own lobbying shop.[110] It would have been churlish to refuse.

From day one, taking on the lobbyists was central to Obama's campaign. The moment he launched his bid on February 10, 2007 —from the same steps in Springfield, Illinois, that Abraham Lincoln had started his own journey 148 years earlier—Obama zeroed in on "the cynics, and the lobbyists, and the special interests who have turned our government into a game." That game was going to come to an end. "They think they own this government," Obama said. "But we are here today to take it back."

As he progressed on his epic twenty-month journey to the White House, Obama finessed and weaved that line into his campaign's core message. In most of his speeches he blamed Washington's decline on two forces: the typical politician who used "the same old tired cynical games" to get elected; and the lobbyists, whose "money and influence drown out people's voices." In practice they were two sides of the same coin: one needed money to get reelected; the other wanted something in exchange.

"Politicians come to your cities and your towns, and they tell you what you want to hear—then they go to Washington," said Obama. "Lobbyists spend millions of dollars to get their way. The status quo sets in." Having identified the culprits, Obama showed what they had wrought: the Iraq war, the subprime mortgage crisis, the soaring cost of health care, and a "planet in peril." Then Obama would synthesize them all into a grand whole.

Along the way, he would point out that his campaign had "not taken a dime" from lobbyists or political action committees (PACs), a vehicle through which special interests donate funds. In contrast to the others, Obama had been funded by ordinary Americans who had flocked online in their millions—"the working men and women who dug into what little savings they had to give five dollars and ten dollars to this cause." Now, in 2008, Americans had a once-in-a-generation chance to say, "Not this year. Not this time." If they were willing to join forces with Obama, together they could bring about: "A nation healed. A world repaired. And an America that believes again."

That was the often electrifying oratory that had helped bring Obama to Denver. And these were the words that would help carry him through to Washington. It was undoubtedly a historic moment. Not only was Obama the first ever African-American to get the nomination. He was also one of the most articulate and intelligent men to get the chance. It might therefore have been an inopportune moment for the Podestas to host their mischievous champagne reception. But it was too juicy a target. Helpless against their own sense of irony (and flair for publicity) the Podestas had succumbed to what Obama might have called "the fierce urgency of now."

Their throng of guests seemed to take the party in the spirit that was intended. Dozens of Democratic U.S. senators and lawmakers also showed up. In a couple of days people would listen to Obama's soaring address at the Mile High stadium. Today, they were at the ground level clinking glasses and swapping business cards. "Obama doesn't really mean it, we're not taking any of it personally," said Tony Podesta, who is known for his tongue-in-cheek humor. "We'll be back to business as usual after the election." That proved to be an understatement.

Only "blood relatives and paid staffers," as the saying goes, or perhaps an ostrich, would reject Obama's description of how Washington works. Decisions of all kinds routinely go in favor of the highest bidder, and big corporations are among the town's best-funded players. Among Tony Podesta's clients are Walmart, Lockheed Martin, and BP. Heather's include Boeing and HSBC. Yet it might be a stretch to describe the Podestas as a problem for American democracy, if only because of their disarming openness. "I'm trying to figure out how I can represent both Albania and Serbia at the same time," Tony Podesta once said to me, with a mischievous twinkle. Sometimes, however, public relations intrudes. In 2012, Podesta ended his firm's contract with the government of Egypt after the military had raided the offices of U.S.-backed civil society groups in Cairo.

Lobbyists often also provide a good reality check on what politicians are saying. With some emphasis, Podesta told me that in

2005 he had hosted a fund-raiser for Obama's Senate war chest. "Obama seemed very happy to come to our house then," he said. As lobbyists, the Podestas hold fund-raising events for politicians they like. Yet it seems willfully abstruse to isolate their profession as the core problem with how Washington does business. In reality, it is more of an effect than a cause.

On a typical deal, the lobbyist plays the role of broker rather than buyer or seller. For the most part, lobbyists act on behalf of their clients: companies such as GE, which secrete lucrative breaks and exemptions into the code that are comprehensible only to their tax lawyers. Obama did not accept election money from lobbyists or PACs. But he took a lot from events hosted by senior corporate executives. In the 2008 campaign he stacked up $71 million in checks from people who worked on Wall Street, the largest Wall Street donation in American history.[111] The sums he raised from all corporate employees were far higher than what he took in small donations from ordinary Americans. Overall he raised more than double the $367 million George Bush had in 2004, which at the time had shattered previous records.

In some ways Obama is to election finance what George Bush had been to tax cuts— a bonanza. It was inevitable then that lobbyists would feel unfairly targeted. Among Obama's top ten donors in 2008 were Goldman Sachs, J. P. Morgan, Citigroup, Microsoft, and Time Warner.[112] "Obama talks about the special interests and their hired guns but then he only bans the hired guns," another lobbyist told me. It was like boycotting a criminal lawyer then going partying with the defendant, he added.

Having covered Obama's 2008 campaign and spent a great deal of time on his plane as it zigzagged from one swing state to another, I suppose it's hard for me to be objective. The gulf between Obama's poetry, which both Hillary and then McCain tried and largely failed to lampoon, and Obama's prose, which involved a lot of stops in the big cities for fund-raising events, was often awkward. "On this January night, at this defining moment in history, you have done what the cynics said we couldn't do," said Obama when he defeated Hillary in the opening Iowa Caucus in January 2008. After that, the gulf got steadily wider.

A lot of the mainstream American media, which Obama later jokingly—but nearly accurately—said had all voted for him,★ were prepared to give Obama a pass. Given how detested Hillary's team was among most journalists, and in light of the fact that Obama was under siege from a vicious rumor mill that called him an apologist for terrorism and a follower of black liberation theology, their reluctance was understandable. But it meant his campaign finance doublespeak was treated far more deferentially than it should have. After Iowa, Obama pushed his formidable skills to full throttle, raising $35 million the rest of that month alone, more than half of which came from big donors.

His boldest maneuver came at the start of the general election. Having agonized over whether to tap the post-Watergate era public funds for those who agree to forgo private money, Obama in June 2008 became the first candidate since Richard Nixon to go for broke. The gambit surprised some of Obama's supporters since McCain had accepted Obama's hypothetical offer (made long before he became the nominee) to conduct the campaign on a "level playing field" if his opponent were also to agree to public financing. Rather than admitting he was capitalizing on an unforeseen cash advantage, Obama presented his U-turn as reform-minded.

Obama's staff argued that his campaign was fed from the grassroots, which was far more democratic than relying on a broken public system. It was not as if Obama would be taking money from lobbyists, they added. Taking the cue the media, particularly the cable channels, continued to accentuate the small donor story. Obama promised to pursue election finance reform once in office (he never did). Most advocacy groups were still upset. "This is hypocrisy at its worst, and I'm bitterly angry about it," said Craig

---

★"Some of you covered me," Obama told a media audience in a lighthearted speech after he took office. "All of you voted for me."

Holman, head of campaign finance at Public Citizen, a consumer rights group, who worked closely with Senator Obama on public ethics reforms. "The only reason he's done this is because he can raise more money than McCain."[113]

In opting for private financing, Obama also ensured that money would continue to absorb every spare minute he had. Obama spent roughly a third of his time during the campaign looking for cash and another third writing or giving speeches. Most of the rest went to media interviews or campaign meetings.[114] That did not leave much for crafting policy solutions or discussing America's challenges with his legions of policy advisers. That scheduling dilemma would only get worse. So, too, would the prose-poetry gap.

Many of the 2 million people who came to Washington for Obama's magnificent snowy inauguration, which Steven Spielberg described as a scene he could not afford to shoot in one of his movies, came to affirm their ideals. Obama's volunteer army of activists, door knockers, and small donors hoped he would usher in a new era of public service, in which the money changers, as Franklin Roosevelt had promised, would be banished from the temple. It is questionable if that many would turn up for another. As Bill Galston, a former Clinton official and one of Washington's most acute political analysts, observed, "Hope is a soufflé that doesn't rise twice."

After he took office Obama kept that distinction between lobbyists and their clients. Corporate leaders frequently visited the White House. Lobbyists were not allowed near the entrance. "From my first days in office, I am going to launch the most sweeping ethics reform in history," Obama said after he was elected. It was a good start. The day after entering the Oval Office, Obama unveiled a new ethics code that would jam the revolving door between the White House and K Street.

Obama appointed Norm Eisen, a classmate from Harvard Law School, as his first "ethics czar." Eisen, a Washington-based lawyer, had cohosted a Democratic fund-raising event in Denver with the Podestas (Obama had no power to ban Democratic lawmakers from taking lobbyist money). No one who had recently worked as a lob-byist would be allowed to work in the Obama administration. Nor, "for as long as I am president," would anyone who had previously worked for his administration be allowed to lobby it.

After drawing up Obama's new rules, Eisen started to issue waivers. The most egregious was for William Lynn, the new dep-uty head of the Pentagon, whose previous job was chief lobbyist for Raytheon, the defense giant. Then came Ashton Carter, who became the Pentagon's head of acquisitions. He had been lobby-ing for Mitretek Systems, another defense company. In all, Eisen issued twenty-three waivers to former lobbyists. "We wanted to be really tough, but at the same time we didn't want to hamstring the new administration or turn the town upside down," a senior official said.

It was a candid admission, and perhaps also a practical one. K Street employs hundreds of highly qualified people who have worked in government before and wish to do so again. Meanwhile, Washing-ton was adapting easily to the new rules. Some lobbyists reregistered themselves as lawyers in order to get around them. Since most lobbyists are lawyers, and since a lobbyist is defined as someone who spends more than 20 percent of his or her time lobbying government, the switch was easy for most.

In spite of the dwindling pool of lobbyists the amount spent on "official" lobbying still rose by almost a fifth to $3.5 billion in 2009 and rose again in 2010.[115] Estimates of the number of "nonregistered advocates" were 100,000 (more than seven times the number of formal lobbyists). Spending on real, as opposed to official, lobbying activities was $9 billion that year, according to an estimate by James Thurber, a leading scholar of the U.S. presidency. That makes lobby-ing the third largest industry in America's capital after government and tourism. "Obama has changed the rhetoric but not the way Washington's political culture works," writes Thurber.

Almost three years after Obama was elected, I asked Tony Po-desta how much impact Obama's new broom had had on Wash-ington's Augean stables. Dressed in a trademark deafeningly loud tie—depicting what seemed to be a golden urn against a Mediterranean backdrop—Podesta said that his industry had never had it so good. Mostly this had been because of the frenzy of lobbying both for and against Obama's signature initiatives during his first two years, health care and Wall Street reform.

The big banks, hedge funds, health insurance, and drug companies all broke Washington spending records in 2009 and continued to match them for the next two years. In 2010 the Podesta Group, the town's third largest lobbying group, posted record profits. Partly, though, the boost to lobbying revenues was an unintended side effect of the reforms Obama had put in place. Those who retained their tag as registered lobbyists picked up even more business because of the scale of some of the legislation Obama put forward. Obama's busy agenda also provided a boost to business at Washington's law firms.

Podesta, whose brother John was head of Obama's transition team and White House chief of staff to Bill Clinton, was irked by what he described as the hypocrisy. He cited a number of Obama people, such as Anita Dunn, former head of White House communications, whom he said were lobbyists in all but name. Dunn, whose husband, Robert Bauer, was Obama's senior legal counsel until mid-2011, works at a firm that advises clients on public and government affairs, which is the polite term for lobbying. Among Dunn's clients are major players in the food industry, the "sensible food coalition," which includes General Mills and Kellogg's. Dunn, who frequently visited the White House, represented them as an adviser.

Then there was David Plouffe, the architect of Obama's campaign, who took a break for two years before returning as the senior White House adviser in early 2011. During the interlude Plouffe earned $1.5 million in book, consultancy, and speaking fees, including $50,000 for an address to members of Azerbaijan's authoritarian government. It was arranged by Bob Lawrence & Associates, a Washington-based lobbying firm. Technically none of this broke Obama's ethics pledge. In the brouhaha, Plouffe said he would donate the fees to charity.

Perhaps the best example was David Cohen, the senior vice president of Comcast, the cable provider, whose controversial merger with NBC in 2011 was approved by Obama's regulators. In spite of the conflict of interest, in 2011 Cohen was Obama's second largest bundler (someone who arranges and collects other people's donations, often from colleagues).[116] He raised $1.2 million for Obama's reelection campaign. Cohen was not a registered lobbyist. He, too, was a regular at the White House. "Cohen employs lobbyists, he supervises lobbyists, just don't call him a lobbyist," said another lobbyist, who wanted his name withheld. "It is all about following the letter of the ethics pledge and then trashing its spirit."

As Obama's term progressed it became obvious that his ethics reform rested largely on a technicality, which hinged on whether or not you self-identified as a lobbyist. If Obama's purpose had been to limit the influence of money in American politics, as opposed to its appearance, then he would have taken more radical measures. Norm Eisen, who set up the White House effort, was appointed as the U.S. ambassador to the Czech Republic in 2010. By then little was being heard about ethics. "Is there a new ethics czar? Does anybody care?" asked Podesta. "We still can't find any fingerprints."

Obama's White House gives off just as strong an aura of money as its predecessors. George W. Bush once told a gathering of fundraisers that they were his political base. "This is an impressive crowd: the haves and have-mores," said Bush. "Some people call you the elites. I call you my base." Obama would be unlikely to speak so candidly. But their differences are mainly cosmetic. Bush raised most of his money from the defense industry, fossil fuel companies, and doctors—traditional Republican donors. Obama raised more of his from Wall Street, Silicon Valley, and lawyers, as Democrats mostly do. In their different ways, both presidents adopted policies that benefited their big donors.

As is the tradition, both handed out plum ambassadorial posts to people who had helped them in their campaigns. To the chagrin of the State Department, many of whose employees did little to conceal their delight at Obama's election victory, America's forty-fourth president was just as prone to treat foreign postings as campaign thank-you notes as its forty-third. According to Open Secrets, the watchdog, a quarter of Obama's overseas appointments went to campaign donors. These included ambassadorships to Brazil, France, Japan, Ireland, Britain, and Argentina, none of which could be described as obscure.

Louis B. Susman, the Chicago investment banker, who was posted to the Court of St. James in London, was known as the "vacuum cleaner": once he had been through a room full of people there was no money left. Susman raised $300,000 for Obama's inauguration. John V. Roos, a lawyer, raised $500,000 for Obama's campaign and then became ambassador in Tokyo. And so on. Few had prior diplomatic experience. "Too often ambassadorships have served as political rewards for unqualified candidates," stated the American Academy of Diplomacy in a letter to Obama in 2009. There is no record of Obama's response.

Some may think it unfair to highlight Obama's anemic record considering that Bush and Clinton were arguably much worse. Clinton infamously invited many of his largest donors to stay in the historic Lincoln bedroom in the White House. As he left office Clinton also issued a flurry of "midnight regulations" that included absolving anyone who worked for him from the weak ethics code they had originally signed. Those who wished could return to K Street. Just under a third of former Clinton officials did exactly that.[117] Many will be banking on Obama to do the same.

In his campaign Bush promised to restore "character and honor" to Washington. With hindsight this meant only that he would continue to go to bed early and avoid female interns. Money was a different matter. Bush scattered jobs, emoluments, and dispensations to donors like so much spring cherry blossom. One beneficiary was Michael Brown, who infamously headed up the Federal Emergency Management Agency during Hurricane Katrina.

Brown's only credential had been to lead the International Arabian Horse Association, a job from which he had been ejected.

"You are doing a heck of a job, Brownie," Bush said memorably to Brown as New Orleans was falling to pieces. Bush also took money from people he then invited to cowrite policy. In spite of its secrecy, Congress and the media eventually obtained the names of those who sat on Vice President Dick Cheney's 2001 energy task force. It was stacked with executives and lobbyists from the big energy donors. Nothing that blatant has occurred under Obama.

Unlike Obama, however, neither Clinton nor Bush promised to "change the way Washington does business," let alone make it a centerpiece of their campaigns. In his classic book *American Politics: The Promise of Disharmony*, Samuel Huntington identified America's key fault line as the gap between the ideals of America's national creed—based on the values of political equality—and its reality, which often fails to live up to them. Whenever the gap becomes too glaring, as it seems to have done in the early twenty-first century, Americans are prone to bouts of "creedal passion."[118]

During such periods, Americans tended to respond in one of four ways—with hypocrisy, moralism, cynicism, or complacency. Huntington saw these tendencies as sui generis, given that America was uniquely founded on a creed rather than on shared history or ethnicity. Polling showed that the outlook of wealthy Americans more often fit Huntington's definition of hypocrisy, while small town and blue-collar Americans were more prone to cynicism. When combined, these mentalities tended to "perpetuate the status quo."

For Huntington, hypocrisy was the most insidious of America's creedal vices: once seen in their leaders it would tilt the broader American public toward cynicism. It is no accident that Bush, who appeared to care little whether money was seen to be influencing his agenda, started with far lower expectations than Obama. Following Huntington, Bush would have qualified as complacent (with some moralism). Obama would appear to be hypocritical (with a lot of moralism). "If you are extraordinarily high-minded in your political pronouncements," wrote Huntington, "then you are bound in the nature of things to be more than ordinarily hypocritical."[119]

It was only after Obama's first few months in office, after people had observed the money-drenched battle over health care and Wall Street's uninterrupted influence over policy, that a widespread cynicism began to take hold. Following his inauguration, Obama said he would give a weekly address on YouTube. The early ones attracted more than a million viewers each. By the end of the year his audience had dropped to just 42,000.[120] By the time Obama kicked off his reelection campaign in early 2011 the spirit of the previous one was all but forgotten.

Obama's team began its reelection efforts by making it known that the plan was to raise a billion dollars for 2012, a third higher than in 2008. To many Obama supporters that seemed mighty brazen. "Imagine if Obama had begun his first campaign saying he wanted to break all money records," said a Democratic advocate who runs a think tank in Washington, D.C. "Isn't that what Hillary did?"

Matt Damon, the Hollywood actor, crystallized the mood of Obama's liberal base, without whose enthusiasm he would have had little hope of winning the nomination. "I really think Obama misinterpreted his mandate," Damon said in 2011. "A friend of mine said to me the other day, and I thought it was a great line, 'I no longer hope for audacity.'" In the next section we will look at how money affected Obama's key reforms and what that tells us about how tough it is to bring about meaningful change in Washington.

Mark Hanna, the legendary political operator of the Gilded Age, said, "There are two things that are important in politics. The first is money and I can't remember what the second one is." If Hanna had asked his progressive opponents they probably would have added "good government." Mocked at the time as supporting a "goo goo" (good government) fantasy, progressives were often dismissed as "mugwumps," a defunct term that derives from a native American word meaning sanctimonious. A slightly more contemporary version of the mugwump might be Jason Donovan, the Australian soap star, who was once celebrated for having asked: "Why can't we all just get along?"

Barack Obama arrived in office promising two conflicting things, change and bipartisanship. The first, "change," is usually divisive and painful. The second, "bipartisanship," depends on people getting along or acquiescing with what you want to do. If change requires a stiff upper lip, bipartisanship often displays a quivering lower one. Whether you are talking about a campaign tableau or a very peculiar facial expression, something must give.

Obama continued both these lines into office. But as he tried to navigate the most polarized Washington in memory Obama's mantra of change was gradually displaced by the rhetoric of bipartisanship. "This is what change looks like," said a steel-jawed Obama after he signed health care reform into law in March 2010. It was arguably his last piece of true defiance. Judged by its content, however, the health care act looked an awful lot like the status quo.

People asked what had happened to Obama's agenda of far-reaching change. The answer was Washington. Transaction had supplanted transformation. Process replaced substance. "Let's be honest," Obama's chief of staff Rahm Emanuel told the *New York Times*. "The goal isn't to see whether I can pass this f***ing bill through the executive board of the Brookings Institution [the liberal think tank]. I'm passing it through the United States Congress with people who represent constituents."

A generation ago, the great American political economist Mancur Olson offered a brilliant insight into why "stable nations tend to wind down over time." Long periods of stability gradually sap a nation's will to alter how the game is played. As success and prosperity become normal, it gets ever more difficult for proponents of reform to dislodge the coalitions that control their nation's resources. Olson was thinking primarily about Britain's sluggish response to the Great Depression and its sclerosis in the postwar years.

He was also talking about Washington in the 1970s. Like an old cruise liner encrusted with layers of barnacles, the propellers of government move ever more slowly. Rather than boosting wealth creation, politics turns into an increasingly elaborate machine for capturing rents and dividing them. "Stable societies with unchanged boundaries tend to accumulate more collusions and organizations over time," he wrote. "As the benefits secured by groups accumulate, the economy rigidifies."[121]

What Olson observed in the 1970s is acutely more relevant in Washington today. In promising to overhaul both America's health care and its financial service sectors, which together cover more than a quarter of the U.S. economy, Obama ran up against the established way of doing things. Obama's health care blueprint was to extend coverage to the one in six Americans who were uninsured, reduce costs for the five in six who were already insured, and improve the quality of health care for all six of them. Some were skeptical whether Obama could realistically promise to make a thing universally available, higher quality, and cheaper all at the same time.

His plan of action also ran straight into the jaws of Olson's paradox: When those who stand to benefit from a proposed change vastly outnumber those who will lose, the latter have an organizing advantage, particularly if the former's gains are modestly divided among many while the latter's are richly split among few. The smaller a group's size, the more easily it can organize itself. And the smaller it is, the larger the gains to each member. The logic of collective action helps explain why America's farm owners, who number in the hundreds of thousands, are good at maintaining their large government subsidies, while those living in poverty, who number in the tens of millions, are woefully bad at it. Farmers can easily organize. People on welfare cannot. "Small, narrow groups have a permanent, inherent advantage," Olson wrote.

His insight also explains why America's health care providers have such an edge over their customers. Whether it is the hospitals, drug companies, insurers, or even the doctors, their numbers are relatively few and the gains from acting together are great. America's Health Insurance Plans (AHIP), the insurance industry's lobby group, has thirteen hundred member companies. Their customer base is 308 million. The Pharmaceutical Research and Manufacturers of America (PhRMA), the drug industry's main lobby group, has sixty-one member companies. Its customers cover half the planet. It should come as no surprise, therefore, that Obama, whose proposed health care benefits would be spread among most Americans, ran straight into the few whose losses would be proportionately large.

At the start of Obama's term opinion polls and K Street spending trends suggested the American public was lukewarm to reform and the health care industry was highly motivated against it. Obama had a simple choice. Either he could follow the logic of what he outlined in the campaign, which would mean confronting an ominous phalanx of special interests; that fork could lead to the mother of all Olsonian battles. Or he could work with the special interests to make sure that he got a bill passed. With the exception of the health care insurers, with whom Obama eventually fell out, the president chose the latter. In so doing he ensured that people like Tony Podesta would have a very busy year. The health care industry's lobbyists were many and its public defenders few. But in Max Baucus they had a singular legislative champion.

"Obama has just caved without firing a shot," said a senior, non–White House adviser to Obama in early June 2009.[122] Instead of drafting his own legislation, Obama had announced he would out-source its contents to Baucus, a six-term senator from Montana and a paragon of bipartisan Washington. Baucus, the chairman of the powerful Senate Finance Committee, was the health care industry's favorite politician. According to Open Secrets, Baucus had received $3.8 million in donations from the health industry, which put him among the top five recipients on Capitol Hill. He took more money from health care groups in 2008 than any federal lawmaker that year.

Baucus's office maintained a busy revolving door with the health care industry. Two former Senate chiefs of staff to Baucus,

Jeff Forbes and David Castagnetti, were prominent health care lobbyists.[123] Both had meetings with Baucus when he was drafting the bill. The main author of Baucus's draft bill was Liz Fowler, Baucus's health care adviser, who had previously been a vice president at WellPoint, America's largest health insurance company. Fowler's predecessor in Baucus's office was Michelle Easton, who was by then lobbying for WellPoint. During the three months it took Baucus to come up with his draft bill—and without having secured the support of two out of three Republicans in his bipartisan "group of six"—the senator intensified his fund-raising schedule.

Critically, Baucus then clinched two deals with the health care industry. First, he gutted the bill of its public insurance option, which, because of the government's scale, would have forced insurers to reduce their rates in the marketplace. Instead they could anticipate as many as 32 million formerly uninsured customers who would be mandated by law to buy their products at the taxpayer's expense. In exchange they would no longer be able to refuse coverage to—or withdraw it from—people with "preexisting conditions," such as a diabetics, or people with heart conditions. They would also face more competition in the new health care exchanges.

Second, Baucus struck a deal with the pharmaceutical industry in which he forfeited the federal government's right to negotiate lower drug prices for Medicare, the government-backed program for seniors, which accounts for nearly half of the health care economy. Baucus also threw in a ban on the import of much cheaper drugs from Canada. In exchange drug companies would chip in $80 billion in extra tax over the next ten years, a bagatelle versus what many forecast they stood to gain from the right to charge the same high prices on far higher volumes.

With these two concessions, most of the health care sector would swing behind reform. The drug industry spent $67 million on advertisements backing the bill. Hospitals and doctors also came out in support. Only the insurers remained hostile. With those same concessions Baucus also deprived the U.S. government of its two most powerful levers to overhaul the nation's health care system, both of which Obama promised on the campaign trail.

From Canada to Japan, in one form or another, every rich country's government negotiates cheaper drug prices and offers their citizens public insurance. The absence of both is largely what makes America's health care system the "wallet biopsy" it has become. They are a big part of the reason why other countries' health spending consumes on average roughly half the resources of their American counterpart while achieving higher life expectancy and covering their entire populations, the three goals Obama had originally set out.

This is also why U.S. employers, who continue to provide insurance to most Americans, will remain just as keen in the future to look for technology that can further reduce their head counts. The C minus grade that Carl Camden, the head of Kelly Services, awarded the bill might still have been better than an F. After Baucus came out with his bill in September 2009, liberal Democrats had no hesitation in awarding it a K—for K Street. "Seldom have so many waited so long for so little," said Lloyd Doggett,[124] a Democratic lawmaker from Texas. "This isn't negotiation, it is capitulation to the insurance industry." Lynn Woolsey, the chair of the Congressional Progressive Caucus, said, "We wouldn't vote for that for anything." In the event, they had little choice.

It took another six months for the Affordable Care Act to be enacted. The final version differed only in minor ways from Baucus's 2,300-page blueprint. The market's verdict was clear. On the day it finally passed in March 2010, Wall Street stock prices hit an eighteen-month high. Insurers did not do so well. Among the big gainers were Pfizer, Merck, and Tenet, one of the largest private chains. "They're certainly going to get a very high return on that investment," said Henry Waxman,[125] a senior Democrat in the House.

It was a pattern that repeated itself often during Obama's first term. First he set out his terms. Then, with the aide of someone like Baucus, he appeared to concede half the battle before it had begun. After 2010, when the House was taken over by Republicans, Obama faced much steeper odds. Until his turnabout in the autumn of 2011, when he swung back to the left with his proposed "mini-stimulus" on jobs, Obama's climb-downs came faster. Yet the bills passed during the previous two years in a Democratic-controlled town were in line with what non–Tea Party Republicans could have accepted in saner times. When he was the Republican governor of Massachusetts in 2005, Mitt Romney pushed through a health care reform that most analysts considered to be slightly to the left of "Obamacare."

During his 2008 campaign Obama frequently warned that lobby groups would "throw everything they've got" at Washington to defend the status quo. By choosing to go the bipartisan route, perhaps Obama was giving in to reality. If Obama had been realistic on the campaign trail, of course, he might never have been elected. "When Washington is this polarized, the status quo is everybody's second choice," said Andy Stern,[126] the trade unionist who was in alliance with Carl Camden, Walmart, and other employers to overhaul the health care system. He was disappointed. "There were good things in the bill. But nothing fundamental was changed."

Shortly after Obama signed health care reform into law, he made a little noticed but telling appointment. Liz Fowler, the lawyer who had drafted Baucus's bill, was selected to head up an office that would implement large chunks of the law, a role possibly more important than drafting the bill. Fowler had worked on and off over many years for WellPoint, America's largest health insurer. Critics accused Obama of trashing the spirit of his ethics code, rather than the letter, since Fowler had not technically worked as a lobbyist for WellPoint. "Her appointment is completely in line with the stringent ethics standards that President Obama put in place, and we're thrilled that she's willing to do the job," said Reid Cherlin, Obama's spokesman on health care. Such were the ins and outs of health care reform.

Like health care, the story of Wall Street reform continued well beyond its enactment and into a more obscure battle of the rules within the bowels of Washington's bureaucracy. Both bills were passed in the first half of 2010. But the amounts spent by Wall Street banks and the health care companies on lobbying actually rose after they were enacted and then stayed at those levels. There was as much, if not more, to be won or lost in the follow-up regulations.

Interested parties need no reminder that a law often finds its true expression in the rule-writing phase after it has passed. The largest beneficiaries of any alteration usually find a good hiding place within complexity. By then, politics has often moved elsewhere. There was only muted protest, for example, when Obama's treasury secretary Timothy Geithner proposed in 2011 that foreign exchange derivatives be excluded from the law's new requirements. That would cover many large cross-border derivatives.

Raghuram Rajan, the economist who clashed with Alan Greenspan in 2005, argued that the government's financial regulators already had the authority to address the problems behind the financial bubble. They chose not to. What was missing was the political will to make sure they did their jobs. "It is a problem of modern complex economies that the only people who understand its most important parts are often captured by them," says Rajan.[127] To judge by the Dodd-Frank bill, the name by which the Wall Street reform is often called, those lessons still had not been learned, he said. "Thinkers tend to think in herds and I am not sure the herd has changed direction," said Rajan. "Our problem is not so much rugged individualism as undifferentiated groupthink."

About a year after Dodd-Frank was passed, HBO released *Too Big to Fail,* its widely praised docudrama on the collapse of Lehman Brothers in 2008. Its characterizations were good—William Hurt got Henry Paulson's rasping diction exactly right, and Paul Giamatti's mournful Ben Bernanke was close. The big exception was Tim Geithner, who was played by a way too Hollywoodesque Billy Crudup. "I haven't seen it," Geithner told me in an interview a few months after the movie was released. "There's way too much happening in real time to watch these movies or read all these books."

He might want to make an exception for *Too Big to Fail,* I suggested. It portrayed Geithner and his colleagues as the heroes who saved the day. "I'm told it gets me wrong," Geithner added. "I'm always jogging and never swearing. They should swap that around." Geithner swears even more than the legendary Rahm "F★★★king" Emanuel. But his vocabulary is belied by his demeanor, which is unfailingly polite and self-effacing.

After Summers's departure in late 2010, Obama relied increasingly on Geithner as his chief economic counsel. Gene Sperling, who replaced Summers and had already once done the job under Bill Clinton, was seen as more of a tactician than a strategist. Sperling received $887,000 in fees from Goldman Sachs in 2008 for advice on charitable work. Compared to the charity going rate it was nice work. Peter Orszag, Obama's budget director, did it the other way round. After Orszag left the White House in mid-2010 he became a vice president at Citigroup in New York. "Sometimes these guys get stipends before they go to Washington, sometimes afterward," a former Clinton official said to me. In Gene Sperling's case it was both.

Geithner has never held a private sector job on Wall Street. But he was president of the New York Federal Reserve when Lehman collapsed. Many saw him as a mouthpiece for people such as Lloyd Blankfein, Goldman's chief executive, and Jamie Dimon of J. P. Morgan. Many were also expecting Geithner to cash in when he left the Obama administration, something that by mid-2011 had become a constant rumor. He ducked the question. "Let's try to get through this next month," said Geithner, who was in the middle of the titanic battle over raising the U.S. debt ceiling. "Maybe I'll play tennis after this. I don't know." Shortly afterward he acceded to Obama's pressure to serve out a full term.

In contrast to most of Obama's legislative efforts, where the White House was usually happy to abdicate the contents to Congress, Geithner was asked to play the starring role in getting Wall Street reform enacted. On other bills, including the "resolution" of the debt-ceiling crisis in August 2011, Obama was eager to outsource the drafting to Capitol Hill. This raised the chances of a bill's success. But it also, inadvertently or otherwise, opened a much wider crack in the door for K Street. Congress did not adopt Obama's ban on meetings with lobbyists.

Obama had in fact settled on this trade-off (ceding control of a bill to lift the chances of passage) before reaching office in January 2009 with the drafting of $787 billion in stimulus to revive the economy. After that—and with the exception of Geithner's Wall Street bill—outsourcing became the norm. During the debate over the ill-fated carbon cap and trade bill in 2009, on which the world's hopes for the coming global warning summit in Copenhagen largely rested, Obama watched special interests stuff the draft with carve-outs, exemptions, and old-fashioned boondoggles. If the stimulus was somewhat unfairly labeled Porkulus, the carbon bill could accurately have been called Pork and Trade.

"What I didn't get was that the White House barely lifted a finger," said Robert Shapiro,[128] a former Clinton economic adviser, who now runs his own Washington consultancy. "They just wanted to check the next box and move on." Many, including Shapiro, began to view Obama's presidency as "transactional." Given that Emanuel, David Axelrod, Valerie Jarrett, and Obama were all from Chicago, the national headquarters of machine politics, perhaps that wasn't surprising. "There may have been a transactional quality to some of the bills," said Peter Orszag,[129] a few months after he had left. "Sometimes that is how you get things done in Washington."

That was the approach for all the other bills. The strategy for what eventually became the Wall Street Reform and Consumer Protection Act was very different. Reforming Wall Street was too important to be left to Capitol Hill. Instead of letting Congress write the first draft of the bill, Geithner produced a white paper, which was later expanded. The Obama administration needed to keep close tabs on each and every clause of it, and Geithner did. "We felt it was important to be closely involved at every stage," Geithner said.

The bill offered a mild overhaul of Wall Street regulation, including the creation of a new systemic regulator and a consumer financial regulatory bureau. Under the so-called Volcker rule, named after the former chairman of the Federal Reserve, it also forced banks with publicly insured deposits to separate proprietary trading divisions into separate entities. Most derivatives would also have to be registered through clearinghouses. But it stopped short of breaking up the "too big to fail" banks. And it shied away from consolidating Washington's alphabet soup of regulatory agencies and their counterpart committees on Capitol Hill. By maintaining Washington's balkanized regulatory arrangement, it ensured that the regulated would continue to have opportunities to play off one regulator against another.

During the bill-writing process, interested parties, such as Blankfein who had provocatively hit back at Wall Street's critics by saying it was doing "God's work,"[130] kept up a near continual conversation with Geithner. This may have been aided by the fact that Geithner's chief of staff Mark Patterson had previously been Goldman's chief Washington lobbyist. Geithner and Blankfein met or spoke no fewer than thirty-eight times between January 2009 when Geithner took office and the passage of the bill sixteen months later. This was four times as often as Geithner saw Harry Reid, the Senate majority leader, or Nancy Pelosi, the Democratic Speaker. The final bill, which, like health care exceeded two thousand pages, was praised by some and attacked by others. There seemed to be no ideological litmus test predicting where a person stood on its contents.

Some, such as Nicholas Brady, the Republican former U.S. Treasury secretary under George Bush senior, were outraged at Geithner's failure to consult more widely. "As far as I can tell Geithner just talks to the investment bank chiefs," said Brady,[131] who himself had not been consulted. "This is largely their bill." Others, such as Brooksley Born, the former derivatives regulator who had fallen out with Larry Summers in 2000, were happier. Born had been consulted by Geithner. "Given how much money there is in Washington and how difficult it is to get anything done, I was surprised by how good Dodd-Frank was," Born told me. She was less complimentary about the rule writing that followed.

The most important dispute was between those who thought the bill enshrined "too big to fail" and therefore boosted the likelihood of another systemic crash, with all its unthinkable fiscal consequences, and those who thought Geithner and Congress had stitched together an effective straitjacket for the banks. A smaller group of bank chiefs and Alan Greenspan complained that the bill was an overreaction. Interestingly, there appeared to be many more pessimists in Britain than in the United States. The British economy arguably had peered into an even deeper abyss during the 2008 meltdown.

I asked Geithner about Andrew Haldane, the Bank of England economist, who in 2009 had written a chilling paper in which he identified an escalating "doom loop"[132] that threatened to end in the crash of all crashes with the bursting of the ultimate bubble: the full faith and credit of the United States. September 2008 had been but a dress rehearsal (and the political debt crisis in August 2011 perhaps another). Haldane's paper probably got more online attention than any other central bank publication in recent years. Many distinguished economists, including Rajan and Joseph Stiglitz, the former Clinton adviser and Nobel Prize winner, shared Haldane's forebodings about a doom loop. Geithner did not. "I like Andrew, he's a really intelligent guy," said Geithner. "I just do not agree with him."

Geithner set out why the Wall Street bill had "fundamentally changed the game" rather than simply having reshuffled the status quo, as others argued. He pointed out that the bill had set up an unprecedented mechanism for coping with the failures of large financial institutions, almost any one of which "we could comfortably handle" were it to go bankrupt, he said. "We are not like Switzerland where they could never afford to let UBS go bankrupt," he said. "We have many banks in the United States."

Thus, if America were to be hit by anything between a five-year flood and a twenty-year flood, the U.S. taxpayer would be able to cope, he insisted. The big question was what would happen if a once-in-a-century flood struck, as it had in 2008. Then everyone had been submerged. Unlike Haldane, who fears the next crisis will strike much sooner than that, Geithner sounded confident about the future. "We have a much more robust mechanism in place to cope with the once-in-a-century scenario," he said. "I am pretty optimistic."

Others, of course, are not so sure. So who is right—the pessimists, such as Rajan, Simon Johnson (a former chief economist at the IMF), and Nouriel Roubini; or those who take their cue from Geithner and who, like Dr. Pangloss, sound as though they expect the best from the best of all possible worlds? Obviously the future will tell. But if it is anything like the past, official pronouncements should be treated with the utmost skepticism. In evaluating Geithner's upbeat prognosis, it is worth remembering he has spent most of his career in jobs that demand unwavering optimism in virtually any scenario. Markets respond to even the tiniest insinuations in language.

Geithner's talk of floods had also reminded me of what Elizabeth Warren (the Harvard bankruptcy scholar turned hopeful politician) had said. The 2008 crisis, she insisted, was man-made, not a natural disaster. Those who still thought of it like a flood, or a tsunami, did not think there were culprits. The key people, including Geithner, responded to the meltdown as though it were a freak event. They poured cash into the disaster zone. Unlike GM, where the chief executive was sacked after Obama took it over, using the same bailout vehicle that saved the financial system, Washington demanded no scalps from Wall Street. No boards were dismissed.

In the 1929 Wall Street crash, many of those who lost their shirts famously jumped to their deaths from office windows. In 2008 it was accountability that jumped. It still hadn't been found. Fairly or not, Geithner has often attracted the blame for its absence. "If you leave aside Bernie Madoff [the Ponzi fraudster, now in prison], how many people were sent to jail?" asked Warren. The answer, of course, was none.

Fear of the public's combustible mood was one reason Geithner and the White House kept such a tight rein on the Wall Street bill. Congress nevertheless found ways to contaminate the process. Just before the meltdown Chris Dodd, the Connecticut senator, chair of the Banking Committee, and later coauthor of the Wall Street bill, was exposed as having benefited from "VIP" mortgages on both his Washington and Connecticut homes.

Dodd, who ran for the Democratic presidential nomination in 2008 (he dropped out early), did not disclose either loan in his annual statements. His benefactor was Countrywide Financial, possibly the most egregious pusher of subprime loans in the market. Dodd was in the "friends of Angelo" club, which was named after the notorious Angelo Mozilo, chief executive of the now bankrupt bank. Members got below-market rates. Dodd's dodgy mortgages were revealed only in mid-2008 when he proposed a measure in the Senate to keep troubled subprime lenders afloat.

The scandal did not prevent Dodd from playing a lead role in the drafting of the Wall Street bill. Dodd retired from Congress in 2010. Few were surprised when a few weeks later he landed a big job as a lobbyist. Dodd had been insisting he would never take that kind of job. "Dodd forswears lobbying," said a headline in the *Hartford Courier*. Then he announced he would take the $1.2 million a year position as president of the Motion Pictures Association, possibly the most glamorous lobbying slot in Washington, D.C. The fact that Dodd would technically be disallowed from lobbying for two years seemed irrelevant.

Such are the biographical niceties of some of the Senate's most senior members.*Yet there were comparatively few allegations of ethical irregularity against the Wall Street bill compared to those

---

*My favorite was Evan Bayh, the centrist Democratic senator from Indiana, who had been on the short list to be Obama's running mate. Bayh also retired from the Senate in 2010. "If I could create one job in the private sector by helping to grow a business, that would be one more than Congress has created in the last six months," Bayh said. No one thought he meant it literally. Shortly after Bayh retired, one new job was created when he accepted a seven-figure salary at a large lobbying firm in Washington, D.C.

flying around about healthcare and cap and trade. The criticisms made of Geithner, who in interviews often volunteers his disquiet about how badly Congress functions, dwell on his intellectual predilections, rather than his own pocket book.

Many of Geithner's detractors, including Rajan, viewed him as an example of "cognitive capture" by Wall Street. Whether that allegation persists will largely depend on what job Geithner decides to take when he quits the treasury. Geithner also has many defenders. "You won't find anyone who has worked harder, longer, or had more demands placed on them than Tim," says a friend of Geithner's, who previously worked at the U.S. Treasury. "He has always been a public servant."

Cognitive kidnappers or not, Wall street spent more than $1 billion on lobbying in the eighteen months before and after passage of what should have been called the Geithner bill. What Wall Street spent added up to more than $2 million apiece for each of the 535 members of Congress. Goldman Sachs and many other banks also stepped up their contributions to both political parties. In one quarter of 2009 alone, the U.S. Chamber of Commerce spent $77 million on campaigns opposing all three of Obama's big reform efforts.[133]

The contrast with the small sums spent by proponents of Wall Street reform was gaping. Americans for Financial Reform, the largest group in favor of a tough reform bill, raised a grand total of $2 million for its advocacy.[134] Whatever the merits of AFR's arguments, most viewers would not have glimpsed their commercials. As for the media, most major players quickly lost interest in the details of the bill. It is hard to sustain a viewer's attention with too much talk about Basel capital adequacy ratios.

The American public also seemed to tire of all the battles in Congress. True to Huntington's prototype, people became cynical about Obama's Washington, and especially the bits to which he had entrusted so much of his agenda. In one 2010 poll, 88 percent of respondents said they believed "money buys results in Congress."[135] One can only guess at what the other 12 percent were thinking.

A few months later Obama launched his reelection campaign. Casual observers could be forgiven for thinking it had started long before then. It is to America's ever more ubiquitous permanent campaign that we now turn.

Strictly speaking, I was not meant to be there. It was a "closed door" fund-raising event for Obama's 2012 reelection campaign and journalists were not invited. But in my contact, who is a stalwart fund-raiser and gatekeeper to a wealthy archipelago of donors, the organizers had met their match. "Just act inconspicuous," she advised.

The event, which was hosted by the Women's Leadership Forum, an arm of the Democratic Party, aimed to raise at least $2 million. If Obama were to hit his target of a billion dollars, he would need to find that much every day of his remaining eighteen months in office. A smart gathering of about three hundred women had turned up. Many of them, like my host, were bundlers, people who collect the maximum individual donations ($38,500 a year) from friends and contacts and combine them in one sum.

In addition to opening their checkbooks, it was a chance for the Democratic women to hear about what the 2012 campaign planned to do. Michelle Obama kicked off the event in the morning. Her husband would drop by to address it in the evening. The real star of the day was Jim Messina, chairman of the 2012 campaign, and the man on whom Obama was relying to secure him a second term in office.

Messina and his colleagues spent most of the day alternating between pep talks to raise everyone's morale and power point presentations to reassure them the campaign had a plan. No speaker referred explicitly to the sharp decline in enthusiasm for Obama in the Democratic base since he came to office. But it hung in the air. The first objective, therefore, was to project a sense of optimism. Messina, who had quit his job as White House deputy chief of staff (Emanuel's number two) to run the campaign, was well practiced.

Messina told the crowd that he and Obama were swimming off the coast of Hawaii on vacation in December 2010 when the president asked him to spearhead his reelection campaign. Messina said that he would accept on one condition: "Only if you promise, Mr. President, that this will be the best grassroots campaign in modern history." Obama agreed. Now Messina was putting it into practice.

Messina clicked on a chart that showed how this goal would be achieved. The Obama campaign would have a full-time staff of some three thousand people who would help to create an army of one million "supervolunteers," who in turn would recruit 4 million ordinary volunteers. The 2008 campaign would look prehistoric by comparison. "The technology we used in 2008 is now obsolete," said Messina. "We had no Twitter then and no iPads and we had only one full-time staffer doing Facebook." This time Obama would need a small army of smart social media professionals. "We need to fundamentally change the way we campaign," he said.

Messina then turned to the main business of the day. Setting up a campaign of this nature would require lots of money. Everyone needed to be imaginative about finding ways to "leverage relationships" with people they knew, such as their Facebook friends. Campaigns were no longer just about knocking on doors. They were about finding "key validators in your communities" who could inspire others, such as leaders of their Parent-Teacher Association. Everyone should keep good databases, he said. "If you cannot measure it, then it doesn't count."

It was an impressive performance. Messina projected a mix of folksy and geeky, with enough anecdote to leaven all the data. He was also good at setting out the stakes. With the help of guest speakers, such as Gene Sperling, Obama's chief economic adviser, Messina underlined the gravity of what they were doing. If you transposed the 2010 midterm trends onto the key 2012 battleground states, the electoral map started to look very challenging, he said. Obama's Republican opponent would reverse all that had been gained in Obama's first term. As the day wore on Obama's $1 billion target started to feel like a levee that would keep out the next Katrina.

Yet there was something puzzling about what Messina laid out. My host, a veteran of many campaigns and a woman with a much sought after Rolodex, thought so, too. On the one hand Obama needed money to build the most professional campaign ever. On the other, it would be powered by the largest volunteer surge in history. "What they are doing is making Astroturf [building fake grass roots]," she said. The trademark groundswell of 2008 had gone. They needed a new one. Obama would not be Obama without a grassroots.

A few weeks later Messina announced the results of Obama's first quarter of fund-raising (ending in July 2011). They hit the ball out of the park. The Obama Victory Fund had gathered $87 million, almost half as large again as the combined total raised by the crowded field of Republicans. Furthermore, Obama achieved all this "from the ground up," said Messina in an online video address. The Obama surge had returned. In all, 98 percent of the donations were below $250. Obama had gathered only a third as many donors at the same point in the last cycle. "It is a monumental achievement," said Messina. "Congratulations to you all."

In reality, it was Messina who deserved it. The largest share of money (as opposed to individual donations) came from wealthy bundlers at closed-door events, including the one I had attended. Between April and June, Obama attended on average two fund-raisers a week around the country. Just before the launch of his campaign, Obama even hosted a reception in the White House Blue Room for a group of his largest bundlers, which included Jon Corzine, the former chief executive of Goldman Sachs, and several Wall Street investors. Because they were not asked for money at the event, the reception was still legal (it is illegal to use federal property to raise election funds). In the next three months, Obama's Blue Room guests raised $3.9 million for him.[136]

Yet it was the ordinary folk that Messina wanted to highlight. There were indeed more small donors than ever. But the Obama campaign had used every ruse to pad them out. Just before the quarterly deadline, Messina sent a mass e-mail reminding everyone that one lucky donor would get to dine with Obama. All you had to do to enter the lottery for "dinner with Barack" was donate $5. In his e-mail, Messina added that he had received an "unexpected update" from Obama in a video that had just landed. Messina had a feeling any undecideds would throw their hat into the ring after seeing it. In the attached video, Obama revealed that Joe Biden would also join him and the lucky donor. Now it was "Dinner with Barack and Joe." In the next quarter that lottery ticket dropped to $3.

On this occasion, Obama technically broke the law since the video had been shot in the Oval Office. Either way, the strategy worked. More than half a million people donated $5 or more to the campaign and Messina stamped that message on the coverage. My Democratic friend was less impressed. As a commentator on the money side of the campaign she was hardly neutral. She was a close friend of the Clintons, and especially with Hillary. During the 2008 campaign many of Hillary's friends developed an intense resentment of Obama. There were still residues.

But business was business. She was still a Democrat. And the Obama campaign was keen to get access to her lucrative database of three thousand donors. "It is unbelievable how often these Obama people keep calling me," she said. "It's all so cloak and dagger." In April 2011 Obama made a state visit to Ireland. The campaign wanted to convert the trip into a fund-raising opportunity with Irish-Americans. An Obama genealogical thread had been traced to the small town of Moneygall, where the president took a pint of Guinness with some of his closest relatives. It was a good photo op and an amused Obama played it tongue-in-cheek.* Before the

---

*Obama was even offered a CD by a local band that wrote a song about him. The refrain of the song: "There's no one as Irish as Barack Obama," says it all.

photo op had ended, she got a call from a Democratic official. The party wanted her to issue a statement saying what a success Moneygall had been. They would mail it to potential donors.

As the head of a super-PAC (a new type of vehicle that is allowed to raise unlimited sums of money without disclosing donors), Obama's people were legally debarred from coordinating with her. "Have you lost your mind?" she responded. "You are not supposed to be talking to me." She eventually agreed to issue a "noncoordinated" statement.

Whether it was phone calls or handwritten thank you notes, Obama was working the conventional donor base hard in 2012. The only similarity with 2008 was that Obama banned both campaigns from taking PAC and lobbyist money. "Money will always find a channel," said the fund-raiser.

Money and American politics are indeed familiar coconspirators. But the relationship has grown much stronger in recent years. In terms of appearance, nothing Obama was doing in the 2012 campaign could yet compare to how President Bush ran his 2004 reelection effort. Bush pulled out all stops. His ways of raising money were much less subtle than Obama's. Yet he raised only a third of what Obama was aiming to get. If the cost of U.S. elections were included in the consumer price index, America would be suffering from hyperinflation.

Perhaps more disturbing is the degree to which election money has secreted into the governing agenda. From one president to the next, the permanent campaign has become an increasingly accepted part of the way Washington works. Everybody, including the electorate, is responsible to one degree or another for the round-the-clock election that American politics has become. Most of the media prefer to cover horse races than policy making. Except for business and trade publications, the few organizations that still treat governance seriously continue to bleed audience share and circulation.

Nor is it taboo for campaign specialists any longer to be involved in the highest levels of decisions; White House inner circles sometimes comprise few others. Karl Rove, George Bush's electoral maestro, was top dog in Bush's White House. So powerful was Rove that some even thought he had integrated the terrorism alert system within the electoral calendar.

At all stages of his presidency, Obama's closest advisers have been professional election consultants rather than Washington hands. David Axelrod, one of Obama's two electoral maestros, was Obama's senior adviser for the first two years in office. Rarely did a meeting take place when Axelrod was not in the room.[137] When Axelrod left for Chicago in 2011 to help prepare Obama's reelection bid, he was replaced as senior White House adviser by David Plouffe, manager of Obama's 2008 campaign.

Plouffe and Axelrod were the only two names singled out by Obama in his 2008 victory night speech in Chicago. Arguably they were also Obama's two most important advisers during the next four years. Among the other members of Obama's inner circle were Robert Gibbs, Obama's campaign and White House spokesman, who left the White House in 2011, and Valerie Jarrett, the Obamas' close friend from Chicago. All were campaign people. None, including their boss, had any governing experience.

Since he joined the 2008 campaign only late in the day, Jim Messina was the most recent arrival to the inner circle. He was also among its most useful. Unlike most of the others, Messina had an extensive Washington background. Messina had worked for Max Baucus almost continuously since 1995 and was Baucus's chief of staff when he left to join the Obama campaign. As Baucus's top man, Messina kept tight control over the senator's election campaigns.

"He ran very top-down operations," said one former colleague. Messina's relationship with Baucus, which they both describe as "father-son," proved critical to Obama's fortunes on the health care bill. Liberal groups (otherwise known as Obama's grassroots) complained that Messina shut them out of the conversation. But "the fixer," as Messina was called in the

White House, did what was asked of him. Who better, then, to run Obama's campaign?

At the end of the Obama fund-raiser that I attended, people lined up to ask Messina questions. A number of questioners wanted to know what the contents of the 2012 campaign would be. They did not seem happy. "I have been sitting here all day and I haven't heard what the Obama campaign message will be," said one woman. "All we've been hearing about is organization and money." Most of those in the audience seemed to agree. Messina promised that the answer would be fleshed out during the campaign.

At that point, the only sure thing either the audience or the American public knew then was that Obama wanted a billion dollars. In terms of his vision for how to rejuvenate the U.S. economy, tackle a planet in peril, mend the festering house mortgage crisis, or bring change to Washington, people seemed confused about what Obama believed. Still, they had been asked by Messina to give up more time and money than ever to get him back into office. "I wonder why I still do this," said my fund-raiser friend. "There must be a hormone that makes you forget what it was like the last time around." Perhaps everyone in Washington is taking it.

The permanent campaign is said to have been devised by Patrick Caddell, an influential Democratic operative, in a 1976 memo to Jimmy Carter. Caddell argued that it was the only way of governing in an increasingly direct democracy, where the power of the old party boss system had declined. "Essentially," Caddell wrote, "it is my thesis that governing with public approval requires a continuing political campaign." Little did Caddell know how quickly his idea would turn into conventional wisdom.

Now older and more jaded, Caddell sounds like he regrets the memo, or what he says are people's misinterpretations of what it said. "I wasn't recommending the permanent campaign," Caddell told me. "I was describing it." He was also rueful about his coauthorship of Carter's notorious 1979 "malaise speech" in which the be-cardiganed president warned his fellow Americans that their country was gripped in a vice of potential decline. A much sunnier

Reagan defeated Carter a few months later. Since then, presidents have avoided talking to the American public about malaise, sacrifice, or any associated negatives. "That speech was also mischaracterized," said Caddell. "Carter never used the word 'malaise.'"

Ironically, these days Caddell appears to be among those in greatest despair about money's grip on Washington. Like some other anti-Obama Democrats, Caddell is a paid contributor to Fox News, the conservative channel. "Fox News Democrats," as they have been dubbed, harbor diverse gripes against Obama. Chiefly, though, they share a vocabulary with their host channel that depicts Obama as an almost satanic force in the land. "Obama is the most disingenuous president since Richard Nixon," said Caddell. "He is more of a slave to money than any president since then."

In Caddell's view, Obama has taken the permanent campaign and the money that goes with it to its ultimate breaking point. "Washington today is like St. Petersburg on the eve of the Russian revolution," he said. "The American people are disgusted and the old order does not yet know that it is finished." Unable to give me examples of when, or how, the American people would storm the ramparts of Washington, Caddell then offered a more plausible forecast.

The more alienated America's voters become from the two major political parties, he said, the more positively they will respond to whackos who emerge from nowhere to exploit their resentment against Washington. Such types included Ross Perot, who was the third-party presidential candidate in 1992 and 1996, Pat Buchanan the Republican with a "pitchfork" in 1996, or even Donald Trump, the property and reality TV mogul, who flirted with a presidential bid in 2011.* One day one of them would win. "Nobody with any decency goes into politics any more," said Caddell. "America is entering a period of great danger."

---

*"I'm glad someone told me Donald Trump is running as a Republican," the comedian Seth Meyers told the White House correspondents dinner in April 2011. "Because I thought he was running as a joke."

In comparison to Caddell's prognosis, Jimmy Carter's malaise speech seemed like Reagan's "Morning in America." Yet among his more far-flung imaginings, there were kernels of truth. Caddell pointed to the Supreme Court's radical and momentous 2010 ruling in which it had opened the floodgates for unlimited corporate spending during elections. Companies, unions, and other organizations could now spend what they like and say what they want. The Citizens United ruling, which squeaked through in a five to four majority, undid almost a century of precedent over the role of corporate money in politics.

Citing the First Amendment, which guarantees free speech, the Court redefined companies as legal persons with rights. Thus, corporate freedom of expression could no longer be restricted. Groups such as American Crossroads, which was run by Karl Rove, George Bush's former man Friday ("turd blossom" was the nickname Bush gave him), were set up to exploit the ruling. They raised tens of millions of dollars. These were the newfangled super-PACs.

Against this growing flood of corporate money, Obama's billion-dollar election target might look more justifiable—although that campaign target began to look ambitious as the cycle wore on. As, too, might his reaction to the Supreme Court ruling. But by then Obama was already sounding formulaic. "The Supreme Court has given a green light to a new stampede of special interest money in our politics," said Obama in a statement. "It is a major victory for big oil, Wall Street banks, and health insurance companies . . . who drown out the voices of everyday Americans."

Obama's condemnation contrasted with the standing ovation the ruling got from the Republican Party. It gave an instant lift to the conservative war chest ahead of the midterm elections that year. Rove's group flourished. The liberals were outspent. "For too long, *some* in this country have been deprived of full participation in the political process," said Mitch McConnell, leader of the Senate Republicans. By "some," McConnell meant "these groups"—his only other description of the entities that would benefit from the ruling.

Within these two statements was the cartoon of each of America's parties today: the cynical and bad-tempered elephant and the hypocrical donkey that often doesn't mean what it says. These caricatures were again on full display in the war over the national debt ceiling and the size of government that erupted after the Republicans regained control of the House of Representatives in January 2011. To judge by America's deteriorating fiscal projections this battle may continue for years.

It is not a recipe for intelligent governing. But it contains all the ingredients of a rolling banquet for money. Just five days after the November 3 midterm election, Tony and Heather Podesta sent out an e-mail with a forthcoming calendar of fund-raising events: "It's time to start looking forward to the 2012 elections!" It then listed five events the Podestas would be hosting for individual senators over the coming few weeks. My fund-raiser friend was also in demand. That same postelection week she got calls from several lawmakers in the House asking if she could help replenish their war chests. "I have no problem with money in politics," she said. "But can't we at least lay off it for one week?"

In a book that he wrote when he was a young congressman, Don Riegle, the former Michigan senator, complained about the growing role of money in politics. Back in 1972, Richard Nixon's campaign consultants were busy preparing for his reelection. Apart from burgling the Democratic Party's offices in the Watergate complex, this involved raising what passed in those days as unprecedented sums of money. Riegle kept a diary of that year, later published as *O Congress,* a celebrated book on the political circuit. In one entry he noted that Nixon was talking about raising as much as $30 million. "The cost of these sums has just skyrocketed out of sight," he wrote. At today's prices Nixon's sums would barely get you out of the starting block.

For Riegle, the growth of money in politics has exacted its highest toll on the changing perspectives of America's leaders. Federal politicians spend an inordinate amount of time trying to gauge what the public is thinking. Yet in Riegle's view Washington has rarely been more remote from the concerns of everyday Americans, perhaps in particular under Obama. Even the capital's economy seems to have become detached from the rest of America. While every other housing market in America saw a decline in prices, Washington, D.C., continued after 2008 to see rises. Ten out of the top twenty richest counties in America are in the Washington, D.C.–northern Virginia–Maryland catchment area.[138] Mancur Olson's Washington is booming. Businesses and national associations keep ratcheting up their investment in America's capital city.

Riegle was among those many senior Democrats to catch Obamamania during the Democratic primaries. Then he lost his enthusiasm. It happened when Obama spoke at an event of blue-collar supporters on the lakeside in Detroit. One of his introducers was an out-of-work single mother with a heartbreaking story. Her husband had recently died. In the tent behind the podium after the event had ended, Riegle noticed the woman standing around with her children. She was clearly hoping to speak to Senator Obama. Riegle approached Obama to suggest he take a photo with them. Obama walked over to get it taken.

"He made no pretense that he wanted to be there," said Riegle. "Here was a chance for Obama to show a voter that he appreciated her words and understood her struggles." Obama posed wordlessly for the snap and then carried on. Riegle was still upset by that otherwise unremarkable moment. Doubtless Obama was exhausted. It was the middle of an epic and grueling campaign. As Messina reminds his audiences, a candidate's schedule is precious. Campaigns live by the data—the bundlers, the turnout metrics, the voter intensity measures, and the finances. There isn't the time to stand around chatting. "If you can't measure it, then it doesn't count," Messina said.

Riegle's anecdote reminded me of a story that took place at the funeral of Franklin Roosevelt, whose death in 1945 prompted a national outpouring of grief. Roosevelt had taken his country through the Great Depression and a world war. He created work for millions on the breadline. Vast audiences tuned in to listen to his radio fireside chats. As FDR's cortege passed by, a man was spotted weeping on the sidewalk. Did he know Franklin Roosevelt? the man was asked. "No," he replied. "But Roosevelt knew me."

7

An Exceptional Challenge

WHY THE COMING STRUGGLE TO HALT AMERICA'S
DECLINE FACES LONG ODDS

The greatest danger in times of turbulence is not the turbulence; it is to act with yesterday's logic.

Peter Drucker

THERE WAS A time when most educated Britons would imbibe a mild variant of anti-Americanism with their mother's
milk. Some still do. The other teat contained a pro-American
hormone. My experience growing up in Britain in the 1970s and
'80s captured some elements of both. America was seen chiefly
through two lenses.

The first, experienced mostly in the abstract, was through the
"special relationship," which derived from the recognition that the
United States had been, and would continue to be, indispensible
to Western freedom. Not only had the United States helped rescue
Britain from the Nazis, it was also the essential bulwark against
the spread of Soviet power. This was a geopolitical Americaphilia
that was personified by Winston Churchill. I grew up on a diet of
Second World War movies that glorified the two main branches
of Churchill's English-speaking peoples.

Then there was the cultural critique, often laced with a strong
undertone of snobbery. Americans were long-winded, sentimental,
self-obsessed, money worshipping, and self-righteous. The same
people were generous, pragmatic, warmhearted, civic-minded, and

they did their best to speak our language, even if they ensured that Shakespeare would be turning in his grave. They also stole our talent. As the actor Michael Caine remarked, "The British film industry is alive and well and living in Los Angeles."

I mention these early caricatures not to damage my credentials regarding America, but in the hope of transcending them. Living for many years in America, working briefly for the U.S. government and raising a daughter who is mostly American in her culture, has lent me a very different perspective. In spite of Hollywood's best efforts to put me off (most notably Mel Gibson's *The Patriot*) my heart is with the American revolutionaries against the redcoat bayonets. It is also with Dwight Eisenhower the day he pulled the plug on what remained of British and French global power in 1956 after they launched the invasion of Egypt's Suez Canal.

My head tells me that if I were an immigrant escaping oppression or poverty my first choice would still be the United States. It also tells me that regardless of America's faults, some recent, some of longer pedigree, to which this book alludes, America's biggest challenges are not unique. In one form or another all Western democracies face a deepening crisis of competitiveness and governance, including Great Britain. What we used to call the West is going through a broadly shared crisis of confidence. As the last of the West's hegemons following half a millennium of world domination, America's actions will largely answer whether and how the West will respond to the rise of others, the Great Convergence, or however else we describe the shifting tectonic plates of the twenty-first century.

One nagging concern is that America's obsession with what Zbigniew Brzezinski, the former national security advisor, calls "the politics of now" will continue to divert Washington's policy makers from the domestic problems that this book has tried to capture. That applies in particular to American's shifting perceptions of their place in the world. Sometime in the near future, China's economy will experience a sharp slowdown and possibly worse. At which point America's serried ranks of optimists may conclude we have reached another Japan moment, whereby predictions of America's relative decline are comprehensively disproved—as happened after the "Japanic" of the late 1980s. This would be a mistake. China's ascent will not be linear. Neither was America's. Nor should the Walter Mittys derive false confidence from Europe's troubles. The EU and its neighbors may well face a worse growth outlook than the United States in the coming years. That does not make America's challenges any less serious.

The rise of dynamic economies in much of the world that was once under Western colonial domination ought to be an unalloyed cause for moral and self-interested celebration: moral because so much of the world is escaping poverty and enjoying freedom; self-interested because, in joining the vast global middle class, Asians, Latin Americans, and increasingly Africans are expanding the arena for mutual enrichment. Economics is not supposed to be a zero sum game. Geopolitics almost always is. In this concluding chapter I will look at the tension between the two. In the process, I will also address two questions that are at the core of how America will respond to the rise of others.

The first is economic. Can the United States sustain an open economy while simultaneously renewing income growth for the majority of its population? Whether via the Tea Party or a more broad-based descent into apathy and cynicism, middle-class Americans are losing faith in their country's direction. As Jeff Immelt, GE's chief executive, recently said, "If globalization were put to a referendum in America, it would lose." The second, and interrelated, question is cultural. Can America forge the consensus it would need to respond effectively to its growing challenges? From the Shays' and Whiskey rebellions of the 1780s and 1790s to today, America is no stranger to antitax populism. Nor is it unacquainted with nativism. Yet by all modern measures the United States has never suffered as much polarization as it does today.

Neither question can be answered conclusively. Nor is history much of a guide. Churchill famously said that Americans always do the right thing after exhausting all the alternatives. He was principally alluding to America's intervention in the two world wars. America's biggest challenges in the early twenty-first century are not deadly like those that were posed by the menaces of Nazism and Stalinism. Yet they are much less susceptible to a coherent, or unifying, response. What would be the right thing for America to do in light of its relative decline? Assuming there is a good answer—and it is not clear that there is—for how much longer can America afford to explore the alternatives?

In mid-2011 I was invited to a small conference at an elegant English country house in Buckinghamshire. The organizers asked me to give an outline of my planned book to the thirty or so mostly European business leaders and officials in attendance. My skepticism about America's prospects triggered a small debate. On one side were those who stridently disagreed. Phrases such as "America always does the right thing eventually" and "No one ever made money betting against America" cropped up. On the other, a number of people spoke less vehemently of their mounting concerns over American power and competitiveness. The first group outnumbered the second.

Faith in America's promise is at the heart of America's story. Disappointment over the gap between reality and promise is a constant feature of both America's and the world's way of thinking about America. Right now that sentiment is acute. Many foreigners and liberal Americans reassure themselves that everything had been fine up until the election of George W. Bush, his trigger-happy reaction to 9/11, and the years of squandered fiscal surpluses that followed. Had the hanging chads of Florida been fully counted—if the Supreme Court were tilted 5-4 the other way—things would be continuing now much as they had in the 1990s. The United States would remain an unparalleled example to the world.

It is a tempting counterfactual in which to indulge. It is hard to imagine President Al Gore frittering away the hard-won surpluses of the Clinton years on wars of choice and tax cuts for the already thriving wealthiest elite of Americans. And it is impossible to imagine President Gore denying the phenomenon of man-made global warming. But it would also be overstated. George Bush certainly exacerbated America's deepest problems. But he did not invent the rise of China and others. Nor did he cause the decline in U.S. manufacturing or the deep problem of middle-class income stagnation, which goes back forty years. Wall Street was already in the saddle when Bush took office. America's education system was already underperforming and other countries were already innovating. Bush did what he could to help most of these trends along but he did not cause them.

Yet the extraordinary rapidity with which they became visible in the first decade of the century means that Bush's place in history is ensured, perhaps to an unfair degree. Had anyone at the turn of the century forecast that the United States would lose it triple A credit rating by 2011 he would have been dismissed as a Cassandra. Had a forecast been made in the mid-1990s that by 2009 China would be the world's second largest economy, it also would have been disbelieved. Most important, had Americans been told that their economy would have ceased to be the model for the rest of the world by 2008 they would have laughed it off.

In 1956, at the tail end of the Suez crisis, Harold Macmillan, Britain's prime minister, described the debacle as the "last gasp of a declining power." He added that "in two hundred years perhaps Americans would know how we felt." History is speeding up. China may have roared up on the United States and the world in the past twenty years. Barring a cataclysm China's next twenty are likely to bring an even greater impact. In his thought-provoking 2011 book *Eclipse: Living in the Shadow of China's Economic Dominance,* Arvind Subramanian, a former IMF economist now at Washington, D.C.'s Peterson Institute for International Economics, makes plain how rapidly this shift is occurring.

Subramanian makes two assumptions. First, China's growth will slow in the next twenty years from 11 percent to 7 percent a year. This would include a debt-induced crisis of growth in China in the next few years. Second, the United States would beat all expectations and attain an average annual growth of 3.5 percent a year in the next two decades, which is between a point and a point and three-quarters higher than most economists would predict. Taking these two together—a relatively modest assumption for China and an optimistic one for the United States—would result in the following: China's GDP would be a quarter higher than America's by 2030. It would account for twice America's share of world trade. And the yuan would have long since displaced the dollar as the world's reserve currency. And this was a conservative forecast.

Whether Subramanian's time horizon proves wrong or right is secondary. His key insight, and one that is very hard to dispute, is that China is the big variable in the equation. America's scenarios range from sclerotic, which looks troublingly more likely as time goes on, to robust. Even under a robust assumption, the United States will lose world economic domination to a growing China within a very short period of time. Unless China goes off the rails, or the United States goes to war with China, there is little the United States could do to alter, or even delay, that outcome. To underscore the speed of change, think of it as follows: The distance between the fall of the Berlin Wall and the election of Barack Obama is far greater than that between his election and America's likely displacement as the world's top dog.

The scale and imminence of the big shift is hard to digest. It remains understandable that both conservative and liberal Americans share the view that it is ultimately within America's power whether she keeps or loses her preeminence. But it is largely an illusion. Such assumptions, in Subramanian's words, "reveal a one-sided, U.S.-centric perspective: that world dominance will be determined mostly by the actions of the United States, not those of China. In fact, the outcome of this race is far more likely to be shaped by China." Nor is this futurology. In 1999 the United States brought China into the World Trade Organization on terms largely dictated by America. By 2011 none but Walter Mitty would dispute that China held at least as many cards as the United States. Witness

America's consistently ineffectual attempts to wean Beijing from its mercantilist currency stance.

It cannot be overstated how bewildering this change is becoming for American policy makers. In my conversations with former and current policy makers, none has better captured this disorientation than Jeffrey Garten, who was Bill Clinton's undersecretary of commerce in the early 1990s and later became dean of the Yale School of Management. Garten, who still teaches at Yale and sits on the board of directors of Aetna, CarMax, and Credit Suisse Asset Management, is one of America's foremost scholars of U.S. corporate leadership. As a former managing director of both Lehman Brothers and Blackstone, you would be hard-pressed to find a better sample of the type of policy maker who espoused America's worldview in the 1990s. It would also be difficult to find someone with a more objective view of how completely America failed to see what was coming. It is a tale of very understandable hubris.

On the geopolitical plane, America had just won the Cold War without spending much ammunition. Conservatives believed America had prevailed because of "peace through strength." Democrats put more accent on the Soviet Union's realization that its model was failing. In their view the victory has more to do with the "soft power" of American wealth and freedom than with the Pentagon. But these were questions of shading. Virtually all colors of the political spectrum bought copies of Francis Fukuyama's book *End of History* and extracted an America-centric—and often quite unrepresentative—caricature from its nuanced thesis. It was perhaps the high noon of American exceptionalism on the world stage. And who, in all honesty, can blame them?

In his own words, Garten was part of a group in the Clinton administration that traveled the world "telling everybody how it should be done." Its most prominent faces were Alan Greenspan, Larry Summers, and Robert Rubin. These were the vanguard of the Washington consensus that handed out free copies of its manual on how to achieve wealth, freedom, universal admiration, *The Simpsons,* and pareto optimal efficiency—or messages to that effect. "It didn't really matter where I was, the theme was the same," said Garten. "The constant message was that we had figured it out and you in China and you in Brazil and you in Germany don't have to reinvent the wheel. America is the model. All you need to do is be more like us."

Broadly speaking that model prescribed the economic retreat of the state, free trade, deregulation, including in the capital account, and the combination of strict fiscal balancing and accommodative monetary policy. It was boosted greatly by the collapse of the Japanese property bubble in 1989, which led to an era of subpar growth and stagnation in Japan that is yet to end (twenty-two years and counting). The growing realization that Japan was not about to supplant the United States, and that the losers of the Second World War were not therefore the actual victors of the Cold War—as those suffering from Japanic had warned—resulted in fifteen years' worth of American bragging.

The pessimists had cried wolf once too often. Garten still winces at the memory. "To look back on what I said, the absolute certainty with which I believed it and the fact that we often weren't taking into account the local history and character of the countries we were visiting . . . ," he said. "I feel genuinely embarrassed at how arrogant we were."

The main reason I wanted to speak to Garten was to discuss the future rather than the past. Memories of hubris are one thing. Prospects of nemesis are another. In particular I wanted his views on the expectations made of U.S. business leaders, whom (according to numerous opinion polls) Americans see as either the solution to America's difficulties or the problem, depending on their politics.

There is barely an American—or global—chief executive whom Garten does not know. From Lloyd Blankfein of Goldman Sachs to Mukesh Ambani in India, CEOs file into Garten's classroom to address one of the world's elite management schools. Others sit down for Garten's books, of which *The Mind of the CEO* (2001) is probably his best known. Few have a better grasp of the type of person who runs a big company.

Many Americans look to business leaders as people who can get things done far more capably than professional politicians. Others, mostly on the left, blame corporate leaders for selling out America's interests by shifting to China. Both, in their different ways, see business leaders as the key to America's future. They are equally misplaced, says Garten. The first, which uses a language of moral betrayal, understates how imprisoned corporate leaders are within their mission to achieve short-term return on equity. The latter ascribe to business leaders an aptitude they don't usually possess. "This is how chief executives get to the top: they hit performance targets, quarter by quarter, and if they don't hit them they're out," said Garten. "Why should you expect them to know how to fix America's problems?"

Likewise, the more one looks at the pressures facing American business leaders in today's ever more supercompetitive world, the more futile the language of moral blame seems. Garten's view is reinforced by Robert Reich, the Berkeley professor and Rhodes scholar friend of Bill Clinton who, as labor secretary, was Clinton's chief in-house critic during his first term. Reich is as impatient as Garten with the politics of making either scapegoats or heroes-in-waiting out of U.S. business leaders. Both want to return accountability to the larger arena of American society.

Take the celebrated case of Walmart, which, depending on your perspective, is either one of the most ruthless or one of the best-managed corporations in America. According to Reich its average employee was paid $17,500 in 2008. Only a small minority had health care or pension benefits. Imports from Walmart's vast global supply chain accounted for 7 percent of America's trade deficit in 2008. Mike Duke, its chief executive, gets paid more in a month than his employees do in an entire lifetime. On top of which Walmart has virtually destroyed the character of small towns and urban communities across America—and now in large parts of the world. What is not to like?

On the other hand, Walmart's profit margins account for just 3 percent of its revenues. Crucially, it also reduces prices by an estimated $600 billion a year for American consumers. If Duke woke up one morning and decided to give a $6,000 health care and pension benefit to each of his one million employees—and raise labor costs by a quarter—Walmart would cease to be profitable. If, however, Duke passed those cost increases on to the consumer, shoppers would switch instantly to another big box retailer. Either way, Duke would get hammered by shareholders and probably lose his job. Since 1995, the proportion of CEOs who are forced out of their jobs has risen sharply to 35 percent, according to Booz Hamilton. The rate of annual turnover has almost doubled to 15 percent.

The driving force behind what Garten calls this "tsunami of pressure" on businesses comes from the big pension and mutual funds that make up for the bulk of shareholders. Yet they, too, are cogs in a machine. Fund managers have to meet their own performance targets or they will also be fired. It makes no difference whether you manage the private wealth of the world's most avaricious tycoon or whether, like Calpers, the California fund, you take care of the retirement savings of the state's granola-crunching liberal class. Fund managers will always chase the highest returns. "Pension funds are always yakking about long-term value," said Garten. "But their fund managers are rewarded on the basis of short-term results. Watch what they do not what they say."

Shoppers behave no differently. I know of one union leader in Washington, D.C., who always tries to fly Southwest Airlines or Virgin America because they are so much more reliable. That is because they are nonunion: they are free of the legacy pension and health care costs that plague their competitors. Bob Reich's favorite example of ruthless liberal shoppers comes from the jeans maker Levi Strauss, which pulled out of China following the Tiananmen Square massacre of 1989. Its jeans got more expensive and the company lost customers. It returned to China shortly thereafter. More recently, no consumer boycotted Cisco when it sold surveillance technology to China, or Google when it forwarded Beijing the e-mail addresses of hundreds of dissidents.

Should Apple for patriotic reasons decide to manufacture its iPhones and iPads back in the United States rather than in Asia, consumers would not think twice about buying a cheaper alternative. As Reich points out, "In the marketplace virtue is always punished." I have environmentally conscious friends who would never buy organic detergents. Even if green detergents were less useless, I doubt they would pay more for them. And, of course, shoppers are increasingly letting the computer select their purchase by finding the cheapest price. Swimming against this tide is expensive. "Lonely forbearance can be the last refuge of the lonely fool," says Reich.

Some, including Reich and Garten, hoped that the 2008 meltdown would trigger a wider questioning of the model. They underestimated how deeply entrenched it was. Whether they know it or not, America's consumers strengthen globalization every day with their actions. "If you had told me in 2008 that we would be back to where we were before, I would have been incredulous," said Garten. "The fact is that shareholder capitalism is stronger than it has ever been and in the next ten years global integration will only intensify."

From where, or whom, can solutions be found? Many still yearn for the golden age before the Internet and the Reagan revolution, when business leaders acted like corporate statesmen and shareholders were one of many stakeholders rather than the only ones that mattered. In the 1940s and '50s, America's political and business leaders agreed on basic standards for workers, including wage increases and nonwage benefits. It was an age of oligarchic capitalism, in which three or four companies controlled each of America's big industrial sectors and where they were able to sit down with politicians in Washington and carve up the economy. Companies had pricing power. Employees got higher wages. And consumers had to tolerate higher prices.

What was good for GM, which, at its peak, accounted for 3 percent of American GDP, really was good for America. It had few foreign competitors and most of the company's employees were

American. Such an arrangement is hard to imagine today. Even assuming there was political support, it would be unrealistic to believe another New Deal could work. In a globalized economy most companies lack pricing power. The only scenario in which the United States could trade off higher prices in exchange for higher wages would be if it decided to shut out its competitors. Pulling up the protectionist drawbridge would result in a cure far worse than the disease. Even then it would not be enough. New technology has drastically lowered barriers to entry in almost every market. Washington would have to turn technophobic as well as xenophobic.

Others, including Obama's economic team, hope a lot more realistically for a return to the 1990s when there was full employment and a four-year respite from middle-class income stagnation. But that may give too much credit to the actions of the Clinton administration and far too little to the one-off positive shock the IT revolution and the end of the Cold War did for America's prosperity. It is true that Clinton's economic team, which has made up the core of Obama's, deftly exploited those huge windfalls to set the United States on a robust fiscal course. But Clinton was no more responsible for the Internet, or the fall of the Berlin Wall, than Abraham Lincoln. It would be hard to engineer something equivalent to that.

Then there is the early-twenty-first-century competitiveness agenda, which was outlined by President Obama in his 2011 "Winning the Future" speech and the 2012 "Built to Last" address, which differ only marginally from the platform on which Clinton was elected in 1992. It came close to capturing the intellectual consensus among economists of all stripes, even if its contents was instantly rejected by the Republican Party. It recommended a lot of familiar but badly needed steps to upgrade the U.S. economy, such as increasing federal investment in R&D, revitalizing America's public schools, and upgrading the quality of American infrastructure.

Together these steps would help improve wage growth for America's middle classes. Each would also boost America's comparative advantage as a destination for investors. Without doubt, they would be necessary to tackle the problem of median wage stagnation. It is unclear whether this would be anywhere near sufficient. And it is hard to imagine it would be enough to stave off America's relative decline, or whether anything realistically could. "This isn't just a question of others catching up with us," said Garten. "America's trajectory is not flat, it is down. Some of our deepest capabilities as a country are now called into question."

I did not ask Garten what he meant by "deepest capabilities." On reflection I did not need to. America is losing its ability to tackle problems. Beginning with the Winning the Future agenda, America has no lack of "starter pack" ideas on how to respond to its growing crises. It mostly lacks the will to implement them. In areas where Washington does find the will, such as education, its ideas have not had the desired effect. Most important, though, America's economic crisis has grown alongside a mutually rein-forcing polarization in politics that has badly disabled the federal government's ability to offer solutions. Just when intelligent gov-ernment is most needed, it seems to have been put beyond reach, at least for the time being. It is to this potentially destabilizing problem that we now turn.

In American politics there is a saying: "If you are explaining, you are losing." Simplicity of message is a skill at which Republicans have often proved better than Democrats. With the rise of the Tea Party, the conservative movement may have gained something of a monopoly on clarity. It has not yet cornered the market on sanity. I once attended a Tea Party convention in Colorado Springs at which Samuel Wurzelbacher—otherwise known as "Joe the Plumber"—was one of the featured speakers. Since confronting Obama in the 2008 election, and alleging his tax plans would "kill the American Dream," Wurzelbacher became an early hero of the Tea Party move-ment. He is now a staple motivational speaker at Tea Party events.

The Plumber, in jeans and a cap, was greeted like a pop star. He keyed straight into the Tea Party's deep resentment at being belittled as stupid by many in the mainstream media. It was a neurosis that ran through the evening. "Don't let them call you stupid," said the speaker before him. "Just you wait until the election. It will be like the rapture. All that will be left is their shoes." Wurzelbacher pumped his fist at those words and then added his own. After praising the Founding Fathers as "Godly men who gave us these Godly words," the Plumber launched into an attack on knowledge. His philippic, which swiped at pretty much anyone who had read anything other than the Bible or the Constitution, produced a standing ovation. "I am not an expert," the Plumber said. "Look at where the experts have got us. They are crooks and thieves."

There was an even more emphatic ovation at the end of the evening when the final speaker, a minor conservative television commentator, hit back at the accusation that Tea Partiers were ignorant. "We have a thirst for knowledge," she said. "When we watch Glenn Beck we learn something your wife doesn't know, or your smart-ass kid didn't know either . . . with Beck we learn things that go way over the heads of the MSNBC people." At the mention of Beck, the speaker may have somewhat undermined her case. In an episode of Beck's daily show on the Fox News Channel a few months earlier, the cult-leader-like talk radio teacher tried to explain the concept of oligarchy. It was pretty clear he did not know what it meant.

On his ubiquitous blackboard, Beck had scribbled six bullet points: Obama, Left Internationalists, Graft, Acorn Style Organization, Revolutionaries, and Hidden Agenda. Beck then circled six letters one by one to spell out the word "oligarh." Beck said, "Why did I select these words? Because they [pointing to the corrupt leftists on the board] all select their words first. Then they tie them into one word—oligarh." By this stage the viewer must have been mesmerized. "But one letter is missing, the letter y," Beck continued. He then spelled out the new word "oligarhy" on the board. "I don't know whether we are going to turn into an oligarhy or what we're turning into. But unless you ask 'Y' [sic] then we are going to transform into something."

Beck, as is his wont, then launched into a generalized attack on Obama. "I am tired of being a sheep. I am tired of being a victim. I am tired of being pushed around. It is time to take the gloves off." Anywhere from five hundred thousand to a million people attended Beck's "Restoring Honor" rally in Washington a few weeks later. It was no fringe event. More so than the big Fox News anchors, such as Sean Hannity and Bill O'Reilly, more so even than Rush Limbaugh, Glenn Beck was the most pervasive early influence on the Tea Party. As David Frum, a former Bush speechwriter and now dissident Republican, observed, "If Beck learned how to spell he'd be unstoppable."[139]

Beck was eventually sacked by Fox after straying into all-too-predictable anti-Semitism. In addition to black theologists, Beck's world is full of Jewish oligarhs. Beck's radio show continued to attract more than 6 million listeners a day—that's more than five times the circulation of the *New York Times*. Four of his books in 2010 alone reached number one on the *New York Times* best-seller list. One of them was called *Arguing with Idiots: Why Small Minds Want Big Government*. The CD audio version was helpfully shortened to *Idiots Unplugged*.

Every electorate suffers from ignorance. It would be as easy to poke fun at the British electorate by citing opinion polls on gaps in UK public knowledge as it is for America. But in the form of the Tea Party movement, and in its echoes of the America First movement of the 1930s and even the nineteenth-century Know Nothings, America is today suffering from a signficant case of organized ignorance. Richard Hofstadter called it the "paranoid style in American politics." Huntington, as I have mentioned, pointed to America's periodic "moral convulsions." The timing of this latest one could hardly be worse.

Those who still argue that the Tea Party threat has been exaggerated emphasize polls showing that much less than a quarter of Americans support the Tea Party's declared aims. Their big goal is to dismember most of the key functions of federal government ("repealing the twentieth century," in the words of one commentator).[140]

Given America's separation of powers, the Tea Party needs to be only a majority of the majority of one half of one branch of government to have a pretty good shot at ensuring nothing significant can move in Washington, D.C. The only threshold that matters is to be a majority of the minority party in the Senate (where forty votes can block almost all legislation), and to remain the largest and most powerful faction in the majority in the House. Even if Republicans lost control of the House, the Tea Party could still get by on the minority veto in the Senate.

In light of such a low bar, and given its organizational prowess, it is hard to see a neat end to the Tea Party's "tyranny of the minority" in the near future. Given also that its overarching aim is to restore what David Frum describes as the "pure ancestral faith" of conservatism, it would be rash to assume that it will drift into the spirit of compromise. This would go against every tenet the Tea Party holds. At the Take Back America rallies, one of the most popular banners quoted Thomas Jefferson: "When injustice becomes law, resistance becomes duty." A couple of popular Tea Party bumper stickers read: "America was founded by right-wing extremists" and "Legalize the Constitution!"

This book is not the place to explore the history of constitutional originalism. For insights readers should go to Tim LaHaye's best selling *Faith of Our Founding Fathers* or W. Cleon Skousen's equally widely read *The 5000 Year Leap*, which explains the providential "leap" God gave to humanity through the U.S. Constitution. Both have sold more than 5 million copies. Their approach to history bears as little relation to scholarship as the daily meanderings of Glenn Beck (whose foreword begins the latest edition of *5000 Year Leap*).

Jefferson, Hamilton, Madison, and Benjamin Franklin were among the boldest and subtlest thinkers of their age. And they devised an extraordinary blueprint for a democratic republic. But it was not flawless, and neither were they. "Set loose in the culture and tangled together with fanaticism, [constitutional] originalism looks like history, but it's not," wrote Jill Lepore, a Harvard historian, in her book *The Whites of Their Eyes,* on the Tea Party. "It is to history what astrology is to astronomy."

Some readers may wonder why this book accentuates problems posed by the conservative right rather than the liberal left. For a start there is no such thing as a liberal "movement"; angry liberals are not as unified as angry conservatives (witness the difference between Tea Party rallies and the Occupy Wall Street movement that erupted in September 2011). And they are not nearly as numerous. At a reception honoring E. J. Dionne, the liberal *Washington Post* columnist, a Brookings scholar, Bill Galston, whispered only half jokingly to me, "A well-targeted cruise missile would wipe out half the American intellectual left."

Galston, like most political scientists, argues convincingly that the United States is suffering from "asymmetric polarization," wherein the right has moved much further to the right than the left has moved to the left. This trend has been at work for forty years. Under any measure of voting patterns, the 112th Congress (elected in 2010) was the most polarized in modern American history—the most conservative Democrat lawmaker was to the left of the most liberal Republican. The previous most polarized was the 111th. And so on.

Much like the crisis of America's middle class, the rise of polarization in Washington dates from the early 1970s. The two have entirely different causes. The backlash against the Civil Rights Act of 1964 and the counterculture effectively began in 1968 with Richard Nixon's so-called Southern Strategy (in which he sought to win over disaffected southern whites to the Republican banner). In contrast, the escalating impact of technology and globalization has been the main cause of rising inequality and declining income.

Although unconnected in their origins, the two trends have become mutually reinforcing, according to a seminal recent study. In their book *Polarized America,* Nolan McCarty, Keith Poole, and Howard Rosenthal, track the tightly correlated growth of income stagnation and political polarization in the United States and the "two-way interaction" between them. When in the minority, the

Republican Party has used its veto power to block the government from taking countermeasures against the market's increasingly bifurcated outcomes. When in the majority, Republicans have actively assisted those inequalities by skewing tax cuts and tax breaks toward the wealthiest.

As the middle-class crisis has become more entrenched, the electorate's mood has understandably worsened. Some of that disaffection has fed into the rage behind the Tea Party. Much of the rest shows up in growing apathy. The longer this feedback loop persists, the more troubling the consequences. The outcomes of federal elections have become far more volatile. This, in turn, has helped to enshrine a permanent campaign in which every election could tip the congressional balance the other way. Since the Gingrich era in 1994, the two chambers have changed control with a frequency not seen in a century.

All of which creates a highly inauspicious climate for long-term policy making. And it makes it particularly hard for Americans to hold the realistic debate they need on the challenges posed by the rapid shift of gravity to Asia. This also troubles many thoughtful Republicans. "We need to find that grit that we used to have as a nation," said Tim Adams, who served as a senior official in George W. Bush's Treasury Department for six years. Adams was also policy director of Bush's 2004 reelection campaign. "When I was at treasury I traveled the world two hundred days a year and I still do [Adams works for an economic consultancy in Washington]," he said. "Other countries are investing, saving, innovating, and planning for the future. And we're stuck on these ridiculous talking points."

America's economy as a result may also be stuck in an unnecessarily prolonged state of neutral in an era when the United States has hit a post depression high for joblessness—in terms of both scale and duration. Tea Party opposition to any new spending forced Obama after 2010 to discard the sharpest weapon in Washington's armory—countercyclical fiscal policy—which he could have used to fight what economists were already calling the "Great

Contraction." Demand continues to languish and the U.S. Treasury's borrowing costs are zero or negative. There could be no better, or cheaper, moment to refurbish America's infrastructure or to embark on a massive retraining program. In the circumstances it is a particularly egregious handicap for America to have imposed on itself. It may well come to be seen as a seminal missed opportunity.

Writing before the embittered 2011 national debt showdown, the authors of *Polarized America* admit there are no simple ways to bring Washington back to its nobler traditions. Some remedies, such as ending the practice of district gerrymandering, may spread slowly from state to state.[141] Others, such as ending the Senate's large bias toward representation from small rural states, are virtually inconceivable. The likelihood is continued stasis. "We have no easy cure," they state. "We wish we did as we find this trend deeply disturbing. As citizens, we hope moderation returns before serious cracks in our institutions occur."

Which parts of the edifice might be cracking the authors do not spell out. But the cannonballs keep getting larger. For the first time in decades, the word "un-American" is being thrown around. Once detached institutions, such as the U.S. Federal Reserve, are increasingly turning into political targets. Some Tea Partiers and libertarians want to abolish the constitutional amendments that set up the Federal Reserve and the federal income tax. Others, notably Rick Perry, the Texas governor and hapless Republican presidential candidate, view Bernanke's attempts to make up with monetary policy what Congress has renounced on fiscal policy as "almost treasonous." The fact that Bernanke is a Republican and a leading scholar of the Great Depression apparently counted for nothing.

In his description of America's bouts of "creedal passion," Huntington said such moments were inherently backward-looking. The Protestant sects, voluntary associations, Minutemen, Sons of Liberty, and committees of correspondence of earlier bouts set the pattern for today's Tea Partiers: they stumble into a new consciousness of old principles. If things are going wrong, America must have strayed from the path laid out by the founders. The impulse is both traditional and radical. And it is rigidly parochial. Rarely does it pause to observe the experience of other countries, or pick up examples worth following. "The American mission of the future was always to realize the values of its past," said Huntington.

Against this, and for all his campaign skills, Obama has become steadily more impotent. In Obama's defense, even Franklin Roosevelt would have had a tough time talking the Tea Party off the ledge. But Obama has also made profound tactical errors. Instead of drumming on his "Winning the Future" speech, which laid out a sensible path for America within a context Americans could understand, Obama allowed that conversation to drift out of the headlines. It was replaced for most of 2011 with a rowdy debate over the fiscal deficit, a subject on which, bizarrely, Obama acquiesced with his opponents in treating as America's most urgent threat.

Doubtless Obama's advisers told him that U.S. voters usually reward the party that comes across as more bipartisan. Appearing to be the side that is ready to make concessions would play well with that key block of independent voters in 2012. But as Jim Morone, a scholar at Brown University, pointed out, the most successful presidents, such as Ronald Reagan, used bipartisanship in service of clear agendas rather than in place of them. They also kept control over the conversation. "Bipartisanship is a tone, not a path," said Morone.[142] "Obama seems to think it is a path."

If you pitch a professorial tone against a crusade the outcome will be in little doubt. Scant surprise then that Obama's agenda kept getting dragged further rightward. By the time the United States was downgraded by Standard & Poor's, America's president had become so disoriented that he launched into another campaign against Washington, D.C. Only this time he was almost three years into his presidency. Obama's frustrations were richly justified. But if U.S. voters disdain one thing more than reckless partisanship it is a weak leader.

Asking voters to assist you by writing letters to their members of Congress might strike them as a giveaway. "I need you to send a message to your representatives that we're tired of the games,"

Obama told voters in his home state of Illinois.[143] "We're tired of the posturing. We don't want more press releases. . . . Think about the next generation instead of the next election."

Had events played differently—had Obama inherited a less turbulent situation—perhaps another conversation may have been possible. But as Hyman Roth says to Michael Corleone in the movie *Godfather II,* you play the hand you are dealt. Obama misplayed his hand and with it lost a golden—and perhaps once in a generation—opportunity to revisit the U.S. economic model. Obama will be praying that a better hand be dealt sooner than that.

In the meantime, uncertainty about America's future keeps piling up. Measures such as labor productivity that were once reliable indicators of the economy's vitality are bouncing all over the place. The worse America's labor force is hit, the stronger the productivity gain. That may be the least of it. What to make of growing U.S. trade deficits in a world where half of America's imports are intracompany transfers? How to read a U.S. stock market that so often booms when Main Street is sagging? Since so many of New York's listed companies draw most of their revenues from overseas can the Dow still be viewed as a viable barometer of America's health?

More fundamentally, to what degree should we continue to see GDP as a proxy for what is happening in the economy? During the great recession between 2007 and 2009, U.S. median household income fell by 3.2 percent to \$53,518, a tough blow after years of stagnating incomes.[144] In mid-2009 the U.S. economy officially went into "recovery." Most Americans could be forgiven for having thought otherwise. Their manifold "personal recessions" actually deepened between 2009 and 2011. Median household income fell during that period by an astonishing 6.7 percent to \$49,909.

To be sure, the usual yardsticks no longer tell us as much as they did. In the case of America's GDP numbers, however, they are becoming dangerously misleading. When two years of economic growth bring about two recessions' worth of income decline for most households something is very wrong with the signals on the dashboard. It seems increasingly hard to deny that there has been a breakdown over the past ten to fifteen years of the link between America's great wealth-creation machine and the fortunes of a critical share of its people.

The American economy is going through a phase of great uncertainty and of "low visibility," as market forecasters say. Perhaps the last occasion the reigning paradigm looked as redundant as it does today came during the 1930s. Alas, our age has yet to produce a figure of the caliber of Franklin Roosevelt or a vision to match the New Deal. Unlike FDR, who ran the gauntlet of "bold, persistent experimentation" to grapple with a world that had turned upside down, Obama has never strayed far from economic orthodoxy. Even in autumn 2011, when he pivoted away from the austerity debate that had swallowed most of the year, the move was half-baked. Though it is true that the U.S. economy could have benefited from a $450 billion shot in the arm, such as the one Mr. Obama proposed.[145] But America's economic quandary requires more than that; it needs new thinking. America has lost a paradigm and has not yet found a replacement.[146]

In times of deep confusion, says Jeffrey Garten, leaders should remember their basics. There is nothing more fundamental to America's health than the economic condition of the majority of its people. The well-being of the middle class is perhaps the truest measure of an economy's value. And their prospects are the ultimate gauge of a democracy's strength. When the middle class is strong America is strong. And vice versa. "Maybe because it is so obvious, we keep missing it," said Garten. "If we can find a way to raise middle-class living standards again, other things will fall into place."

Recapturing middle-class prosperity is much easier said than done, particularly during the aftermath of a financial—or "balance sheet"—recession, when households and individuals typically take years to pay off their debts. It is even harder when grappling with the supply shock of the arrival on the global market of vast new armies of workers from China, India, and Brazil, and elsewhere.

Globalization continues to undercut labor's bargaining power in America and around the world. So, too, does new technology.

The challenge is immense. The goal must be to ensure that the large majority of Americans once again benefit from global trade and changing technology, rather than see both as a continual threat to their economic security. The alternative is too troubling to contemplate: the gradual rejection by Americans of the open economy that has served the United States, and the rest of the world, so well. Neither foreigners nor Americans would benefit from a new era of U.S. isolationism. What then is to be done?

This is not the kind of book that ends with shopping lists of policy prescriptions; my aim has been to report and analyze. Apart from being unearned, such an exercise would also be hard to limit. Issues that have not been addressed in this book, such as America's approach to global warming, would surface without preface. More to the point, America's challenges merit something better than a journalistic manifesto. It requires new ideas. As this book has tried to capture (along with many other books and studies), imaginative thought is missing at many critical levels, from the quality of U.S. public education and worker skills training to the functioning of the federal bureaucracy and the direction of American democracy.

Yet to stray momentarily into prescription, there can be little doubt that Garten's goal is right: America will ultimately stand or fall by the health of its middle class. The best thing an aspiring FDR could do is to channel Americans' frustrations into a more constructive and coherent force—not by appealing to old social democratic orthodoxies, or to the mood of injured national superiority that exists in parts of the heartlands, but with a renewed pragmatism that can see the world afresh. As stated, it is so much easier said than done. Even recommending such a course sounds utopian. Perhaps in its constant reminder America's political conversation could become relevant again. It would help, in fact, if Garten's advice were permanently tattooed on Washington's forehead.

★ ★ ★

When I arrived in America few things worried me more than knowing I could be sued if we forgot to shovel the snow in front of our house—someone might get hurt. With some reluctance, we would head for the kitchen, boil a large saucepan of water, and pour it onto the sidewalk. That saved a lot on the shoveling. In fact, I don't think we had a shovel. I was also startled by the demands my daughter's nursery placed on our time. Frequently, we were required to turn up at the nursery with home-baked pecan pies or something (a moment when Whole Foods came in handy). Then we were expected to wangle free restaurant coupons, or a weekend in Chesapeake, for the school's silent auction.

What is it with these hyperactive Americans, we wondered? Don't they ever put their feet up and read a novel? As time went on, and as the subliminal worked on our minds, we adapted. In principle, we still expected the authorities to clear leaves from our sidewalk. In practice we started to behave like everyone else. Many of the other parents at the nursery were friendly. Our daughter's playdates were enjoyable. And other people's pecan pies taste much better. We even bought a couple of shovels.

It was only when I got to know the Freeman family in Minneapolis on an assignment for the *Financial Times*,[147] however, that my skepticism began to break down. Unlike our neighborhood, which is in one of Washington's leafier urban spots, the Freemans live in a community that is suffering from creeping rust in its soul. Once a bastion of solid middle-class living, the home foreclosure crisis has spread gradually across their neighborhood. Boarded-up homes are stripped for copper. Just a block from where the Freemans live there is a crack house. Friends in the area keep losing their jobs.

After a three-year freeze Mark and Connie Freeman, who both work at the Nicolett-Methodist hospital in one of the city's suburbs, finally got a pay raise. It amounted to $3 a day. To look at the time sheet of how each spends a typical day is to realize that they have little time to pause for breath. "I don't know whether it is me, or whether I'm getting older, but we both seem so exhausted all the time," said Mark, fifty-three, a born and bred Minnesotan who works as a warehouse packager at the hospital. They could be forgiven for putting their feet up.

In the best American spirit, the Freemans are the types who shovel your snow, stick their hand up to volunteer for school events, do the neighborhood crime watch, and coach the Little League. Mark, who belongs to the Service Employees International Union, also tries to recruit part-time service workers to the union. Connie, who is an anesthesia supply technician, fears her husband may be wasting his time. Mark has also joined a civic group that is lobbying the Minneapolis government to build the city's next light rail extension through their neck of the woods. Together the Freemans give twenty hours a week in voluntary work.

Mark spends a lot of time knocking on doors. But he finds it increasingly hard to stir people out of their apathy. People are tired, he says. "If I were honest, I would say a lot of people are too cynical or just plain exhausted to join in," Mark said. Sometimes he also feels he is wasting his time. But he always goes back. "If we stand back and watch this neighborhood disintegrate then we only have ourselves to blame," he said.

Recently Mother Nature had done her best to help things along. In April eastern Minneapolis had been ripped up by a tornado, the worst in years. The storm cut a trail through the nearest main street and headed for the Freemans' suburb. Five people died within a few blocks of where they live. Apart from the missing trees, it didn't look much different than before. "It already felt like a tornado had been through our neighborhood," joked Connie.

The following day the Freemans gathered spare clothes, tins of food, kitchen rolls, and whatever else was at hand and headed to a nearby church. They were among the last to arrive. "We couldn't believe it," Connie said. "It was piled high with donations already." The disaster had brought people together. The atmosphere reminded Connie of what life used to be like. "People were helping out. Strangers asked each other if they were okay," said Connie. "It felt good to be here."

More than a decade ago Robert Putnam, the Harvard sociologist, drew America's attention to the decline in volunteerism. Because of television, the growth of suburbia, women's mass entry into the workforce, and the computer, Americans were ceasing to be joiners. Tocqueville's society of busybodies was keeping its doors shut. Were Putnam to write a sequel, it is hard to believe that America's atomization would not have intensified since then.[148]

Mark and Connie are swimming against the tide. But their son Andy, twenty-two, who suffers from severe autism, is battling against a much stronger current. Until he was ten Andy barely spoke. At his birthday parties he would retreat into his room, turn out the light, and put his face in his hands. "When I think of how frightened Andy was it makes me so sad," said Connie. Year by year, Connie and Mark tried to build up Andy's confidence. They searched out special needs educational programs, filled in the endless forms, and became adept at making the most of what was available.

Since it was Minneapolis, which carries a whiff of Scandinavian social democracy, the options were quite wide. To the amazement of Andy's social workers, who had seen many severe cases, he began to grow in confidence. He started to make friends, mostly with other autistic children. He built the confidence to take public transport, took up singing and acting, and now fills in his own paperwork for educational assistance. "The odds are already so heavily stacked against Andy," said Connie. "We wanted to make sure he could be independent."

I went back to visit the Freemans because I wanted to see how they were doing. We were twenty-four months into the economic "recovery," which began officially in mid-2009. I had last seen them one year into it. In contrast to how recoveries are supposed to work, things had got markedly worse since my previous trip. Mark had lost his part-time job running the karaoke machine at the local Veterans of Foreign Wars club. He also had fewer hours from his other part-time job at the local liquor store. Mark retained his full-time hospital job. But in the space of a year their joint annual income still fell from $70,000 to $50,000.

Local property values had continued to nosedive. At the end of Mark and Connie's street sits a nationally protected house designed by Lawrence Fournier, a contemporary of Frank Lloyd Wright. It is listed on the National Register of Historic Places. It went on the market in early 2011 at $330,000. It sold for under half of that. The Freemans were stunned. That would make their modest, 700-square-foot single-story home, which they bought for $50,000 in 1989, practically worthless. Mark said they had spent over twice that on the mortgage already.

Then there was the stark mathematics of their looming retirement. At just $70,000 their savings would not get them very far. Combined with the value of their house, their financial assets are still higher than the American median.[149] But by the Freemans' calculations they would never be able to retire. The value of Social Security is dwindling and their mortgage still has to be paid off. In the past people would go by the "rule of eighty," which says your wages should amount to years of service plus your age. "The new rule of eighty is that you work until you're eighty," said Mark.

Naturally, both worry about whether they will maintain the health to keep on working. But their greatest concern is Andy. Their combined legacy would keep him going for barely two years. "What would happen to him if we fell under a bus?" said Connie, who has a friendly apple-cheeked face that triggers associations in me of the best in country pub cooking. "I worry myself sick thinking about his future."

The previous week, Andy had graduated with a GED (General Educational Development), a fallback for those unable to get a high school diploma. Andy had climbed a mountain to get the certificate. It was a triumphant moment. He was also studying theater at the local community college. In both cases, he was assisted by a special needs fund. Minnesota, which shut down for two weeks in 2011 when its legislature failed to agree on a budget, had just cut the GED funding from three years to one. The college program was hanging by a thread. "There is no way Andy could have got a GED in one year," said Connie. "That was his lifeline."

For his excitedly awaited GED graduating ceremony, Andy composed his own five-minute speech, which he delivered without notes. He talked of a future in acting, directing, and even scriptwriting. Nor was this fanciful. He had already performed at the college in a short play that he wrote. Talking that day about all his dreams of the future, Andy's optimism was infectious, said Connie. "I sat there watching him and thought of this little boy who was too scared to be with other children," she said. "And there he was, with his hands on the lectern, speaking to an audience of a hundred and looking everybody in the eye." Connie laughed because her own eyes had started to water as she recounted it. "I know it's stupid," she said. "When I talk about Andy I can't help myself."

I think about the Freemans a great deal, not because they are unfortunate but because in today's America their situation is disturbingly normal. They both work their hearts out. They rarely have the money left over to go to the movies or eat at their local pizza joint. They live in dread of a medical crisis. And however fast they run they find it impossible to stand still. Regardless of Mark's politics, which is a mix of hard-nosed and dreamy, it is impossible to deny their foreboding. Their neighborhood once teemed with voluntary associations, trade unions, community churches, and American Eagle clubs. Most are now boarded up. In their place has arisen a rootless culture, in which most people work on contract, spend their evenings in front of the television, and try to move out if they can.

One or two, including a local Protestant pastor, abandoned their homes after failing to find buyers. The Freemans used to hear loud Baptist singing from his home a few doors down. Now empty, they found a bullet hole in its front door. Yet by some miracle the Freemans still have the optimism to volunteer. Others are not so resilient. The growth of "bowling alone" and the rise in economic insecurity have led to a sharp rise in the frequency of mental illness in America over the last generation. Every year, one in four

American adults suffers from some kind of mental illness that keeps them from work, ranging from mild depression to nervous breakdown.[150] By some margin this is the highest rate in the world. Here, too, America is an exception.

In fact, on pretty much every social indicator you check, America is off the charts. An American baby is twice as likely to die in its first year as a Scandinavian, German, or Japanese.[151] More than twice as many Americans are obese as is average for wealthy nations. And America's prison population is more than five times the ratio of the next highest developed country, the UK, which conveys a near-pathological gap with other countries, which has become considerably wider in the last twenty years. For the generation leading up to the Great Contraction, most of the wrong trends had almost been steepening. Many are now metastasizing. Four years after the housing collapse, one in four American mortgages is still underwater. One in seven Americans is on food stamps. Even Americans' life expectancy is starting to look wobbly. And America's once stratospheric economic participation rate has collapsed to the European average (an astonishing development given how much longer European welfare benefits last). There is only so much neighborhood volunteerism can do to keep such powerful forces at bay.

How long can this go on before something gives? As the richest country in the world, almost 150 years after it became the largest, can America really do no better? There are no easy answers to these nagging questions. Some will fall back on the nation's long history of resilience. America is the exception; it stands apart from the normal cycles of history. Her fate is solely in her hands. The more thoughtful exceptionalists may quote Samuel Huntington: "Critics say America is a lie because its reality falls so far short of its ideals. They are wrong. America is not a lie; it is a disappointment. But it can only be a disappointment because it is also a hope."

The less thoughtful, including many who run for public office, simply reiterate the American exception when they get the chance. During a Republican presidential debate Mitt Romney said, "The rest of the world doesn't admire America because of her wealth. They admire us for what is in our hearts." Given what they had been put through in Iraq in the previous few years, most of my military friends at the National Defense University would probably have been rolling their eyes. In the 2012 race Romney and most of his fellow Republican contenders were unbowed. They insisted that the United States should confront Iran, actively contain China, and intervene wherever necessary to maintain America's worldwide supremacy. Romney also led the field in calling for a large expansion in U.S. military spending. I doubt very much whether this reflects what is in American hearts.

The truth is that America's stock has been falling around the world for quite a while.[152] At home, opinion polls register mounting disappointment minus Huntington's hope. Simply proclaiming the superiority of the American model is not helping anyone's credibility. That also applies to Democrats. I recently listened to a liberal anchor on MSNBC say the following: "Whatever else is happening in America we're still the country where anyone can make it, no matter what their origins." As Huckleberry Finn said, "Saying so don't make it so." Were America's politicos to peer closer into American hearts, I imagine they would be more circumspect. They would find rising fear and anger. They would also come across a growing sense of boredom; Americans are increasingly turned off by politics. And they would surely meet families like the Freemans, who know the difference between saying and doing but who fear their country has forgotten.

Acknowledgments

I took a nine-month leave of absence from the *Financial Times* to write this book—six months travel and research and three months of writing. I want first and foremost to underline my gratitude to the *FT,* and in particular to Lionel Barber for encouraging me to do this book and also for reading key parts of it. Without having worked for the *FT* and gaining the kind of access and respect it affords, this book would have been far harder to write.

A project such as this is necessarily selective—the subject is simply too broad and imponderable for any one person to address comprehensively in a single volume. Many Americans might be even more skeptical of a foreigner embarking on such a task, and particularly someone from Britain. Happily for me, almost everyone whom I approached was enthusiastic about the subject matter and ready with advice and introduction.

In particular I would like to mention the following people for going out of their way to help me with the kind of generosity that comes like manna from heaven: Bill Miller in Austin, Texas, David Beier in Santa Monica and D.C., John Calhoun in Portland, Oregon, Gerald Abbot in D.C., Derek Shearer in L.A., Clyde Prestowitz in D.C., Francisco Sánchez at the Department of Commerce, Brian Toohey at the SIA, and Tony Podesta and Don Riegle—all in D.C. I would particularly like to thank David Rothkopf, an always insightful friend and frequent lunch companion, who has encouraged and advised me on this project from the start.

There are many people, particularly in Washington, D.C., whom I am unable to name since they assisted me off the record. In the following list, I apologize if I have accidentally omitted any names.

With a few exceptions I have left out those who are formally interviewed and quoted in this book. An undertaking such as this would not be possible without your kindness: Mark and Connie Freeman, Stella O'Leary, James McIntire, Carl Camden, Anuradha Basu and Shanker Trivedi, David Price, Luke Albee, David Smith, Liaquat and Meena Ahamed, Kenneth Fong, Kim Walesh, Neeta Bidwai, Bob Hormats, Vint Cerf, Chuck Hagel, William Morin, Jonathan Davidson, Bill Wicker, Larry Rosenstock, Dick Shaink, Rosario Palmieri, Bryan Ashley, Ronald Brownstein, Simon Rosenberg, Bill Galston, Norm Ornstein, Thomas Arnold, Andy Grove, Craig Barrett, Paul Mandabach, Rob Atkinson, Geoff Lamb, Michelle Smith, Larry Summers, Sheryl Sandberg, David Autor, Katherine Miller, John Hofland, David Gergen, Larry Katz, Robert Gordon, Tom and Ginger Luce, Peter Orszag, Michael Bennet, Tom Davis, Gregory Tassey, Peggy Hamburg, Vicki Seyfert-Margolis, Tim Adams, Naren Gupta, Jeff Garten, Diana Farrell, Daniel Price, Anne and Jim Rierdon, Bob Reich, Jared Bernstein, George Scalise, Brad Delong, Arati Prabhakar, John Thornhill, Carl Giordano, Andrew Williams, Rolf Elkus, Irwin Jacobs, Tom Daschle, Leo Hindery, Alan Platt, John Podesta, Rob Shapiro, Tom Friedman, and Robert Kahn.

I would also like to thank my New York agent, Scott Moyers at Wylie, whose support and sage advice were critical rocket boosters for this project. Scott has since moved onto greater things at Penguin. By the same token, it would have been hard to imagine doing this book without the unstinting enthusiasm and support of Morgan Entrekin, publisher of Grove/Atlantic. Every author should have a publisher like Morgan. They would also be blessed to have Morgan as their editor. I would also like to thank Peter Blackstock at Grove/Atlantic, for his attention to detail and unwaivering responsiveness. Finally, I would like to thank my wife Priya Basu, who put up with my prolonged absences, eccentric mood changes, and nocturnal writing habits with very cheerful forbearance. Had it been any other way, this book would not have been written. I know Priya would agree that this volume should be dedicated to our beloved daughter, Rashmi, who rules over our present and future.

Notes

1. Charlie LeDuff, "Riding Along with the Cops in Murdertown, USA," *The New York Times,* April 15, 2011.
2. Ranking by the Aspen Institute, September 2011.
3. Self-Storage Association (SSA).
4. "Economic Security at Risk," findings from the Economic Security Index, July 2010, by Jacob Hacker et al.
5. Robert B. Reich, *Supercapitalism: The Transformation of Business, Democracy, and Everyday Life* (Alfred A. Knopf, 2007).
6. "The Evolving Structure of the American Economy and the Employment Challenge," March 2011, Council on Foreign Relations.
7. See Michael Mandel, "How much of the 2007–2009 productivity surge was real?" Innovationandgrowth.wordpress.com, March 28, 2011.
8. "An Economy that Works," McKinsey, June 2011.
9. "Striking it Richer: The Evolution of Top Incomes in the United States," Emmanuel Saez (lecture, University of California Berkeley, July 17, 2010).
10. Ron Chernow, *Alexander Hamilton* (Penguin Books, 2004).
11. David Kocieniewski, "But nobody pays that," *The New York Times,* March 24, 2011.
12. Both quotes from Clyde Prestowitz's excellent *The Betrayal of American Prosperity* (Free Press, 2010).
13. Andy Grove, "How America can create jobs," *Bloomberg Businessweek,* July 1, 2010.
14. Aaron L. Friedberg, *The Weary Titan: Britain and the Experience of Relative Decline, 1895–1905* (Princeton University Press, 1988), 67.

15. "The Need for Public Investment and Increased Revenue," December 13, 2010, at the Economic Policy Institute, Washington, D.C.

16. In a 2011 interview with the author.

17. In a 2010 interview with the author.

18. Alan Greenspan, "Dodd-Frank Fails to Meet Test of Our Times," *Financial Times,* March 29, 2011.

19. Steel Works—the American Iron and Steel Institute.

20. Business Innovation Factory, Kamen profile.

21. Rising Above the Gathering Storm, Revisited: Rapidly Approaching Category 5 (National Academies Press, 2010).

22. *Austin-American Statesman,* November 29, 2006.

23. Jean M. Twenge and W. Keith Campbell *The Narcissim Epidemic: Living in the Age of Entitlement,* (Free Press, 2009).

24. Lori Gottlieb, "How to land your kid in therapy," *The Atlantic Monthly,* July/August 2011.

25. Ibid.

26. The College Board, July 2010.

27. Steve Brill, "The Rubber Room," *The New Yorker,* August 31, 2009.

28. Edward Luce, "US School Reform Report Awaits Grades," *Financial Times,* July 28, 2010.

29. Diane Ravitch, *The Death and Life of the Great American School System* (Basic Books, 2010), 88.

30. According to the U.S. Department of Education.

31. Round Rock, Texas, district superintendent's office.

32. *The Death and Life of the Great American School System,* 207.

33. Rising Above the Gathering Storm, Revisited: Rapidly Approaching Category 5 (National Academies Press, 2010).

34. U.S. Department of Education, National Center for Education Statistics.

35. See Robert Gordon, Northwestern University, The Recession and Recovery, AEA panel, Denver, January 11, 2011.

36. In an interview with the author.

37. Bureau of Labor Statistics, September 2011.

38. Bureau of Labor Statistics and the U.S. Census.

39. Michael Mandel, "The State of Young College Grads, 2011," Innovationandgrowth.wordpress.com, October 1, 2011.

40. "An Economy that works," McKinsey.

41. David Rothkopf, "The Myth of the Innovation Nation," *Foreign Policy,* January 25, 2011.

42. Information Technology and Innovation Foundation (ITIF), Washington, D.C.

43. Rising Above the Gathering Storm, Revisited: Rapidly Approaching Category 5, National Academies Press, 2011, Washington, D.C.

44. In 2011, Solyndra's bankruptcy would cause a minor storm over at Obama's Department of Energy, which had extended it loans that were funded by the 2009 $830 billion stimulus.

45. National Venture Capital Association, July 2011.

46. Peter Kedrosky and Dane Stangler, "Financialization and its entrepreneurial consequences," Kauffman Foundation, March 2011.

47. Henry R. Nothhaft with David Kline, *Great Again* (Harvard Business Review Press; eBook edition, June 2011).

48. Ibid.

49. ITIF.

50. Alcatel press release, 2008.

51. "Rising Tigers, Sleeping Giant," report by ITIF and the Breakthrough Institute, November 2009.

52. Clyde Prestowitz, *The Betrayal of American Prosperity: Free Market Delusions, America's Decline, and How We Must Compete in the Post-Dollar Era.* (Free Press, 2010).

53 Oregon had a jobless rate of 9.6 percent in August 2011, compared to a U.S. rate of 9.1 percent (BLS).

54. Information Technology and Innovation Foundation.

55. Interview with the author.

56. http://www.whitehouse.gov/sites/default/files/microsites/ostp/pcast-nano-report.pdf.

57. Jonathan Rauch, *Government's End: Why Washington Stopped Working* (Public Affairs, 1999), 148.

58. Gregory Tassey, *The Technology Imperative* (Edward Elgar Publishing, 2007), 311.
59. *Government's End,* 134.
60. The Cato Institute puts the total number of tax pages plus legal opinions at 72,000. The actual tax code is much shorter.
61. "The Joy of Tax," *The Economist,* April 8, 2010.
62. Paul C. Light, *A Government Ill Executed* (Harvard University Press, 2008), 58.
63. Scott Shane and Paul Nixon, "In Washington, Contractors Take on Biggest Role Ever," *The New York Times,* February 4, 2007.
64. *A Government Ill Executed,* 192.
65. Ibid.
66. This was related to the author on background by two separate officials at the Department of Commerce.
67. *A Government Ill Executed,* 88.
68. Terry Sullivan, "Fabulous, Formless Darkness," Brookings, spring 2001.
69. Interview with the author.
70. Interview with the author.
71. Semiconductor Industry Association.
72. Ibid.
73. Interview with the author.
74. This was related to the author by two industry executives who attended the meeting.
75. http://online.wsj.com/article/SB123142562104564381.html.
76. "Venture Wire," *The Wall Street Journal,* November 18, 2010.
77. Ibid.
78. Interview with the author.
79. "FDA Confronts Challenge of Monitoring Imports," *The New York Times,* June 20, 2011.
80. Peggy Hamburg, interview with the author.
81. Interview with the author.
82. "Opportunities to Reduce Potential Duplication in Government Programs," GAO (Government Accountability Office), March 2011.

83. Economic Mobility Project, Pew.

84. Ibid.

85. Ibid.

86. "Ever Higher Society, Ever Harder to Ascend," *The Economist,* December 29, 2004.

87. GAO "Opportunities" report, March 2011.

88. Jacob S. Hacker and Paul Pierson, *Winner-Take-All Politics* (Simon and Schuster, 2010), 242.

89. Ibid., 251–52.

90. Ibid., 242.

91. Rick Shenkman, *Just How Stupid Are We? Facing the Truth about the American Voter* (Basic Books, 2009).

92. Ibid.

93. Ibid.

94. Ibid.

95. http://www.gallup.com/poll/5392/trust-government.aspx.

96. NYT/CBS poll, October 25, 2011.

97. See Jane Mayer's superb *New Yorker* article "Covert Operations," August 30, 2010.

98. Rush Limbaugh, *See, I Told You So* (Pocket, 1993).

99. In a telephone interview with the author in November 2008.

100. Chernow, *Alexander Hamilton.*

101. In an interview with the author.

102. In an interview with the author.

103. "The Gray and the Brown: The Generational Mismatch," *National Journal,* July 24, 2010.

104. "The People's Will," *The Economist's* special—and very well researched report on democracy in California, April 23, 2011.

105. Ibid.

106. Ibid.

107. Ibid.

108. Dennis Cauchon, "Texas wins in US Economy Shift," *USA Today,* June 21, 2011.

109. U.S. decennial census (2000–2010), U.S. Census Bureau.

110. Tony's is called the Podesta Group and Heather, who is twenty-six years Tony's junior, owns Heather Podesta + Partners.
111. Center for Responsive Politics, Publicsecrets.org.
112. Ibid.
113. In an interview with the author.
114. This is my best but unscientific guess from the hundreds of candidate schedule e-mails during the campaign.
115. *Obama in Office,* ed. James Thurdber (Paradigm, 2011), 136–37.
116. In Obama campaign disclosures to the Federal Election Commission, July 2011.
117. *Obama in Office.*
118. Samuel Huntington, *American Politics: The Promise of Disharmony* (Belknap Press of Harvard University, 1981), 64.
119. Ibid., 66.
120. *Obama in Office.*
121. Mancur Olson, *The Rise and Decline of Nations* (Yale University Press, 1982).
122. In an interview with the author.
123. Edward Luce, "Baucus's well-placed friends give prescription greater potency," *Financial Times,* September 21, 2009.
124. In comments quoted by the *Congressional Quarterly.*
125. Ibid.
126. Interview with the author.
127. Interview with the author.
128. Interview with the author.
129. Interview with the author.
130. In an interview with John Arlidge of the *Sunday Times,* November 8, 2009.
131. Interview with the author.
132. http://www.bankofengland.co.uk/publications/speeches/2009/speech409.pdf.
133. *Winner-Take-All Politics,* 277.
134. Ibid., 292.
135. Lawrence Lessig, "How to Get Our Democracy Back," *The Nation,* February 2010.

136. "Obama raised $86 million, 40 percent from bundlers," *Politico,* July 15, 2011.

137. Edward Luce, "The Fearsome Foursome," *Financial Times,* February 3, 2010.

138. U.S. Census 2011 American Community Survey.

139. In an interview with the author.

140. Harold Myerson, "Whose Hurt by Paul Ryan's budget proposal?" *The Washington Post,* April 5, 2011.

141. At the time of writing it is too early to assess the impact of California's move to a nonpartisan system of drawing district boundaries, and likewise its embrace of the open primary, which is designed to weaken the polarizing grip of the party bases on the selection of candidates.

142. In one of many interviews with the author.

143. In a presidential town hall at the Wyfells Hybrids production facility in Atkinson, Illinois, August 17, 2011.

144. Numbers from U.S. Census broken down by Sentier Research and first cited in the *Wall Street Journal,* October 31, 2011.

145. Presidential address to Congress, September 8, 2011. Though some of the bill did eventually pass in broken-up pieces after the bill in whole failed to overcome its first hurdle in the Senate.

146. I was half tempted to call this book "paradigms lost" but thankfully got the better of that pretension.

147. Edward Luce, "The Crisis of Middle Class America," *Financial Times,* July 30, 2010.

148. Robert D. Puttnam, *Bowling Alone* (Simon and Schuster, 2000).

149. According to the Pew Research Center's breakdown of U.S. Census income survey data, the median wealth for white Americans was $113,149 in 2009. For Hispanics and African-Americans median wealth was at a shockingly low tally of $6,325 and $5,677, respectively.

150. Kate Pickett and Richard Wilkinson, *The Spirit Level: Why Greater Equality Makes Societies Stronger* (Bloomberg Press, 2009).

151. Ibid.

152. Anti-Americanism around the world has eased off a little under Barack Obama, compared to that under George W. Bush. But it

remains at a very low level. In the 2010 Pew Survey on global attitudes, only 32 percent of those surveyed globally believed the United States considered their country's interests in policy making. This was 6 percent higher than the last number under Bush.